CW01496380

Common Denominators

Global Issues

General Editors: Bruce Kapferer, Professor of Anthropology, James Cook University and John Gledhill, Professor of Anthropology, Manchester University

This series addresses vital social, political and cultural issues confronting human populations throughout the world. The ultimate aim is to enhance understanding – and, it is hoped, thereby dismantle – hegemonic structures which perpetuate prejudice, violence, racism, religious persecution, sexual discrimination and domination, poverty, and many other social ills.

ISSN:1354-3644

Previously published books in the series:

Michael Herzfeld
The Social Production of Indifference: Exploring the Symbolic Roots of Western Bureaucracy

Peter Rigby
African Images: Racism and the End of Anthropology

Judith Kapferer
Being All Equal: Difference and Australian Cultural Practice

Eduardo P. Archetti
Guinea-pigs: Food, Symbol and Conflict of Knowledge in Ecuador

Denis Duclos
The Werewolf Complex: America's Facination with Violence

Common Denominators

Ethnicity, Nation-Building and Compromise in Mauritius

Thomas Hylland Eriksen

Oxford • New York

First published in 1998 by
Berg
Editorial offices:
150 Cowley Road, Oxford, OX4 1JJ, UK
70 Washington Square South, New York, NY 10012, USA

Berg is the imprint of Oxford International Publishers Ltd.

Library of Congress Cataloging-in-Publication Data

A catalogue record for this book is available from the Library of Congress.

British Library Cataloguing-in-Publication Data

A catalogue record for this book is available from the British Library.

ISBN   1 85973 954 7 (Cloth)
          1 85973 959 8 (Paper)

Typeset by JS Typesetting, Wellingborough, Northants
Printed in the United Kingdom by Biddles Ltd, Guildford and King's Lynn.

Habit of seeing opposites. – The general imprecise way of observing sees everywhere in nature opposites (as, for example, 'warm and cold') where there are, not opposites, but differences in degree. This bad habit has led us into wanting to comprehend and analyse the inner world, too, the spiritual-moral world, in terms of such opposites. An unspeakable amount of painfulness, arrogance, harshness, estrangement, frigidity has entered into human feelings because we think we see opposites instead of transitions.

Friedrich Nietzsche, *Der Wanderer und sein Schatten*, § 67

It takes at least two somethings to create a difference. (. . .)

There is a profound and unanswerable question about the nature of those 'at least two' things that between them generate a difference which becomes information by making a difference. Clearly each alone is – for the mind and perception – a non-entity, a non-being. Not different from being, and not different from non-being. An unknowable, a *Ding an sich*, a sound from one hand clapping.

Gregory Bateson, *Mind and Nature*, p. 78

Contents

Preface   ix

      CHAPTER ONE   1

Introduction

      CHAPTER TWO   7

Mauritius Past and Present

      CHAPTER THREE   22

Fields and Levels of Mauritian Society

      CHAPTER FOUR   47

Dimensions of Ethnicity

      CHAPTER FIVE   75

Contested Symbols: Language and Religion

      CHAPTER SIX   103

Cross-Cutting Ties: The Non-Ethnic

      CHAPTER SEVEN   137

Mauritian Nationhoods

CHAPTER EIGHT   167

The Mauritian Dilemma

CHAPTER NINE   183

Conclusions and Prospects

Bibliography   190

Index   199

Preface

Can multiethnic nations be stable and meaningful imagined communities? Are multiethnic societies necessarily multicultural ones, or is the very term 'multicultural society' a contradiction in terms? To what extent do processes of modernisation lead to an obliteration of ethnic boundaries, and in what ways are the very same boundaries strengthened through social change? Is it possible to avoid discrimination against minorities in multiethnic society? How can ethnic conflict be avoided? And what does the word 'we' mean?

These are some of the questions raised in this book – questions that have occupied much of my intellectual attention for the last decade, not least with respect to Mauritian society. As this book will make clear, the recent historical experiences of Mauritians can provide a profound and nuanced understanding of multiethnic societies. This can serve as a counter-example to the depressingly numerous cases of violent ethnic conflict of recent years, and can provide fresh and sometimes unexpected premises for ongoing debates on 'multiculturalism' and minority rights worldwide.

The book is written in a comparative spirit. I have sought to use the example of Mauritius to make sense not only of fundamental processes of identification, ethnic and non-ethnic alike, but also to shed light, albeit indirectly, on tensions and conflicts in other societies. Mauritius, which has often been described as a 'laboratory of diversity', has a story that deserves to be told, about the possibilities and predicaments characteristic of complex multiethnic societies. In Western Europe, in particular, it is only recently that identity politics has become an issue of national concern; but Mauritius has been self-consciously multiethnic since its inception as a society nearly three hundred years ago, and may for that reason have a lesson to teach the rest of us.

Parts of this book are identical or similar to work published earlier, to the extent of as little as a sentence or as much as a few pages. Much has been adapted from *Communicating Cultural Difference and Identity* (Eriksen 1988), an early study of ethnicity and nation-building in Mauritius. Much less has been grafted from my doctoral thesis, 'Ethnicity and Two Nationalisms' (Eriksen 1991c), which was a comparative study of nation-building and interethnic relations in Trinidad and Mauritius, very different in scope from the present study. Snippets and excerpts have also been taken from 'Mauritian Society between the Ethnic and the Non-ethnic' (Eriksen 1997a), 'The Cultural Contexts of Ethnic Differences' (Eriksen 1991a), 'Multiculturalism, Individualism and Human Rights' (Eriksen 1997b), 'Nationalism, Mauritian Style' (Eriksen 1994a), 'Multiple Traditions and the Problem of Cultural Integration' (Eriksen 1992b) and 'We and Us: Two Modes of Group Identification' (Eriksen 1995). These articles may often be the fullest sources for the particular issues they raise concerning Mauritian society – for although important research undertaken by other scholars is under way, Mauritius is still seriously understudied anthropologically; but conversely, most of this book consists of original material.

During my long-standing engagement with Mauritian affairs, which has sometimes brought me precariously close to meddling, I have made many friends and no enemies. Very many Mauritians deserve a note of thanks, and I can only mention a few of them. I have a great debt of gratitude towards the Cotte/Jugdhur family, Suren Pamoo and Suresh Pamoo, Alix Koenig and Georges Koenig for their extraordinary hospitality; Malenn and Adi Oodiah, Elisabeth and Gaëtan Boullé, Amrita Suntah and Patrick Bazile and his family – thanks for their friendship and intellectual input; and I am also grateful to Raj Virahsawmy, U. Bissondoyal, Dev Virahsawmy and, in particular, Vinesh Hookoomsing, for their enduring interest in my work. Many others could have been mentioned, Mauritians and non-Mauritians alike – you know who you are.

Oslo, November 1997

CHAPTER ONE

Introduction

Commenting obliquely but accurately on the genre of biography, Virginia Woolf lets the protagonist of her novel *Orlando* (1928) assume an enormous and seemingly unrealistic variety of social roles and identities, right down to the point of changing gender. Yet, the narrator says towards the end of the book, she has written only a small fraction of the possible biographies that could be written about Orlando; in other words, persons have many more dimensions than a single book might reveal.

The people of Mauritius, it is tempting to say, collectively exploit a fair proportion of Orlando's vast role repertoire. Mauritius, a polyethnic island-state in the south-western Indian Ocean, has for historical reasons an ethnically very diverse population of about one million, four major religions, a large but uncertain number of languages, and no indigenous population. Widely considered an economic miracle by the 1990s, Mauritius is also a stable multi-party democracy that has gone through several peaceful changes of government since independence in 1968. Mauritius has, since its independence, consistently failed to fulfil the predictions of gloomy prophets. The island, regarded by its colonial administrators as hopelessly overpopulated, ethnically divided and overdependent on sugar mono-culture (Meade *et al.* 1961), is currently prospering, and its population seems to cope efficiently with problems formerly perceived as insurmountable. In one of the few scholarly books on Mauritius written by foreigners, the anthropologist Burton Benedict ends with a prophetic statement: 'The ethnic divisions of Mauritius are changing. They are no longer mere categories but are becoming corporate groups. The danger of communal conflict increases' (Benedict 1965:67). His argument, which seemed reasonable at the time of its proposal, was not immediately proved wrong, and the first half of the syllogism was correct; but within less than a decade it was clear that Mauritians had chosen another, less destructive, direction, at least for the time being.

Leaving for fieldwork in Mauritius for the first time in early 1986, I had jokingly told my friends that I expected to find a society where postmodern relativism was as deeply ingrained as the faith in technological progress had been in Europe in the 1950s. Instead, it would turn out that I encountered a very wide range of perfectly solid and confident personal identities, often based on qualitatively different premises; some of them were justified with reference to ethnic identity, while others were not. The local approach to identification was puzzling and seemed eclectic; even the basic ethnic classification drew on varying kinds of criteria.

• *Port-Louis.* A first approach to the diversity of Mauritius might be spatial. Beginning in the centre of the capital Port-Louis, the only truly ethnically segregated town in the island, a visitor quickly encounters the Jummah mosque, an imposing white monster of massive stone fringed with beggars, brutally planted in the midst of busy Chinatown; its self-assertive presence a majestic interruption to the strings of small colourful Chinese shops sprouting from the mosque in four directions. The mosque bears testimony to the stability and collective prosperity of the Muslim community in Mauritius. Although three times as numerous, the Hindus have nothing nearly as prestigious.

An ethnically segregated city, damp and aromatic Port-Louis retains the ambience of a busy colonial centre of administration and commerce, domestic and international. A few blocks from the Jummah Mosque is the city market, embalmed in a pungent smell of saltfish – a rancid reminder of Mauritius' past as a slave society. An increasing part of the bustling market, still dominated by trade in basic foodstuffs, is gradually being taken over by vendors of generic tourist curios; tee-shirts, souvenir cups and saucers and flags, as well as globalised local specialities such as tortoise shells and sharks' teeth. Clustered along a palm-fringed boulevard ending at the docks are many of the administrative and commercial nexuses of Mauritius: to the left, one finds the Parliament and the Queen Victoria monument; across the street is the Anglo-Mauritius House, where insurance companies and shipping firms are located – and which for many years contained the only European-style outdoor café in Port-Louis, patronised by foreigners and the upper middle class. Further down along the avenue are several government ministries, the General Post Office and one of the city's bus stations, and at the upper extreme is the Bank of Mauritius, which was for years the only Mauritian building more than six storeys tall.

Starting from Cassis in the west and moving towards Roche-Bois in the east, several distinctively ethnic neighbourhoods can be identified in Port-Louis. All the major ethnic categories of Mauritius except the Franco-Mauritians are represented in one or several distinct neighbourhoods. (Rich Franco-Mauritians fled Port-Louis for the cooler climate in the interior during a malaria epidemic in the 1880s.) The western extreme of the capital is dominated by respectable working-class and lower-middle-class Creoles; in Bell Village, this area merges into an ethnically mixed area, which again merges into an upper-middle-class Hindu neighbourhood near the ominously named Champ de Mars, where horse-racing is a weekly Sunday attraction for thousands of male Mauritians of all communities and classes. Beyond the stadium there is a growing squatter settlement, which is ethnically composed of Hindus, Creoles and Tamils. A few blocks below the Champ de Mars, the commercial centre of the city begins and exhaust fumes take over from the scents of garden flowers. To the immediate east of the city centre lies Chinatown, which in turn merges into the Muslim neighbourhood of Plaine Verte, beyond which is the largely Creole quarter Abercrombie. The north-eastern frontier of Port-Louis is Roche-Bois, a largely Creole and Rodriguan area which rose to national fame during the 1970s because of its militant dockers.

• *Plaines Wilhems*. Approaching the urban centres of Mauritius from the airport near the small south-eastern town of Mahébourg, one passes through immense canefields and the large estate village of Rose-Belle before going uphill to the dark green tea estates surrounding Curepipe. Although only some three hundred metres above sea level, Curepipe has a distinctly cooler and rainier climate than Port-Louis; these microclimatic variations provide an apt analogy to the seemingly great cultural variations of the island. Curepipe and adjacent Floréal were the towns to which the white upper class of Mauritius moved in the 1880s; they still possess a strong ambience of old-world aristocratic Europe. Some of the poshest shops and finest restaurants of Mauritius are found in the Curepipe area, as are most of the embassies and high commissions, as well as the most imposing colonial dwellings, with large, well-kept grounds surrounding them. The miniature Eiffel Tower in the courtyard of one of the French restaurants in Curepipe accurately signifies the positioning of the town in the collective consciousness of Mauritius.

Moving down the Plaines Wilhems from Curepipe, lush and affluent Floréal merges almost imperceptibly into the dusty twin towns of Vacoas-Phoenix, which in turn give way to Quatre-Bornes, Rose-Hill (pronounced *Rozille*, French 'r') and Beau-Bassin; initially three clearly distinguishable towns, they are now virtually continuous. From Beau-Bassin, the Route Royale goes steeply downhill through Coromandel, a new industrial estate reminding the visitor that manufacturing has replaced sugar as the main earner of foreign currency during the 1990s, and eventually reaches hot and humid Port-Louis.

Apart from Curepipe–Floréal and Port-Louis, Mauritian towns are similar in their spatial layout. They are centred around two axes; the main road and the bus station (which was formerly the railway station). Most of the buildings date from the early postwar years; most are single-storeyed, and many are poorly maintained. Although consumerism may not yet have reached European levels in currently booming Mauritius, the number of shops and other commercial establishments in Mauritian towns is impressive and bears testimony to the island's initial *raison-d'être* as a transit port. Most of the shop signs are written in French, although the traffic signs are in English.

Initially, it may seem a stupendous task to try to make sense of social categories and cultural patterns in a society that is simultaneously a member of *La Francophonie* and of The New Commonwealth; where fifteen languages may be spoken, according to official statistics; where the currency is the rupee, whose name is usually pronounced in a vaguely French-sounding language (but the banknotes have text in English, Hindi and Tamil); where people can possess names like Françoise Yaw Tang Mootoosamy; and where the second-in-charge of the Catholic Church turns out to be a man named Amedée Nagapen. The pages that follow, fuelled by human concerns and social science theory as well as by the pedestrian nitty-gritty of ethnographic research, are an attempt to make sense of this apparent chaos.

• *Compromise through encounters.* This introductory chapter apart, the rest of the chapters can be divided into two's. Chapters 2 and 3 introduce the empirical field and the analytical issues, Chapter 2 concentrating on introducing Mauritius, and Chapter 3 delving into conceptual and methodological questions. Chapters 4 and 5 show the ways in which ethnicity is reproduced in Mauritius, giving particular attention to the relationship between instrumental and symbolic aspects. Chapters 6 and 7 present non-ethnic forms of alignment and identity, while the last two chapters discuss the dilemmas faced by democratic multiethnic societies. This book is chiefly a study of compromise, avoidance, merging horizons and collective identification in complex modern society. Its empirical focus is Mauritius, and the material has largely been collected and analysed through anthropological methods;[1] but it is my hope that the book may have a lesson to teach us all – about the need to reconcile opposing interests, the importance of acknowledging both the existence of strong collective identifications and individual rights, and the sheer complexity of personal identification. It seeks to identify the fields and arenas where compromise is necessary, as well as those fields where either indifference or similarity are the only viable options. Writing this book has been a labour of love, as Mauritius, the site of my first ethnographic fieldwork, remains a society I feel strongly attached to. This sentimental attachment may occasionally interfere with academic pretensions, particularly in the concluding chapter; but as a compensation I offer sincerity and engagement.

In other words, this book is unabashedly (and unfashionably) normatively slanted. It must therefore be said that the reader looking for simple formulaic solutions to the challenges of multiculturalism in the New World, to the issue of social exclusion of ethnic minorities in the rich countries of the Old World, or for that matter solutions to ethnic competition and downright ethnic warfare in other countries, will have to go elsewhere, although these issues are also dealt with intermittently by way of comparison. What this study offers is essentially a thorough understanding of the political culture in Mauritius – one of the few stable democracies in the postcolonial world – and a demonstration of the ways in which Mauritians come to terms with their insistently multiethnic social environment.

If the normative orientation is unfashionable, central parts of the theoretical framework are no less so – quite undeservedly in my opinion. In the analysis, I draw extensively on the methods and concepts advocated by the Manchester School of urban anthropology, a group of researchers studying social change in Zambia from the 1940s to the 1960s. This body of work, pioneering in the study of ethnicity (or 'tribalism', as it was called at the time), can today be read as exceptional case studies in how new shared meaning can be developed through interaction between people of discrete cultural origins (see Chap. 3). There is, I hasten to add, a male bias, particularly in the ethnographic description, but also in the analysis of this book. Mauritius is a male-dominated society, and I am a male anthropologist. Complementary analyses, showing important dimensions that I have missed because of these shortcomings, are naturally necessary for a fuller picture. Although fieldwork in Mauritius was carried out in 1986 and in 1991–2, the ethnographic present is used throughout the book except when the temporal setting makes a difference.

Before moving on, it should finally be stated that this book is not primarily intended as a study of ethnicity and nationalism,[2] although the forms of identification analysed most carefully are, for obvious empirical reasons, ethnic and national ones. Its compass is both wider and narrower: it tries to identify the forms of compromise necessary for every complex society to function – compromises in political arenas and in the arena of married life, compromises between ethnic groups, between genders and between classes, between modernists and traditionalists, between Hindus and Christians, and between ethnic and non-ethnic forms of identification. Ethnicity and nation-building are central preoccupations for Mauritians, who frequently experience tensions between the two dimensions; but from this it does not follow that interethnic compromise is the key to peace and prosperity in every society. Other compromises may be more important, depending on the society in question and its internal contradictions.

Of course, when compromise fails, conflict ensues; and certain forms of conflict can sometimes be both necessary and desirable. In choosing to focus, in most of the book, on the integrative processes in Mauritian society rather than discussing the possibilities of future violent conflict, I have been loyal to the current spirit of Mauritian society itself. The focus is deliberate. In the early 1990s, I was temporarily employed as a researcher at the International Peace Research Institute (PRIO), analysing compromise, common denominators and peace in multiethnic societies. Eventually it transpired that I was the only person at PRIO carrying out research on peace. All the other peace researchers were studying conflict, in most cases 'death on a large scale', to quote PRIO's current Director, Dr Dan Smith. Rather than showing what doesn't work, this book shows what works and why.

Notes

1. Some of the ethnographic micro details have been tampered with; notably, some of the individuals presented have been compounded from several actual individuals. Mauritius is a small society, and some of my informants might not appreciate being identified.
2. For critical overviews of the anthropological literature on ethnicity and nationalism, the reader may consult Eriksen (1993b) and Banks (1996).

CHAPTER TWO

Mauritius Past and Present

Historical Junctures

Mauritius, a former British colony (1810–1968) and before that French (1710–1810), has been an independent state since March 1968 and a republic within the New Commonwealth since March 1992. Located just within the Tropic of Capricorn in the south-western Indian Ocean, roughly eight hundred kilometres east of Madagascar, the state comprises the islands of Mauritius and Rodrigues as well as a handful of small to tiny islands to the north, the latter often referred to as the 'outer islands'. Mauritius belongs, together with Rodrigues and neighbouring La Réunion, to the isolated Mascarenes archipelago, named after the Portuguese explorer Pedro de Mascarenha. When speaking of Mauritius in the following, I refer to the island proper unless otherwise stated. Mauritius is by far the largest island in the state, covering 1,850 of its total of 2,074 square kilometres; and of the 1.2 million inhabitants of the state, 96 per cent live on the main island.

Mauritius was unpopulated when discovered by Portuguese explorers in the latter half of the sixteenth century. This makes it one of the last inhabitable territories on Earth to be discovered and settled, seven hundred years after the permanent colonisation of barren Iceland by Norse sailors, and well over a thousand years after the Polynesian expansion had come to include remote Hawaii and Easter Island. The island may have been known to Arab sailors in medieval times, but the Austronesian speakers who became Madagascar's aboriginal population around AD 500 seem to have bypassed Mauritius, like the many tradesmen active in the Indian Ocean for centuries before European colonialism. The nearly constant south-eastern wind is doubtless part of the explanation for its remaining unknown for so long.

Despite its pleasant climate and fertile volcanic soil, the Portuguese never seriously attempted to colonise the island; the Dutch did a few decades later, however, and named it after their Prince Maurits van Nassau in 1598. Sixty years later the Dutch, after infamously exterminating the dodo (that flightless, goose-like bird that was for centuries Mauritius' main claim to fame), introduced sugar-cane and the Javanese deer from the Dutch East Indies to the island, but their colonising attempt must retrospectively be deemed as half-hearted, and it was ultimately unsuccessful. The last Dutch-men left Mauritius in 1710, following decades of slave revolts and a chronic shortage of European colonists and support from the metropole. When they eventually left the island, small groups of fugitive slaves, *esclaves marrons* as they were later called, may have remained in the forested hills of the south-west and south-east; their hypothetical descendants, if they could be identified, would be the aboriginal population of Mauritius.

• *The French and their slaves.* French colonisation began in 1710, but it is generally acknowledged that the colony, then rebaptised Île de France, was settled permanently only under the governorship of Mahé de Labour-donnais (1735–1745). Large numbers of slaves were then brought in from different parts of Africa, from Madagascar and the French colonies in southern India, and freemen trickled in at an increasing rate – skilled workers, traders, noblemen and adventurers from France, the Indian subcontinent and neighbouring Bourbon (which is today the French *Département-d'Outre-Mer* La Réunion). Most of the Indians came from the Malabar coast, and even today, the term *malbar* is used pejoratively about Hindus – although now the vast majority of Mauritius' Hindus are the descendants of North Indians. The capital Port-Louis was founded by Labourdonnais, under whose leadership plantation farming was also introduced, along with a wide variety of non-endemic plants (Toussaint 1971), many of which can be admired today in the botanical gardens at Pamplemousses, also founded by Labourdonnais. Unlike many Caribbean plantation societies, Mauritius was never a net supplier of goods during the French period (Arno and Orian 1986). Its function in the French Empire was chiefly that of a port strategically located between Africa and Mada-gascar on the one hand, and India and the Far East on the other.

The slaves who were brought to Mauritius in this period largely came from Madagascar and East Africa, and the West African component, although present, was thus never as substantial as in the New World. Even today, Mauritians of African or Malagasy origin may speak with resentment about the *tem margoze* – the time of slavery, which is said to have been as bitter as the vegetable *margoze*. During slavery, a French-lexicon Creole evolved, first as a *lingua franca* used in slave–master and slave–slave contexts, and eventually as the mother-tongue of the slaves and free blacks. As Bernardin de St Pierre's travelogue (1983 [1773]) indicates, the Creole spoken in Mauritius during the late eighteenth century was essentially the same language as that which is the main vernacular in contemporary Mauritius (as well as being spoken, with slight variations, in the Seychelles).[1]

A new ethnic category emerged during the French period: the Coloureds, or *gens de couleur*. Often the children of plantation owners and slavewomen, the Coloureds were unable to inherit from their fathers, but might receive an education as a compensation. Educated Coloureds aspiring to membership in Franco-Mauritian society were – and still are – generally rejected (see Dumas 1974 [1843] for an early, fictional account; Humbert 1979 for a more recent description), although they are socially and culturally closer to the Franco-Mauritians than to any other group.

• *British rule*. During the Napoleonic Wars, Britain seized Île de France in a sea battle off the south-western coast of the island (December 1810), and rebaptised it Mauritius (the French version of the name became, and still is, Île Maurice). No attempt was made to discourage the several thousand Frenchmen and Creoles[2] settled there; the prosperous, well-organised community of planters was recognised as a valuable asset. In fact, the capitulation, authored by the British and signed by the French in 1810, guaranteed that the inhabitants should be allowed to keep their customs, traditions and religion (slaves were, naturally, not considered inhabitants proper). Both the English and French languages were – and still are – used in politics and administration. Many British administrators were eventually assimilated into the Franco-Mauritian category, such as the family of the famous Francophone poet Robert-Edward Hart; but the opposite did not happen. When Charles Darwin visited the island on his way home with the *Beagle* in 1836, he expressed dismay at its slight degree of Anglicisation (Hollingworth 1965), as did the Anglican missionary Beaton, arriving a couple of decades later (Beaton 1977 [1859]). Indeed, similar reactions are not uncommon today, after 158 years of British colonisation and thirty years of independence with a constitution written in English.

• *The Asians*. Slavery was abandoned in 1835, and, because of the disappearance of the former slaves from the plantations (for reasons still debated by Mauritian and foreign historians; see Allen 1983; Quenette 1985; Arno and Orian 1986; Bissoondoyal and Servansing 1989) and the continued growth of the sugar industry, large numbers of indentured labourers destined for the sugar fields were brought in from several parts of India, through a grand scheme of labour migration famously described by Tinker (1974) as a new form of slavery (see also Bissoondoyal and Servansing 1986;

Carter 1995 represents a novel perspective on indentureship). Already in the 1860s, Indians accounted for over half the Mauritian population. A few decades later, Chinese immigration, up to then modest, increased and was fairly substantial until the mid-twentieth century, culminating in the aftermath of the Maoist revolution of 1949 (see Ly-Tio-Fane Pineo 1985 for details).

• *Post-independence politics*. Mauritius achieved independence after negotiations with the British, followed by General Elections and widespread social unrest in the towns, particularly in Port-Louis. A remarkable 44 per cent of the electorate voted for the anti-independence coalition. There were scattered incidents of violent ethnic unrest before and after independence (see Chap. 7), but there has been no public, violent ethnic unrest since 1969.

The political system is modelled on the British Westminster system, which ensures stable majorities but not proportional representation. For example, in the 1982 General Election, the winning coalition got only about 65 per cent of the votes but all the contested seats; in the 1996 General Election, the figures were 80 per cent of the votes and all contested seats. Of the 70 seats in the Legislative Assembly, however, only 62 are actually elected, 60 from mainland Mauritius (3 for each constituency) and 2 from Rodrigues. The remaining 8 seats are distributed to runners-up according to an ingenious mechanism known as the 'Best Loser system', on the basis of ethnic membership (the first four) and a combination of ethnicity and party membership (the remaining four). The rationale behind the 'Best Loser system' is the wish to ensure that all ethnic groups are represented in the Legislative Assembly. Its critics (see Chap. 8; see also Nave n.d. 1) argue that it contributes to entrenching ethnic divisions in a situation where class differences have become more important.

Potential ethnic conflicts, issues relating to sugar and the until recently high population growth (3.5 per cent in the mid-1960s, 1.4 per cent in the mid-1990s) dominated public discourse during the first decade of independence, which saw the emergence and immediately high popularity of an ostensibly non-ethnically-based political party, the leftist populist MMM (*Mouvement Militant Mauricien*, see Chap. 7), which was the main opposition to Seewoosagur Ramgoolam's Labour Party/*Parti Travailliste* during the 1970s, until winning the 1982 General Elections. From 1982 to 1995, Aneerood Jugnauth was Prime Minister, first (1982–3) for the MMM, and then for the splinter party MSM (*Mouvement Socialiste Militant*). Other parties include the *Parti Socialiste Social Démocrate* (PMSD). As the Westminster model favours a two-bloc system, coalitions have been frequent.

Official national symbolism in Mauritius is still closely linked to the colonial ideology and its symbols; there has been no popular ideological wave of anticolonial resentment in Mauritius even remotely resembling New World social movements such as Black Power, Négritude or Rastafarianism in impact.

The main foreign issue of independent Mauritius has been the Diego Garcia conflict. Diego Garcia is a part of the Chagos Archipelago, situated roughly half-way between Mauritius and the Indian subcontinent. During colonial times, the archipelago was a dependency of Mauritius; however, one of the conditions of the British–Mauritian agreement over independence was that the islands should be ceded to Britain. Britain then leased the islands to the United States. Today, Diego Garcia is the site of an American naval base of considerable strategic importance (see Bowman 1991:157–62 for details; see also Simmons 1982).

Diego Garcia was populated by some 1,200 persons originating in Mauritius, though some of them were born on the atoll. The *Ilois*, as they are known, were repatriated in the early 1970s. Compensation was paid and accepted, yet the *Ilois* ('Islanders') have experienced serious difficulties in adapting to Mauritian society. They are widely regarded as a social problem, and most of them belong to the very poorest segments of the population, leading precarious lives on the outskirts of Port-Louis (Walker 1986). In addition, it has been established that the ceding of Diego Garcia to Britain was illegal according to international law. Finally, it has been conclusively shown that the definition of the Ilois as 'temporary workers', which justified their 'repatriation', was false; there were actually permanent villages on the island. The case has been brought to international courts, and Mauritius has received much sympathy, notably from Third World countries; but there has been no tangible progress.

• *International connections.* Despite its geographical proximity to Africa, Mauritius cannot be considered an African country proper. Although some 30 per cent of its population is of largely African and/or Malagasy extraction, the actual socio-cultural configurations throughout the island are very different from those in most African areas. Mauritius has been built from scratch since 1715, and has in most respects much more in common with West Indian islands than with virtually any African society of comparable scale (see Eriksen 1991c, 1992a for comparisons with Trinidad). Mauritius is a member of the OAU (Organisation for African Unity), but many maps of Africa exclude Mauritius, and in standard works of African history, Mauritius is more often than not absent from the index (see e.g. Davidson 1978). Mauritius is the only country in the world to be simultaneously a member of La Francophonie and the New Commonwealth

– a characteristic expression of the kind of cultural complexity at work in the island.

The most important trade partners are the EU (notably the UK and France), the USA, South Africa, Australia, Japan and Taiwan, and cultural bonds are healthier in relation to virtually any other region in the Old World other than Africa. The South African transition from apartheid may change this.

Mauritius has an increasing number of air links with the Western world, and is served by frequent cargo ships. The airport at Plaisance was expanded in the late 1980s.

Not sensing that they belong to a continent, Mauritians of non-African origin tend to turn to their real or postulated ancestral homelands for a self-identification of loftier scope, temporally and spatially, than the options locally available. Finally, the western Indian Ocean is a regional unit of increasing relevance, both strategically on a global level (Selwyn 1983; Bowman 1991), and in terms of local cooperation. These processes, which will be discussed in greater detail later, are highly consequential for the development of new social identifications in Mauritius. Despite its physical insularity, it would have been impossible to make sense of any event in Mauritian history without an understanding of its positioning in global and regional systems. In an era of intensified globalisation, this holds true today more than ever before.

The Economy

Mauritius has a population density of more than 500 individuals per square kilometre, which places it among the world's top five (excluding 'mini-states'). Some 52 per cent of the total land area is under sugar-cane cultivation and about 7 per cent is grown with tea. There is little arable land not under current exploitation.

• *Sugar.* Capitalism, regarded as a system of production and not exclusively one of exchange, truly began in Mauritius in the 1820s. Before this period, its main function had been that of a seaport. Mauritius was, in other words, a latecomer to the plantation economy (R. Virahsawmy 1986). This explains why Mauritius (along with Trinidad, Guyana, Fiji and Natal) should receive so many Indian indentured labourers after the abolition of slavery, since other important British sugar colonies, such as Barbados and Jamaica, did not. In Mauritius, the sugar industry was in its initial phase of growth when the supply of cheap labour suddenly became uncertain. Today, Mauritians of Indian origin constitute about 65 per cent of the total population, the highest proportion in any society outside India.

Unlike some West Indian islands, notably Trinidad, Mauritius did not switch to cocoa during the decline in the sugar industry, which lasted from approximately 1860 to 1908 (Toussaint 1971:101), and the island may have been among the poorest colonies in the British empire during this period. Increases in sugar prices in 1920–23 ameliorated conditions somewhat (ibid.:115), but Mauritius was by and large a poverty-stricken society lacking in career opportunities until the early 1980s. In his well-informed, if cynical, essay 'The Overcrowded Barracoon' from the early 1970s, V. S. Naipaul (1973) depicts Mauritius as an absurd island that everyone wants to leave, and an opinion poll carried out by SOFRÈS in April 1977 indeed suggests that 75 per cent of the population would wish their children to emigrate.

• *Diversification*. Sugar prices rose in the early 1970s, followed by a recession in the late 1970s and early 1980s, marked by high levels of emigration and unemployment. Switching to strategies of industrialisation by invitation and tourism, Mauritius has nonetheless experienced uninterrupted and fast economic growth, based on manufacturing and tourism, since around 1983. During 1986, the unemployment rate fell from more than 20 per cent to nil. The political scientist Simmons, writing a few years before the economic take-off, notes that 'just as the waving fields of sugarcane dominate the plateau, sugar – the crop, the industry, the employer – dominates the economic political and social patterns of the island' (Simmons, 1982:7). A few years later, this is no longer the case.

The division of labour has traditionally been strongly ethnically corre-lated, and despite significant changes on the ground, folk notions still tend to associate particular ethnic groups with particular forms of livelihood. Hindus are associated with agriculture (as labourers or small planters) and increasingly with the public service; Creoles[3] are fishermen, dockers, or factory artisans or belong to various other categories of manual, skilled or semi-skilled work; the Coloureds or *gens de couleur* are lawyers, journalists, or teachers or belong to similar liberal professions; Sino-Mauritians are involved in business; Muslims are either merchants or labourers; Tamils are to be found everywhere; Franco-Mauritians are 'sugar barons' or high executives.

These folk assumptions linking ethnicity and class were fairly accurate until the mid-1980s, with a few exceptions, such as the fact that it is not true that a large proportion of the Creoles have ever made their living as fishermen, as is commonly assumed. Indeed, throughout the postwar period there have been more Creoles working in the sugar fields (a kind of work for which Creoles have a proverbial abhorrence) than there have been full-time fishermen in the entire island. It is nonetheless true that a majority of Mauritian fishermen are Creoles, that many Creoles spend their afternoons and weekends fishing, that many of the coastal villages have Creole majorities, and that many unemployed Creoles fish for their own consumption, and these facts may explain the persistence of this mistaken notion.

Settlement is ethnically correlated, but most localities are mixed. As a rule, there is a Hindu majority in rural areas except in certain coastal villages, which are Creole-dominated, while there are non-Hindu majorities in the towns. However, in the Hindu villages there is always a non-Hindu minority, usually including a resident Sino-Mauritian shopkeeper's family, and most of them have ample numbers of Creoles, Muslims and Tamils as well. In any urban neighbourhood, further, whether predominantly settled by Sino-Mauritians, Creoles or Muslims, there are always families belonging to other ethnic categories. Except for Port-Louis, settlement in the towns is differentiated along class criteria and thus does not follow ethnic lines in so far as the two criteria do not coincide. Besides, distances are short and the road infrastructure is good: there is, in other words, necessarily a great deal of casual interethnic contact.

Ethnicity

Mauritian society is, if anything, a plural one. The absence of a clear ethnic majority, aboriginal or not, calls for compromise or coercion; both options have been chosen in various situations in the colonial past. Independent Mauritius is a functioning multi-party parliamentary democracy (the voter turnout at the General Elections in December 1995 was nearly 80 per cent) whose inhabitants are to a remarkable extent aware of the predicaments of multiethnicity in a nation-state. Policies of compromise alternate with policies of avoidance and 'melting-pot' policies leading to identity formation along non-ethnic lines throughout an enormous range of social contexts, many of which will be investigated in the remainder of this book. More than twenty public holidays, representing the entire range of religious and ethnic variation in the island, are celebrated every year. As a rule, symbolic expressions of ethnicity are encouraged by Mauritian politicians, while communalism[4] is overtly discouraged but widely practised.

Although the ethnic groups of 1997 are culturally less distinctive than those of 1897 would have been, Mauritians perceive themselves in many situations as being qualitatively different from members of other ethnic groups. This is a feature so pervasive and multifaceted in everyday inter-action that it cannot be accounted for as a purely political phenomenon.

The very construction of the social person is based on ethnicity in Mauritius. It could be said that, like class in Britain, race in the USA, clan in Somalia or nationhood in Norway, ethnic identity (*apartnans kominoter*) is an ontology shared by the overwhelming majority of Mauritians. The cognitive map dividing the population into ethnic groups is, in other words, *a shared cultural notion that emphasises internal differences.*

• *Local taxonomies*. It is in principle impossible to state 'how many ethnic categories' there are in Mauritius. According to the former official ethnic classification, still often invoked although formally abandoned in 1982, there are four – Hindus (52 per cent), Muslims (16 per cent), Sino-Mauritians (3 per cent) and General Population (29 per cent). It may be noted here that the criteria for dividing the population into ethnic categories are inconsistent: two of the categories are essentially religious ones, one of them is based on geography, and the final one is a residual category. At certain points in the postwar history of Mauritius, the four officially recognised communities[5] have functioned as political entities, but this has not invariably been the case. Earlier classifications, such as the one used in the Census of 1901, were racially based, whereas this one, using neither 'race', religion nor geographical origin as its unambiguous criterion for differentiation, describes potential political alignments; and as such, the classification – its basic logic dating back to the 1944 Census – was obsolete in 1968, and is even more so now. The taxonomy, first used in the 1952 Census (Mauritius 1953), was retained by the first government of independent Mauritius, ostensibly in order to ensure that each community be fairly represented in public bodies. It was abandoned by the 1982–3 MMM government because it allegedly served to reproduce a sense of communal (ethnic) belonging no longer seen as desirable; but in practice it still exists through the Best Loser system. The 1944 classification also remains embedded in shared cultural representations; it is often criticised and opposed, and thereby it is confirmed.

The criterion for membership in the puzzling fourth ethnic community, first used in the 1952 Census (Mauritius 1953), is that the person in question, 'does not appear, from his way of life, to belong of one or other of these three [other] communities' (Constitution of Mauritius, Schedule I, §4). In fact, the category 'General Population' consists of a small group of white Franco-Mauritians (about 2 per cent of the current population, following considerable emigration around Independence); a much larger category of Creoles (usually defined as Catholics of African or mixed African-European, African-Indian and/or African-Chinese descent); and classificatory anomalies, including Christian Tamils,[6] as well as people whose ancestors might have come from as many as eight different geographical regions, and who at least nominally are Christians. Neither the 'General Population' nor its non-white component can meaningfully be said to constitute a socio-cultural entity. Apart from the most fundamental principles of internal differentiation, wealth, education and the 'amount of milk in the coffee', that is skin colour, the Coloured-Creole category is a slippery and elusive one with a great deal of internal differentiation, sometimes even on a situational basis, so that an individual who would be considered a non-Coloured Creole in town could be perceived as a Coloured in the countryside.

The Franco-Mauritians also form socially distinctive groups. Those who claim aristocratic descent have until recently been strongly endogamous; among the 'commoners', further, anybody who marries a non-white person (usually a Coloured) loses considerable social capital despite the obvious cultural continuity represented through the marriage, Coloureds being Francophone Catholics.

The three remaining 'communities' also fail to present obvious cases of tight ethnic organisation. Before the Second World War, the majority of the Mauritian population was simply classified as Indo-Mauritians; then, successively, the Muslims (16 per cent) and Tamils/Telugus (9 per cent) broke away politically; and Hindus from the low castes are not necessarily members of the same ethnic category as members of the 'twice-born' castes (see Chap. 4). Indians of North Indian descent, most of them Biharis, are now sometimes spoken of as 'Hindi-speaking' (although they do not speak Hindi, but Kreol and possibly Bhojpuri). The Muslims are divided into Sunnis, Shi'ites and Ahmadis, as well as having their own endogamous 'high castes', the Meimons and Surtees. The Tamils are divided along caste lines, while the Sino-Mauritian community has been split first along linguistic lines (Hakka and Cantonese), and later along political lines following the Chinese revolution in 1949. As a general rule, moreover, differences between townsmen and villagers potentially divide all ethnic categories except the Sino-Mauritians and Franco-Mauritians.

One cannot, then, speak of ethnic groups as 'objective entities', nor of ethnic membership as a categorical and unambiguous quality of individuals. Group membership is highly conditional, and the actual compass of a particular ethnically-based collectivity depends on the context. Continuous redefinitions of ethnic categories and of the relevance of ethnicity take place responding to changes in situation and context – changes that may occur on local as well as global levels of society.

• *Language issues.* Mauritian language controversies are closely tied to issues of ethnicity. The complexities of the Mauritian language situation have been discussed in a large number of analyses (a comprehensive review of literature appears in the opening chapters of Stein 1983; see also Baker and Hookoomsing 1987). According to official figures, Mauritius bears a strong resemblance to the Tower of Babel; fortunately for the Mauritians, the actual situation is much tidier (see Chap. 5). According to official statistics, about 15 languages are spoken. Their distribution – spatially, numerically and situationally – is nevertheless very uneven. The official language, English, is virtually absent from the linguistic repertoire of the majority of the population. It is used in official documents, in academic writings and to a limited extent in the mass media; English is also an important language in school, but it is generally poorly learnt. French is by far the most important European language in Mauritius. Most Mauritians speak it, many speak it very well, and it is usually the first language in which one acquires literacy. Well over half the national radio and television broadcasts are in French; North American films are dubbed in French; bookshops have extensive selections of French novels (and English ones in French translation); and both daily and weekly newspapers are edited almost exclusively in French. However, English is a language many wish to master, and its prestige is reflected in the English names of several of the French-language publications.

Although it is probably correct that most Mauritians could if they had to, few actually speak French in daily social interaction. The language conventionally spoken by the great majority of Mauritians is *Kreol*,[7] a French-lexicon Creole whose origins go back to slave–master and slave–slave contexts in the first half of the eighteenth century;[8] which later (in the eighteenth and nineteenth centuries) became the mother tongue for the non-white Catholics and a *lingua franca* in the island as a whole; and which today is the mother tongue for a growing majority of the Mauritian population, although it retains ethnic connotations, being still primarily associated with the Creoles.

Other languages currently spoken in informal settings are Bhojpuri (a Bihari/Eastern Uttar Pradeshi variant of Hindi) and Hakka (a southern Chinese language). Tamil, Telugu, Arabic, Marathi, Latin, Urdu, Hindi and English – ritual and sometimes literary languages – are probably no longer languages Mauritians speak with their children. In some cases, they never were. Their main significance is often symbolic, as markers of identity (see Chap. 5).

- *Dilemmas of polyethnicity.* Mauritian society faces predicaments to which there is no solution but compromise, given that democratic procedures are taken for granted – it would for instance have been highly difficult for the Muslim community to introduce *Sharia*, should they have wished to; government decisions about family planning are received less than enthusiastically in strongly Catholic neighbourhoods, but cannot be overruled locally; and there can never be a national religion – and perhaps English is a good compromise as a national language, as Naipaul might have put it, because nobody speaks it.

• *Common denominators.* A general principle that can be extracted from the multilayered functioning of Mauritian society, which is going to be a central concept in this book, is that which I shall speak of as the *principle of the lowest common denominator* in social interaction between members of different ethnic groups. Briefly put, this dictum implies that similarities and shared horizons, or platforms for discourse and interaction, are actively sought in everyday practices as well as in politics. Sometimes the lowest common denominator is a large number, as it were; in other cases, as among close friends, it is a small one. Integration can thus be conceptualised as a matter of degree (in this way, one of the least exciting social science debates of recent years can be avoided): a society is not either integrated or disintegrated, but it is integrated in certain respects and to certain degrees. Processes which lead to common denominators are the very opposite of schismogenetic processes (Bateson 1972), where communication breaks down and customary behaviour patterns mechanically reproduce and deepen conflict. The armaments race is the quintessential example of schismogenesis.

Four ethnic categories are customarily reified at an abstract and general level by Mauritians. But if a common myth of origin is considered an important defining mark for an ethnic group, then the island has at least eight ethnic groups;[9] and if one chooses to stress the endogamy rule, the number may rise to around twenty (depending on the choice of informants, as these things are contested); whereas if ancestral language is to be invoked as a differentiating criterion, at least fifteen ethnic groups may be counted. This ought to make it clear, if there should be any doubt, that ethnicity is and remains a relational and situational kind of social phenomenon, defined from the inside and not by objective criteria (see also Chaps. 3 and 4).

Change

A striking feature of contemporary Mauritian society, which merits some initial comment, is its current pace of social change. At Independence, the island was fully dependent on sugar for foreign exchange; since then, the economy has diversified remarkably, and, by the second half of the 1990s, the country may safely be described as a NIC (Newly Industrialised Country). An industrial 'zone' (the Export Processing Zone, EPZ, called the *zone franche* locally), modelled on similar projects in East Asia, was founded in 1971 and has since then grown at an uneven pace. However, the number of employees in EPZ enterprises doubled from late 1983 to late 1985 (Yeung and Yin 1986, Leffler 1988) and passed the sugar industry as the largest source of employment in the late 1980s, becoming the most important earner of foreign exchange during the early 1990s, representing 45 per cent of the total exports by 1995, compared to sugar's 40 per cent. In addition, tourism has also become an important industry, even if Mauritian governments have hitherto actively avoided the kind of mass tourism encountered in certain parts of the Caribbean.[10] Emigration numbers fell dramatically, and unemployment disappeared so fast that by the late 1980s Mauritian authorities were importing construction labour from Malaysia.

Another factor that distinguishes Mauritius from most Southern countries is the fact that there is no rural exodus; indeed, the urban population is growing more slowly than that of many rural areas. Industry is not restricted to a spatial zone, and many of the new factories are established in large villages, several of which (notably Flacq, Bambous and Triolet) now have the size and complexity of small towns. Only about 43 per cent of the Mauritian population are classified as urban by the World Bank, but less than 5 per cent live more than an hour and a half, by public transport, from the nearest town. As was shown by Burton Benedict (1966), the small scale of Mauritian society is an important factor for analysis: it can never attain the complexity of nations such as Indonesia or South Africa, and single events and individuals can make a big difference. Further, the distance between the élites and the masses is usually much shorter, by way of social networks, in Mauritius than, say, in Great Britain or Kenya.

• *Cultural homogenisation.* Since the beginning of the twentieth century, the Mauritian population has in important respects become culturally homogenised. The spread of the Kreol language into the Hindu/Muslim countryside during the twentieth century (see Chap. 5) is an indication of this. Officially, about 90 per cent of the population is literate, and, although this figure is too high, a majority can read and write French and sometimes English. The largest newspaper, the French-language weekly *Week-End*, has a circulation of about 60,000, and 90 per cent of Mauritian households had a TV set by the mid- to late 1990s. The system of education is nearly uniform, and primary schooling is in theory free and compulsory. There having been no significant peasantry or 'traditional' mode of production in the island, the entire population has since the very beginning of colonialisation been integrated into a capitalist system of production and consumption; but this integration is growing in intensity with increased education, social and geographic mobility (including a growing number of European-educated returnees) and mass media consumption. Although these processes of homogenisation are not necessarily acknowledged by the agents, who may tend still to stress 'how different they are', they can easily be observed – a point to which we will return in a later chapter.

• *Revitalisation*. At the level of actual representations and everyday practices, it can be argued that the various ethnic segments of the Mauritian population are becoming more similar. On the other hand – and that is a common paradox of ethnicity – there has in many regards been an inverse relationship between the development of ethnic self-consciousness and the development of shared culture crossing ethnic boundaries (see Chaps. 7 and 8). The dissolution of boundaries in some contexts leads to the reassertion of boundaries in others.

Notes

1. Although the generic term 'Creole' is used of all languages that have evolved from pidgins, French-lexicon Creoles differ greatly. The Creole spoken in La Réunion is not immediately intelligible to Mauritians, and Haitian Creole, for example, is very different from Mauritian Creole (Jourdain 1956, Goodman 1964, Chaudenson 1979).
2. The word 'Creole', used as a non-linguistic, sociological category, has a large number of different meanings. Here it is used in the late eighteenth-century French sense (identical to the original meaning of the Spanish *criollo*): namely, a white person born in a colony.
3. 'Creole' here and in the rest of the book refers, except when stated otherwise, to a Mauritian wholly or partially descended from African and Malagasy slaves, following Mauritian usage. The terms Coloured and *gens de couleur* are used throughout the text to distinguish a *sociological*, not primarily a 'racial', sub-category of Creoles, although it is a common folk assumption that ethnic categories are 'really' racial ones.
4. The term (*kominalis* in Kreol) is used in roughly the same way as in India, denoting particularistic politics threatening national cohesion by invoking 'primordial loyalties' at a subnational level.
5. Adopting Indian usage, Mauritians describe their main ethnic categories as communities (in Kreol, *kominote*).
6. In some cases, these families have been converts since the mid-nineteenth century; in others the conversion took place last week. Sometimes they are not referred to as Tamils at all nor perceive themselves as South Indians, even if there has been little or no intermarriage with others. They are then lumped with the Creoles as a Creole sub-group of uncertain or 'mixed' origin.

7. This spelling, introduced by Philip Baker (1972), distinguishes the language from the ethnic category. The orthography exemplified in this work, developed by Baker, by the linguist Vinesh Hookoomsing (Baker and Hookoomsing 1987), by the militant group LPT (*Ledikasyon pu travayer*, Education for Work; LPT 1978, 1985) and by the cultural one-man movement Dev Virahsawmy (who since 1966 has insisted on calling the language *Morisiê*, that is Mauritian), is based on the International Phonetic Alphabet (IPA). French orthography is still often used in written Kreol, and many Mauritians, trained to read French, complain that the Baker orthography is difficult to read. However, most scholars agree that if Kreol is ever to achieve status as something more than a poor man's French, it should avoid adopting the idiosyncrasies of French spelling. When citing a Kreol word or phrase, I use the LPT's orthography, which is nearly identical to the *lortograf linite* proposed by Baker and Hookoomsing (1987), the only difference being Baker and Hookoomsing's use of diacritical signs for nasalisation (making the Kreol alphabet identical to the one used locally for Bhojpuri), while the LPT instead double the consonant (*m* or *n*, as the case may be) when it is not nasalised. Since Kreol and French are closely related at the level of vocabulary, readers with a knowledge of French may profit from pronouncing the Kreol words quoted in the text *in French*: many of them will thereby become intelligible (e.g. *bonom* for *bonhomme*, *kominote* for *communauté*, *sakenn* for *chacun/chacune*).

8. For many years, it was held, by linguists and others, that French-lexicon Creoles consisted of 'French words and African grammar'. However, Goodman (1964:138–9), the first to carry out a truly comparative study of French-derived Creoles, admits uncertainty regarding the relative roles played by varieties of French and African languages in the formation of fairly similar French Creoles. Today, the general hypothesis of the 'African substratum' has largely been abandoned, although African languages have clearly played a role in the development of Kreol and other French-lexicon Creoles. For one thing, the presumedly uniform 'substratum' cannot be the same in Haitian and Mauritian Creole, since the largest groups of slaves in the two islands came from different parts of Africa. It seems more likely that many of the similarities that cannot be traced back to standard French derive from seventeenth- and eighteenth-century Breton seafarers' French. See Hancock (1979) for the general scholarly debate on Creole languages; see Corne and Baker (1983) for an updated discussion with particular reference to the Mauritian and Seychellois Creole ('Isle de France Creole').

9. French, African, (North Indian) Hindu, Tamil, Muslim, Hakka-speaking, Cantonese-speaking and *gens de couleur* (mixed Euro-African).

10. For example, it is illegal to build a hotel that stands taller than the tallest coconut palm on the beach.

CHAPTER THREE

Fields and Levels of Mauritian Society

The Duality of Culture

Analytic terms such as culture, ethnicity, nation and identity are no longer as simple and seemingly straightforward as they may have been in the anthropological past. The main reason is probably that apart from forming part of an academic vocabulary, they have entered politics and folk discourses all over the world, often carrying a different meaning from that employed in the social sciences. There is by now a vigorous academic cottage industry grappling with, deconstructing, refining, challenging and defending – as the case may be – these concepts, and they will inevitably have to be discussed critically as the analysis proceeds. Fundamental questions regarding the nature of society and its relationship to its constituent groups, the state and individual agents are raised through such apparently arid and scholastic discussions, which are therefore, at the end of the day, far from unimportant. At the moment, the most pressing task nevertheless consists in beginning to familiarise the reader with social life in Mauritius as it unfolds in everyday interaction, and I shall therefore limit myself to a few – admittedly lengthy – preliminary remarks.

•   *Structure and flow.* There has been a general tendency in the last few decades of anthropological theorising to move from an emphasis on boundaries, homogeneity, stability and fixity to a focus on flux, ambiguity, fuzziness and 'grey zones' in the conceptualisation of culture and social relationships. This is certainly the case as regards the concept of *culture*. In the dominant cultural anthropological tradition from the eighteenth-century Romantic Herder through the founding father Boas to contemporary masters such as Lévi-Strauss, Geertz and Sahlins, culture was conceived of as *stable* through time, sharply *bounded* in relation to other cultures, and *shared* by its members. It is now increasingly seen as a fluid and ambiguous phenomenon, and shared culture must therefore be seen as a matter of degree (see e.g. Clifford 1988; Appadurai 1990; Strathern 1991; Hannerz 1992; Eriksen 1993c; Friedman 1994). In the analysis of Mauritian society,

I will show the usefulness of such a perspective: rather than asking whether or not two individuals share the same culture, we may ask in which respects they share a symbolic universe and in which respects they do not. Likewise, the term *identification* is currently more palatable to many anthropologists than the term *identity*, as the former word connotes something that is dynamic and shifting. However, as the analysis will also show, identification is both chosen and determined; identity is *both* situational and imperative.

• *Degrees of similarity*. Although Mauritius must be considered a *society* in accordance with any reasonable definition of the term,[1] it seems highly problematic to talk of a single, substantial Mauritian form of *culture*. As regards the social distribution of the symbolic and cognitive structures that constitute culture, one can insist, as natives in every society often do, that all individuals are unique and idiosyncratic, or perhaps that ethnic groups differ significantly culturally (this would be the view of 'plural society' theorists, notably M. G. Smith (1965), as well as that of many Mauritians). On the other hand, it may also plausibly be said that anyone successfully socialised into a society either adheres to or opposes certain learnt rules for thought and behaviour, a shared pattern or matrix that intrinsically relates his or her actions to an ambiguous, but universally intelligible system of signification. Culture can in this sense be regarded as *the ways in which one can conceivably lead one's life*. Culture is not to agree on everything, but rather consists in the ability to disagree, since disagreement presupposes shared categories. There are necessarily cultural ways of coping with the opposite sex, finding work or performing a task; there are culturally specific ways of posing the perennial as well as the superficial questions of existence. Culturally specific knowledge may include knowing when to speak French instead of Kreol, how to vote, for whom and why, understanding why a *séga* song is funny, knowing how and when to get into and out of debt – and there are also specific, implicit rules for the cultural expression of spontaneity: the display of emotions, cursing, laughter, shrugging and nearly all forms of body movements. Culture, or *habitus* in Bourdieu's (1977, 1980) overused terminology, is in this way virtually inscribed into the bodies of its carriers. It need not be available to discursive reasoning; when it is, culture is being ideologised and reified, since it becomes negotiable. This, simply put, is why only *communicated* cultural differences contribute to ethnic relations.

• *Duality of culture*. Since cultural differences vary contextually, culture must itself be regarded as a property of particular social contexts (or language-games, Eriksen 1991a). On the other hand, culture is a necessary condition for the context defining it. It is thus necessary to think of culture as something analogous to Giddens' (1979, 1984; see discussion below) conceptualisation of social structure as dual. A thorough deconstruction of culture into the varying meaning-aspects of concrete social relationships, however, deprives us of the possibility of grasping culture as a complete system of signifiers – and this presents us with a problem. On the one hand, culture is neither a property of a person nor an integrated symbolic system; this is never more evident than in polyethnic societies, where competing cultural systems may present themselves within the shared frames of relevance, through competition, as potentially relevant. On the other hand, however, culture *is* a thing, *une chose sociale* in Durkheim's and Mauss's sense, in so far as it provides a context necessary for agency to be meaningful. We must therefore arrive at an understanding of culture that makes it impossible to talk of, say, North American culture, or Mauritian culture, without specifying the context – while at the same time not reducing culture to individual agency.

In so far as our focus is on the communication of cultural differences and identities, which is the underlying concern throughout this work, then a substantial definition of culture, or of 'the culture' under consideration, is not required, since the main object of study consists in demarcating acts signifying cultural discreteness. The cultural difference is postulated by the agent him- or herself and is as such socially relevant. A seeming paradox of the contemporary world, frequently mentioned by non-anthropologists as a puzzling fact, namely that as 'objective cultural differences' diminish, the political importance of assumed cultural differences increases, thus becomes perfectly understandable. This distinction is crucial not only for understanding Mauritian society, but also for a general comparative understanding of identity politics in the modern world.

The political issue contrasting 'national culture' with cultural pluralism and differentiation, an important topic in the ideological discourse of Mauritian society, thus pertains not so much to the distinction between identity (or 'sameness') and difference, but to the *communication* of sameness and difference. The limits of shared culture, conversely, are the limits of shared representations made relevant in a particular situation of interaction.

• *Ethnicity*. The concept of *ethnicity*, although more recent and less central to the discipline than culture, has also undergone profound changes. Despite its ubiquity in the literature, it remains somewhat vague. The word ethnicity, as employed in social anthropology, is becoming increasingly difficult, as it is being used in interpretations of a growing range of social contexts; some displaying strong family resemblances, some highly different. As a theoretical term, ethnicity remains seducingly vague.

Following dramatic social change in many of the geographical heartlands of social anthropological research, ethnicity has somehow become a word of comprehensive connotations, indispensable to those who try to come to terms with these processes of change. It is sometimes, simplistically, reduced to a peculiar form of political organisation. Although politicised, orchestrated ethnicity is more spectacular than the ethnic identity quietly reproduced through ritual and everyday interaction, and more easily depicted through elegant models, the latter is no less significant, socially and culturally, than the former. Indeed, in Mauritius, one of the largest ethnic categories, the Creoles, have a perfectly dreadful political record, partly because of certain enduring particularities in their own social expression of ethnic distinctiveness. This not only implies that ethnicity has many aspects of which politics is but one; it also entails that ethnicity is best conceptualised as something altogether *different* from the 'ethnic political organisation', the latter being a possible *result* of a certain ethnic configuration but being far from a necessary condition for its existence.

Through the anti-essentialist work of, *inter alios*, Edmund Leach (1954), J. Clyde Mitchell (1956), A. L. Epstein (1958), Fredrik Barth (1969), Harald Eidheim (1971), Abner Cohen (1969, 1974a, 1974b), A. P. Cohen (1985, 1994) and Edwin Ardener (1989), the focus of ethnic studies in anthropology has gradually shifted from comparative descriptions of group characteristics to analyses of properties of social process, including acts of signification. Ethnicity is now seen as an aspect of a *relationship*, not as an innate quality of a group. The relationship between ethnicity and culture, as these and many other scholars have noted, is complicated, and since it is crucial for an understanding of Mauritian society, it will be dealt with later. Like culture and social integration, ethnicity is a contextual and not an absolute phenomenon. Handelman's (1977) typology of degrees of ethnic incorporation – from the mere ethnic category via the ethnic network to the ethnic association and the ethnic community – is a good starting-point for investigating the actual significance of ethnicity in a person's life, and even if it is not equally applicable everywhere, it reminds us that 'there is ethnicity and ethnicity', which many books on the subject, including Horowitz' impressive survey of ethnic conflicts worldwide (Horowitz 1985), do not: what it *means to be ethnic* is not at all the same among Swedish-Americans in the Midwest and among Russians in Kazakhstan.

Any fashionable attempt to sanctify 'the native's point of view' as authoritative in a description of Mauritian society or 'culture' would be ridiculous, and in the study of such complex societies (as indeed of any society) it is apparent that there is no such thing as *the* native's point of view if one talks of more than one person, and that there are distinctive levels of social reality relevant for analysis. That, however, does not mean that such shared forms of discourse do not exist, but that shared culture as well as societal integration is a matter of degree. There are realms for sharing and realms for diversity in every society, and a main political challenge, as well as an analytic one, consists in drawing a line between the realms that can be accepted by the members of the society.

The Problem of Integration

Social theorists conventionally distinguish between individualistic and collectivistic (or 'holistic', in Dumont's (1983) terminology) approaches. According to the former, which is often traced to Weber (but could have been traced to Hobbes and beyond), any societal phenomenon can be studied with reference to its manifestations at the level of the individual. According to the latter, which in sociology and social anthropology tends to be associated with Durkheim, Marx and Tönnies, *society* has properties that cannot be reduced to individuals, since there are phenomena that are inherently and irreducibly collective, such as religion and ideology. Using biological (actually anatomical) metaphors in describing the integration of society, collectivists have for decades been criticised for committing fallacies of misplaced concreteness (Bateson 1959[1937]:262–3). Later, structural-functionalism, in its Marxist as well as its non-Marxist variants, has been repeatedly and convincingly demolished by scholars showing its static bias, its circular character as scientific explanation, its dependence on mystical notions of societal causation and, ultimately, a teleological view of social integration.

• *Agency and structure*. Pure methodological individualism is nonetheless as untenable as structural-functional explanation. For it is an indubitable fact that every individual being acts upon a set of circumstances that he or she has not created, and it is equally true that society is not the intentional outcome of sequences of rational action. Society is both a necessary condition for all individual actions and the unintended result of all intentional individual actions. The theory of structuration developed by Giddens (1979, 1984) provides a simple analytical matrix for overcoming the contradiction between structure and agency that may make a simultaneous understanding of both types of social phenomena possible.

The problem of *social integration* is closely related to the problems of accounting for the relationship between agency and structure and the related problems pertaining to the concept of culture. For, in so far as societies change, it cannot be assumed axiomatically that societies are 'integrated' – this would be quite as unjustified as claiming that culture (or 'cultures') is integrated, since human agency is in principle chosen, creative and unpredictable, and there are conflicts, contradictions and inequalities in the distribution of knowledge and skills in any society. Societies and cultures are open systems. Boundaries are largely imposed by analysts and natives, and they are therefore bound to shift according to the perspective.

On the other hand, both society and culture clearly *are* integrated in so far as it is impossible to act intelligibly in an uncultural way, since there are modes of discourse peculiar to specific societies, and since aspects of society and culture are reproduced regularly through institutionalised routine agency. The degree of any particular form of integration is therefore an empirical question, which cannot be dealt with properly if the individualist–collectivist distinction is retained as a strict dichotomy. Rather than arguing the primacy of the individual or of society, which is ultimately a futile exercise, we ought to study how the levels articulate with each other.

A useful blend of actor-oriented and systemic perspectives on social reality was developed by the researchers associated with the Rhodes-Livingstone Institute in Salisbury (now Harare) from the late 1930s, under the successive leadership of Godfrey Wilson and Max Gluckman. Their studies of urbanisation and interethnic encounters rarely deal explicitly with confrontations between symbolic systems or with cultural syncretism, which are concerns central to the present work, but rather focus on aspects of instrumental action and situational selection of statuses taking place between agents of diverse ethnic origins, who were thrown together in a shared industrial workplace (G. Wilson 1941–2; Mitchell 1956; Epstein 1958; cf. also Gluckman 1958 [1940]).

The most remarkable theoretical achievement of this school was perhaps their readiness to deconstruct the then dominant view of societies as bounded and stable entities. It was the nature of their field of study, which could obviously not be delineated other than in an arbitrary way, which prompted the replacement of the term 'society' with concepts like social network (Barnes), action-set (A. Mayer), scale (the Wilsons) and social field (Gluckman and others) – all of which denote the relativity of system boundaries; which remind us that society or society-ness is a matter of degree. It should be noted, however, that Wilson, Gluckman and their successors took certain insights from Durkheimian social theory for granted, frequently without acknowledging this explicitly. They assumed that agents were fundamentally constituted by, and acted upon premises defined within, their societies. They had internalised the premises of societal integration taught by Radcliffe-Brown, Fortes and Evans-Pritchard, and saw no reason to question them. The discontinuity between the life-worlds of agents of differing tribal backgrounds was taken for granted.

However, in actually investigating social process and change on the Copperbelt, they were emphatically actor-oriented. Epstein and Mitchell,

in particular, applied the principle of *situational selection* in order to explain
how conflicting expectations arising from the agent's participation in
different systems of relevance were reconciled, so that 'the individual may
behave as a tribesman in one situation but not in another' (Mitchell
1966:59). Aidan Southall remarks, in line with this idea: 'The switch of
action patterns from the rural to the urban set of objectives is as rapid as
the migrant's journey to town' (Southall 1961:19). Mitchell further makes
the important distinction between *situational* and *processual* change. Only
in the latter case do the social institutions change; in the former case,
individuals adapt strategically to changing circumstances (Mitchell 1966).
In other words, to rephrase Marx's famous statement: agents act inten-
tionally, but they have to act upon social conditions that they have not
themselves chosen. When a larger field of shared meaning than that
immediately available is required for the accomplishment of a certain task,
this is developed through patterns of interaction frequently described as
negotiation. Later in this book, I shall describe such interaction as the search
for *common denominators,* which can be defined as the totality of rules and
symbols adequate for a particular kind of interethnic encounter to be
meaningful for both parties involved. These common denominators, and
any disagreement concerning their content and field of relevance, are
framed in a shared language of discourse, which is thus supra-ethnic.
Interethnic negotiations and competition, and overcommunication of ethnic
differences, can in this way actually be an indication of a high degree of
supra-ethnic cultural integration.

Insights about the relativity of system boundaries, which are sometimes
touted as recent and innovative, were perceived as obvious facts, and were
dealt with in a sophisticated way, by these anthropologists. They knew that
any delineation of a system is arbitrary and ultimately meaningless unless
one delimits the system with a particular analytical problem in mind. Best
known in some quarters for their field methods and quantitative techniques
for handling data, or for their characteristic form of analysis and
presentation known as the extended case study, their contributions to
theoretical ideas about society or society-ness are no less important, to a
great extent transcending the simplistic dichotomy between individualist
and collectivist accounts.

Fields

Another common, simplistic distinction in social anthropology is the
opposition between public and private spheres of social action (famously

associated with gender differences in Rosaldo 1974). This distinction is also too simple for our requirements here, where a finer grid is needed. As it will be shown below, Mauritians (like other people) are integrated into several social subsystems, or fields, of varying scale, and although the public/private distinction is a good starting-point for distinguishing them, it is not sufficiently detailed.

Social organisation in Mauritian society varies crucially with respect to compass and importance in society at large, although this difference may not seem important to the participants. To old *bonom* L'Intelligent in the fishing village of Case Noyale, it apparently makes little difference whether he receives his monthly Rs. 200[2] from the state or from his son; but the two possibilities imply integration on very different systemic levels (state versus household). This difference is important because different sets of norms (implicit and explicit) apply in the different fields delineated through the respective transactions.

In discussing ethnic and non-ethnic identities and forms of organisation, proceeding to discussions of nationalism and social change, I accordingly try to locate the phenomena in two respects: first, we have the actual arenas where action continuously unfolds; secondly, the Mauritian nation-state, itself an 'actor' in both domestic and international politics, but necessarily reproduced by ongoing individual agency, must be related to the concrete fields of interaction.

• *Fields and scale.* Two anthropological perspectives on social reality have proved useful for such an appreciation of the compass of individual action and its inherent relationship to greater society. The approaches are different and complementary: one stresses the significance of the changing *context* of social micro-process, whereas the other presents a matrix for an understanding of the relationship between individual interactions and abstract institutions. Both represent a reformed, or mitigated, method-ological individualism informed by system theory, insisting on the primacy of individual agency, yet admitting that supra-individual phenomena (norms, social structure) have to be fed into the model lest individual agency be misrepresented voluntaristically, as if it were chosen in a vacuum, and the societal level disappear from sight.

The first perspective drawn upon is the kind of sociological analysis departing from concepts of scale and social fields, as discussed by Reidar Grønhaug in a couple of important texts which are, regrettably, difficult to find (Grønhaug 1974, 1978). Social fields are conceptualised by Grønhaug, developing concepts from Godfrey and Monica Wilson (1945) further, like this: 'People pursue tasks, and when they act and counter-act *vis-á-vis* each other, the acts have intended, but eminently a multitude of un-intended consequences, chain-reactions, and repercussions. When series of such implications between events make up delineable implication-systems we can label them *"social fields"'* (Grønhaug 1974, II:16). Social fields are, in other words, an abstraction of the anthropologist and do not necessarily form part of the actors' representations.

Ultimately it is true that only individuals are capable of action, but some are more powerful than others because they act on a larger scale. The actions of sugar factory proprietors and national politicians have greater ramifications than those of the average field labourer, even if the latter may in theory have larger personal action-sets[3] than more powerful agents. Ethnic identity and organisation are produced and reproduced in several social fields, some of which are systemically more important than others in so far as actions at those systemic levels influence a larger number of people and/or are more authoritative than others. This will be demonstrated below, where the status structure of three social persons active on different levels of scale is compared. I then proceed to suggest a typology of social fields to be applied to the analysis later. The aims are to locate agency in social space, and to distinguish between relevant actions of varying content and consequences. Nearly every case of action discussed can be localised to one such field, while enduring processes involving many individuals, and/or processes initiated on a high level of scale, are likely to take place in two or several fields, simultaneously or successively. This kind of distinction makes it possible to see how the situational and relational aspects of identification structure not only the lives of persons, but society as well, and it also show how ethnicity takes on different modes of functioning in different kinds of social setting.

The relations activated in any field can be divided into two vaguely defined types; multiplex and uniplex (the concepts were introduced by Gluckman 1955). The difference refers to the qualitative content of the relationship; whether or not it involves more than one aspect of the social person. The dichotomy is only meant as a regulative idea in the Kantian sense, and has no claim to accuracy.

The distinction between 'small' and 'large' scale is not the same as 'macro–micro' distinctions (Barth 1978:255–6). While macro analysis, departing from a conception of systemic levels, refers to societal properties dependent on a large number of actions for their very existence, analysis departing from a concept of scale presupposes the existence of these properties as conditions for action, and restricts itself to analyses of agency itself in different contexts. Scale is, Barth writes (1978:253), 'a characteristic of the *context of social interaction*' (my emphasis). He further outlines the procedure of sociological discovery logically leading from notions of scale and fields: 'Having observed an action, you seek to discover the field of options to which such an action belongs, and the contexts in which these options are relevant. (. . .) The course of investigation is thus from the event to class, from the singular to population or aggregate' (Barth 1978:256–7). The procedure suggested is purely inductive and therefore an impossible one in principle, yet it is attractive as a methodological device, since it leads the attention of the researcher away from his models, towards an appreciation of social reality itself.

Structural Levels

The kind of socio-cultural complexity peculiar to Mauritius, compared to virtually any ethnically less heterogeneous society, is the kind of complexity that entails more than a score of national holidays. In other words, the complexity is at its most evident at the macro level of society, not at the experiential level. The structure of the individual does not usually reflect this because there are standardised, culturally sanctioned ways of relating to members of other ethnic categories – and the relevant stereotypes are few in every individual case, although they are many altogether. In the discussion of ethnic taxonomies and stereotypes in Chapter 4, it is shown that taxonomies are always most detailed closest to the individual in question, and how the classification of other Mauritians is carried out according to an increasingly simplistic model as social distance grows. In other words, if there are as many as 15 (or 20 or 25, for that matter) categories of Mauritians acting as ethnic categories in one or several recurring contexts, it is rare that more than four or five such categories are relevant in the actual status set-up of any one individual. Even politicians do not seem concerned with internal divisions within ethnic categories other than their own. The workings of ethnicity in Mauritius are such that internal sub-divisions within the ethnic category are rarely interfered with – or exploited – by outsiders.

In their successive participation in different social fields, individuals activate various aspects of their social status repertoire or cultural identity. Each individual possesses, according to his or her status set-up, real or potential membership in several collectivities of varying compass – they can all be represented wholly or partly in one or several of the social fields in which he or she participates, and invoke different aspects of the social person. In the following chapters, we shall explore the forms of integration in groups; the reproduction of collectivities as relevant units of action seen from the perspectives of the participants' 'interests' (utility/meaning), fields of participation (social fields), and normative/representational systems (fields of shared meaning, i.e. taxonomies, norms etc.).

• *The theory of structuration.* The second analytical perspective drawn upon extensively in this study, the theory of structuration (Giddens 1979, 1984), entails that social structure is always in a process of becoming, being constituted by directional, independent agency – yet existing on a different systemic level as necessary conditions for that very same agency. In other words: interaction is the stuff that society is made of, but action is always going on in a context that it did not itself create in the first place. It is in this sense that, say, ethnic identity is simultaneously *imperative* and *situational.* When we begin to act in the world, the world is already there, and it can only partly be modified by our actions and interpretations. This pre-existing context provides the necessary conditions for action, and is in turn reproduced and modified by the ongoing processes of agency. In a methodological individualist framework, the same phenomenon can be described as the reproduction of already existing incentives and constraints as the aggregated outcome of (partly or wholly) unintended consequences of intentional interaction over a long period of time. The road to hell is paved with good intentions: since the accumulated consequences of action are unknown, they may be different from the actors' individual intentions.[4] The whole is, at least in this respect, different from the sum of its parts.

Social structure, then, consists of the relevant, overt or covert, conscious or unconscious factors external to the individual, influencing his or her agency; *and* the accumulated outcome of intentional actions. Actions frequently have unintended consequences at any given systemic level (from the dyad to geopolitics) and structure may well be recursive (have feedback effects) in a fashion not predicted by anybody. But although most lay actors perceive structure as a constant, as a thing as it were (*une chose* in Durkheim's famous words), we must insist that it is but a process, necessarily produced and reproduced continuously by actors who may nevertheless not be fully aware of the actual (immediately and retrospectively viewed) content of their actions, neither at the time of acting nor later; even consummated acts can be and are being reinterpreted with hindsight (see Schütz 1972:159-163). The anthropologist should, on the other hand, be able to identify ramifications of actions even if they remain unknown to the actors themselves.

There are, ultimately, no responses but individual ones to changes on the societal level, and there can be no societal or 'structural' level without individuals to produce and reproduce it. The inclusion of institutional levels of society in the course of analysis is nevertheless necessary in order to account for changes in actors' representations and actions. Change, at the level of individual action, enters first as potentiality or 'definite possibility'[5] for choice, following reconfigurations in one of several 'macro levels', such as changes in the political leadership of the village, in the national legislation, or in the world market.

Claude and Veerasamy

So far, I have discussed fields, levels and the duality of structure in an abstract way. The three examples that follow indicate some of the uses these purely analytical conceptualisations can be put to in the endeavour to understand what people are up to and what it means when we say that they 'have identities'. The action-sets, statuses and fields participated in by the three agents are distinguished between.

Claude (35) is a Creole living in Roche-Bois, a working-class suburb in northern Port-Louis. He is married with two children, and earns his living as a docker, being one of the few dockworkers who was not laid off when the new sugar bulk terminal (the *vrac*) was opened in 1980.

• Work: Daily routine. In his status as a docker, Claude daily encounters a horizontally organised collectivity largely composed by members of his own ethnic category (6 Creoles, 1 Tamil). (Status: Workmate/colleague.) His occupation is stereotypically and statistically linked to his ethnic membership. Vertically, he reports to a Hindu foreman and, further up in the hierarchy, to the Franco-Mauritian administrator. (Status: Employee/ subordinate.)

• Work: Trade unionism. At union meetings he regularly encounters 6 people, 4 of whom are Creoles, with one Tamil and one Muslim.

The union of which Claude is a member is linked to the MMM party, representing Creoles and others. (Status: Union member.) The union leader, a Tamil-Creole, is a personal acquaintance of Claude; they live in the same neighbourhood.

• Leisure. He spends much of his leisure time with four male friends in his locality; three Creoles and a Hindu. One of them is a workmate, and they are all about the same age. Claude has known two of the Creoles and the Hindu since he moved into the neighbourhood ten years ago; the third one, who moved in a few years later, is a former schoolmate of his cousin from the village of Triolet. (Status: Friend.)

Other members of his club, whom he meets at least once a week, include five young Creoles, a Sino-Mauritian, two Tamils and one Hindu. Some of them play football with the local sports club, where Claude was a member as a young man. (Status: Remote friend.)

The local shopkeeper and his family are Sino-Mauritian; Claude encounters them about twice a week and exchanges a few words. (Status: Customer.) He also has many casual acquaintances in the neighbourhood, virtually all of them Creoles; some of whom he occasionally goes to parties with. Favours (money or a helping hand) are sometimes granted neighbours, although it is customary first to turn to one's kin. (Statuses: Neighbour, friend.)

Claude occasionally (although rarely nowadays) takes out a girl to a film in town, her acceptance of the invitation connoting (within the dominant Creole ethic) that she must accept his sexual advances afterwards. (Status: Lover.) Due to variations pertaining to class and culture, no girl from outside the Creole working class would be available for this kind of relationship.

Claude has no television set, but he is free to watch TV at a friend's house, although he rarely does.

• Family life. His wife and children are Creoles. His wife has never worked. (Statuses: Father, husband, head of household.)

• Kin relations. In his extended family, his links are particularly good with his cousin Jean, who lives in a Hindu-dominated village in eastern Mauritius; he sees Jean about twice a month. His father died three years ago; Claude sees his mother, who lives with his elder brother nearby, twice a week. Several of his five remaining siblings, who live in other parts of the island, are not encountered casually; only at rites of passage, that is in practice, about three times a year. (Statuses: Brother, cousin, son.)

• Other sets. Claude goes to Mass with his family about once a month (his wife and daughter go every Sunday). At church, he briefly encounters many fellow Creoles whom he knows, but little information is exchanged. The priest is an expatriate Frenchman, and Claude hardly knows him personally, although they exchange the occasional phrase when they meet. (Status: Member of the congregation.)

About two Saturdays a month, he goes to the horse races downtown with one or several members of his peer group. He bets regularly at a Tamil-owned stall, the proprietor of which was a remote acquaintance of his late father. (Status: Customer.)

Veerasamy (40) is a Tamil from Rose-Hill. Married with four children, he works as a bus driver.

• Work: Daily routine. Veerasamy works with a Tamil conductor. (Status: Workmate/colleague.) Among the mechanics etc. at the garage, about 60 per cent are Tamils, while the remainder are Muslims and Creoles. Veerasamy encounters many of them daily and exchanges brief greetings and perhaps a cigarette. (Status: Colleague.) Veerasamy takes his lunch breaks with fellow bus drivers and conductors, most of whom are Tamils or Tamil-Creoles. (Status: Colleague/friend.) Although not Tamil-owned, the company is run on a daily basis by a Tamil and an office staff of five persons: two Tamils and three Muslims. Veerasamy reports at the office twice a day. (Status: Employee/subordinate.)

• Work: Trade unionism. He is not a member of the union, which comprises employees of companies other than his own as well, and thus is ethnically mixed.

• Leisure. Veerasamy is a regular customer at a bar in Rose-Hill, where he encounters men from virtually every community. (Status: Remote friend.) None of his colleagues frequent the bar; many of them are religious men. His closest friends at the bar belong to the Franco-Mauritian–Creole continuum; virtually every evening he meets, chats with and exchanges drinks with a *petit blanc*, a Coloured and two Creoles. However, he does not visit them nor invite them home, and their friendship depends on reconfirmation in these encounters. (Status: Friend.)

The proprietor of the bar is a cheerful Sino-Mauritian, always ready for small talk. Veerasamy and his friends discuss him behind his back, however, and they agree that his smirking manner is but a technique of maximising his profits ('You know what the Chinese are like: they worship money like you and I worship God!'). (Status: Customer.)

Veerasamy has a television set, and he watches the news and occasionally a non-Hindustani feature film whenever he is at home.

• Family life. His wife and children are Tamils, and his wife belongs to the same caste as himself (roughly in the middle of the hierarchy). (Statuses: Father, husband, head of household.)

• Kin relations. Veerasamy's parents are both dead; all his siblings live within a radius of three kilometres. Two of his three brothers and one of his two sisters are Christian. They still maintain contact, but relations have become somewhat strained since the conversions. (Status: Brother.)

On Sundays, Veerasamy occasionally helps his elder brother cleaning his chicken coop, and is invited for dinner in return. (Status: Younger brother.)

• Other sets. Veerasamy does not frequent the temple regularly, and participates in ritual only when obliged to, as in rites of passage in the family. He does not belong to a club any more. The family lives in a housing estate where most of the occupants are Creoles, and he is on good terms with his neighbours. (Status: Neighbour.) He visits a Creole prostitute occasionally. (Status: Customer.)

• *Networks and ethnic identity*. Both of the men's action sets include individuals from several of the other ethnic categories. However, in Claude's case, there is a clear tendency for it to be easier to form close links with members of own ethnic category than with outsiders. To begin with, Claude's ascribed statuses relating to kin and origins define him as a Creole. The Hindu in Claude's close group of friends overtly undercommunicates his Hindu identity, meaning he does not participate actively in political discussions, and does not talk about his family life nor about religious issues.

Veerasamy presents a less obvious case. An urban Tamil, he perceives himself as a 'real' Mauritian, together with the Coloureds, as opposed to the 'Indian Immigrants', many Tamils having already arrived as freemen during the eighteenth century. Politically, Tamils in Rose-Hill are allied with the Creoles; culturally, they tend to classify themselves under the heading 'real Mauritians' along with Franco-Mauritians, Coloureds and Creoles, rather than under the heading 'Indo-Mauritians'. It is therefore easy for Veerasamy to agree with his drinking comrades' casual criticism of the government, and, in the status of friends, he does not perceive them as ethnic others. However, at the bar, Veerasamy introduces himself as Samy, a more Christian-sounding name than his real one. Thus, in a certain sense, he changes cultural identity when changing status. At work he is known as Veerasamy, and he is freer to speak his mind on certain subjects with his colleagues, who are also Tamils, than with his friends at the bar. Following the dictum of the lowest common denominator, his playing out his various identities/statuses depends, as it were, crucially on the numerator (that is, his interpretation of the context). During a lunch break, Veerasamy once asked for his colleagues' views on conversions to Christianity. (Most of them were violently opposed.) At the bar, the shared meaning necessary for such a dialogue to take place was absent. Conversely, Veerasamy is able to discuss women with his fellow drinkers in a manner not possible during lunch breaks. In this sense, truth is local and relevance relative when we deal with complex action sets like Veerasamy's, common in urban Mauritius.

It should further be noted that Veerasamy's friendship-based set, unlike Claude's, is not directly linked with a locality.

Most of the sets described have potential ethnic aspects that remain latent most of the time. Their becoming manifest as conflict is usually spurred by events on a greater scale. The most spectacular large-scale process of regular ethnic entrenchment is arguably the General Election campaign every five years, but relative ethnic discreteness is also being reproduced in daily, trivial situations of interethnic contact. Two such contexts constitute the cases to be considered now.

- *Ethnicity in the bar.* Veerasamy's relationship with some of the men at the bar became difficult for a while during a court case against a Tamil accused of nepotism. It was claimed, by a remote friend of Veerasamy (a Creole), that nepotism was typical of Tamils – 'in that respect, they're just like Hindus'; the Creole, further, proceeded to strengthen his argument by referring to Veerasamy's working place, well known for being dominated by Tamils. Veerasamy retorted that it was not his personal fault; he needed a place to work like everybody else, and it was not true that non-Tamils were denied employment where he worked – he mentioned a couple of cases where non-Tamils had been employed where there were also Tamil applicants. He gained little support, and for a few weeks, he avoided some of the Creoles, including his mates, although he did not cease to patronise the bar. Eventually, the Creoles in question reached the conclusion that 'Samy is OK even if he is a Tamil', and things returned to normal; but both parties had been reminded of their competitive relationship in the job market.

The example is typical of casual interethnic relations. Low-level conflict usually arises when someone tries to generalise about another ethnic category, thus breaking the dictum of the common denominator; or, more generally, when statuses associated with different social fields are conflated. Non-violent quarrel and eventual mutual avoidance is the usual outcome. The conditional clause invoked by Veerasamy's friends when they understood they had wronged him is probably a universal phenomenon wherever there are minorities. The familiar formula is this: 'Some of my best friends are Jews, but...'; conversely 'He's all right even if he is a queer', etc.

Interethnic unease and latent antagonisms are not the outcome of direct interethnic contact; rather, they exist as abstract models being reproduced within the ethnic category, but as often as not being falsified in actual interethnic situations. To account for non-stereotypical ethnic others as exceptional cases is, obviously, necessary in order that the abstract model should be maintained. To interpret unpleasant events as the cunning scheming of ethnic others is a different method. The second example deals with this.

- *Ethnicity at work.* A process structurally similar to the bar incident took place when a Hindu was appointed foreman at the wharf where Claude was employed. The docks have traditionally been the domain of the Creoles; the employment of the Hindu was unusual and was rumoured to have been monitored by a government minister (which is highly unlikely, given the character of the work). After grudgingly having obeyed the Hindu's orders for a week, Claude eventually refused to carry out a particularly messy task.

Invectives were thrown from both sides, and Claude's fellow workers took his side, claiming that the floor ought to be cleaned by means of a machine. The foreman replied that none of the machines were at the moment free, and the task had to be carried out quickly. Claude, sensing his activity in the union (which was associated with Creole communalism) made him the foreman's scapegoat, left in a fury. The foreman complained to his superiors and demanded that Claude should be dismissed. The union took up Claude's case, and eventually mutual apologies were reluctantly exchanged, both men studiously avoiding each other later.

• *Do unions transcend tribes?* The two cases are in some respects similar; both arise from daily interaction and draw on ethnic antagonism – and in both cases, a higher level of scale is instrumental in creating the actual situation: in the second case cited, the integration of Creoles and Hindus into the same economic system is the crucial structural condition; in the first case, job scarcity is the most important variable. The most important differences are that in the first case the parties were reconciled, but not in the second; and that the first situation (and its context) was voluntary on the part of the participants, but the second enforced, owing to the rules of the labour market. This seems less than arbitrary; thus Philip Mayer's dictum 'Unions transcend tribes' (Mayer 1961) cannot be applied directly to the Mauritian labour market. When several ethnic categories participate in a uniform economic system and there is competition over jobs, antagonisms are just as likely to be accentuated as mitigated, particularly when nepotism is one of the most common forms of communalism. Unions transcend tribes only when there is no general, intersubjective perception of a systematic correlation between occupation and ethnic membership.

At Veerasamy's regular bar, there is no scarcity of important goods (apart from bottles and cigarettes, which are customarily shared through routine acts of reciprocity); thus, the joking relationship is usually more pertinent than the quarrel. At the wharf, on the contrary, people make their living knowing they may well be replaced by an ethnic other should the management wish it, and people are constantly slightly paranoid about other ethnic categories 'taking over the island'. To Claude, the appointment of a Hindu foreman was symptomatic of this process (whether imagined or real); thus, the situation took on a gravity not to be expected in casual intercourse.

But the interpretation of any situation depends on the actors' representations, and therefore it would be inappropriate to consider the working place as a more crucial context in the formation of ethnic identity and groups than, say, the bar. They both provide arenas for encounters and interethnic flow of information, and in this respect they rank equally.

- *Field-dependent identities.* A typical, more general aspect of the cultural content of the men's action sets is the *situational changes in attitudes* towards other ethnic categories.[6] At work, Veerasamy happily chats away with the conductor about the silly ways of the Creoles, and he does, when pressed, admit holding the view that Creoles are somewhat inferior to Tamils. This, he explains, is not contradictory to having Creole friends, since they are exceptional. Similarly, Claude, the Hindu-hater, maintains cordial relations with a Hindu neighbour. Obviously, their accounting for this assumed contradiction in terms of 'exceptions' will not do analytically. Rather, it is more than likely that stereotypes, whether ethnic or not, apply to people with whom one doesn't entertain multiplex, vaguely defined relations: to the faceless mass, as it were, of potentially threatening aliens.[7]

The stereotypes, although experientially false in many actual situations, give meaning and direction to taxonomies and, more generally, make sense of the apparently chaotic diversity of 'races' and 'cultures' in Mauritius. Nevertheless, divisions other than the ethnic ones are often articulated in Mauritius, although their compass is usually more restricted; one such is social class (see also Chapter 6).

In 1971 and 1979, Claude's union joined up with several unions chiefly recruiting non-Creoles in large-scale strikes led by anti-communalist militants urging workers to unite against the exploiters regardless of colour. From this class perspective, Claude and his foreman would possibly have common interests, as would Veerasamy and some, but not all, of his mates at the bar – *against* capitalists belonging to their own ethnic category. The fluctuations in Mauritian class consciousness do not seem to be caused by changes in the actual economic infrastructure of society, but through reinterpretations of the infrastructure. Social reality is ambiguous, and different (native) interpretations are available. Any interpretation must, for it to be intersubjectively valid, depart from a particular perception of *practice*, but it does not emerge unmediated from practice itself.

Runglall

The third person whose action sets and social identities will be outlined is integrated socially in a different way from the two others.

Runglall (45) is a Member of the Legislative Assembly (MLA) and a lecturer at the University of Mauritius. He is a Vaishya Hindu (the most numerous caste in the island), and is married with two children.

- Work. Runglall works full-time as a lecturer in sugar technology. This entails a large set of regular links of varying intensity and content with individuals from all communities. His secretary is a Hindu (female). His immediate colleagues are Hindu (2), Franco-Mauritian (1), foreign white (1), Sino-Mauritian (2), Coloured (1) and Muslim (2). In the tea room, he is liable to meet them and anybody else from a group of fifteen further employees. Some are personal friends. (Status: Colleague.) His students belong to every community and caste, a fair proportion of them foreigners (mostly from African countries). (Status: Teacher.)

• Politics. He belongs to the ruling party. The political milieu is small, and he knows virtually every MLA personally, irrespective of ethnic membership. In committee work, he develops closer links with some. Through the agency of the Chief Whip (the leader of the parliamentary group) his links with fellow party delegates are continuously reproduced; this also regularly takes place at party meetings, during coffee breaks in Parliament and so on. Only two persons participate in both his political and professional networks, but among his political colleagues, too, he has contacts whom he defines as personal friends – as also in the Opposition. (Statuses: Colleague, fellow Hindu, fellow politician.)

Pressure groups include religious bodies, unions and *ad hoc* petition campaigns. Three of Runglall's closest political associates are, unlike himself, members of the largest Hindu organisation.

• Leisure. Runglall's chief Sunday activity consists in gardening at home. He and his wife frequently give parties where from 4 to 40 people are invited, most of them from his professional and political sets; most of them Hindus, but never exclusively Hindus. They are also often invited to similar parties. Although overtly 'just for fun', parties play an important role in maintaining and creating political connections. (Status: Host/guest.)

• Family life. Runglall's wife is a Creole, and their three children are ostensibly raised to embody the spirit of 'Mauritian-ness', free from ethnic prejudice (and membership). (Statuses: Husband, father, head of household.)

• Kin network. Runglall sees his parents, with whom he speaks Bhojpuri, 'much too rarely'. There was a stir in his family when he decided to marry a Creole, but basically his parents, who run a small tobacco shop, are proud of their son. He has 'virtually lost touch' with his two brothers, corresponds irregularly with his elder sister, married in England, and visits his younger sister 'whenever he has the time': in practice, they meet only at rites of passage. As he is not dependent on his wider kin network, it is activated only when a cousin or nephew needs his favours. (Statuses: Son, brother, cousin, uncle.)

• Other sets. Runglall frequently speaks at public meetings, and he is occasionally interviewed in the mass media; thus he communicates unidirectionally to a large number of people. They collectively respond at election time. (Status: National politician.) He corresponds with colleagues abroad, and contributes to international journals. (Status: Colleague/ professional.)

Runglall lives in a upper-middle-class residential area dominated by Franco-Mauritians and Hindus; he has little contact with his neighbours.

• *Levels of scale.* Runglall's action sets are qualitatively – and significantly – different from those of the two other men in that many of his links operate on a *larger scale* than any of the others'. When teaching at the university or giving interviews in a newspaper, he addresses a large number of actors simultaneously; when voting in Parliament, he makes decisions affecting many other people's lives, through defining modes of discourse and structural conditions for action. In a word, Runglall has a much better opportunity to influence Claude and Veerasamy than they have to influence him. Accordingly, Runglall's actions on a large scale are conditioned by social pressures operating on the same level: the *All-Mauritius Hindu Congress*, an important interest group, professes to represent his electorate, but the Christian pressure group *Ligue Ouvrier d'Action Chrétienne* cannot do so.

Runglall has for the last decade been among the most outspoken anti-communalists in Mauritian politics. Nevertheless, he admits probably having been elected on an ethnic basis, and his party, although ostensibly a universalist socialist party, recruits its politicians and voters nearly exclusively from the Hindu community. This, too, he admits in private. Since politics is widely perceived as an ethnic zero-sum game by the electorate and by the pressure groups representing it in tangible issues, a politician is forced to consider this perception when defining his strategies, even if he disagrees with the model. In Runglall's case, this entails a contradiction between his domestic practice and his pragmatic politics, if they should be considered as part of the same system. But as I briefly noted above, discussing Veerasamy's different statuses, relevance is context-dependent. In choosing his spouse and raising his children, Runglall invokes norms and values relating to a certain representation of humanity *tout court*, the level of discourse being private and the meaning-content of links very vague and encompassing. When participating in the professional community, the central norm pertains to scientific progress, and relates to a representation of the state of the art. In politics, then, the level of discourse is public. Runglall's context of reference is his party and his electorate. The Franco-Mauritians can safely be assumed not to form part of his electorate. So, when, in 1983, it was suggested that the export tax on sugar from plantations should be raised, he voted in favour of the proposition, although he might, in a different context, have considered it unjust.

Similarly, Runglall's party has recently been instrumental in improving the lot of the small planters, most of them Hindus, a small minority of whom are very wealthy. As Abner Cohen (1981) and other observers have noted regularly since Marx's critique of Hegel's *Philosophie des Rechts*, particularist intentions must be masked as universalist ones in public discourse. Thus, both the decisions referred to were justified with reference to the common good. Outside the Hindu community, nevertheless, it is commonly agreed that the first decision was an act of revenge against the Franco-Mauritians, and the second an implicit promotion of Hindu economic interests. And it is empirically true that little has been done by the state apparatus to improve the economic conditions of Creole fishermen. In so far as they form an interest group, it is via the agency of Catholic organisations, which are not perceived as relevant pressure groups by a Hindu politician, but which might be perceived as such by the Hindu private man.

Runglall's status as husband to his wife changed meaning during the election campaign of 1983. His party was eager to get votes from Creoles, and Runglall's position as spouse of a Creole thus became an asset in the campaign. In campaigning among Creoles, Runglall the politician exploited this status in a fashion Runglall the husband could not have accepted.

Few of the three men's statuses derive directly from their ethnic member-ship. But ethnicity as a relevant and negotiable social resource frequently enters into their ongoing interpretation of their statuses, and therefore influences their actions in a way it would not have, had an essentially non-ethnic model of greater society been reproduced in a wider range of situations of inter-ethnic contacts.

Fields in Mauritian Systems of Action

The social fields enumerated and briefly discussed below are my abstractions from observed interaction. They have no empirical existence except as abstractions. The actors involved may or may not share the anthropologist's representations of these fields, but they are necessary demarcating devices in the search for a full understanding of the function-ing of Mauritian ethnicity and nationhood.

Local Fields

- *The household.* The most basic social unit in all communities, whether rural or urban. Nuclear, extended or joint. Usually mono-ethnic.
- *The locality.* Never entirely mono-ethnic, whether rural or urban. Comprises a large number of social networks of varying content, intensity and degree of formalisation. Peer groups are often mono-ethnic. 'Non-ethnic' youth clubs are often *de facto* nearly or wholly mono-ethnic, as are, naturally, Hindu *baitkas* and Muslim *madrassahs* (youth clubs). Local religious organisations are more or less mono-ethnic, but local parents' groups (educationally oriented pressure groups) are not. Village councils usually reflect the ethnic composition of the area, but ethnicity is not overtly exploited in local politics.

Extensive kin networks are sometimes localised to a village or a ward, but are more frequently scattered over a wide geographic area. Nevertheless, these and similar personal networks outside the locality are included in this field, since their scope and the consequences of their maintenance define them as voluntarily reproduced multiplex networks on a small scale.

- *The working place.*[8] Often mono-ethnic, but increasingly polyethnic, particularly in recent occupational types within industry and tourism. Local union branches may be one or another. Hierarchies exhibit strong correlations with ethnic membership.

Nationwide Fields

- *The national economic system*, comprising as a field the social networks on top of the entire multiethnic hierarchical system of working places, real or potential, and those actors repeatedly interacting with members, such as high trade union representatives. Unions are often in practice ethnically specific, and policies of employment and promotion are often linked with ethnic membership. (These practices contribute to reproducing the global division of labour (a macro feature), highly correlated with ethnicity.) Organisations such as the Chinese Chamber of Commerce overtly represent sectional interests. This is where a disproportionate amount of allocative power is exerted.
- *The national political system and the state bureaucracy.* Encompasses several multiethnic subsystems, but the actors participating tend to follow ethnic logics in practice. The political parties – which always, owing to the electoral system, comprise two major blocs – are largely ethnically constituted. Whether or not a group is included in the political system at

any time depends on its recognition by the other recognised actors. Authorising power is concentrated here.[9]

• *Nationwide communicational systems.* The public educational system strives to satisfy every pressure group through policies of overt compromise, as does the MBC (Mauritius Broadcasting Corporation) through its multilingual programming. The two largest daily newspapers, as well as many of the weeklies, profess to be 'national' ones; the remaining ones more or less overtly address themselves to particular ethnic segments of the population. Weeklies and periodicals may be classified according to the same categories. There are about 30 cinemas in Mauritius;[10] as a rule, Hindustani films from Bombay dominate in the countryside and North American, European and Hong Kong-made films, all dubbed in French, dominate in the towns, reflecting not only the geographical distribution of the ethnic categories, but also to some extent local variations in the culture of Indo-Mauritians.

• *The importance of levels.* The difference in scale between the two groups of fields is much less spectacular in Mauritius than in most other nation-states, although I shall maintain that there is a difference in kind and that the two must never be conflated in analysis. In the first cluster of fields, based on face-to-face interaction, the individual is perceived as the central acting unit; in the second, anonymity and aggregated systemic properties are central features. Further, any decomposition of the fields into participants' statuses will *by definition* display a predominance of multiplex relationships in the local fields and uniplex ones in the national fields. If Runglall wishes to create close, vaguely compelling bonds with fellow actors in the political field – whether referring to aims defined in his status as 'politician' or as 'Hindu', 'friend' or 'human' – he descends to the locality field in order to do so, while perhaps incorporating his status in the political system in his strategic actions in the locality field. This was apparent during the election campaign mentioned above. Runglall would then visit Creole villages in order to win votes, in his status as a politician. But he was received as a casual actor by strategic allies in the locality field, in a local space of vague mutual obligations. Acting the role of friend (bringing little gifts, buying drinks), he sought to fulfil the aims of the politician (securing votes). This indicates that not only do statuses change when the actor moves between fields, but so does the content of any particular status that one brings along, consciously or not, to the next field. Similarly, Veerasamy acts within different structures of relevance in the three local fields. At home, he responds to family obligations, with friends to the exigencies of manhood, at work to norms defining him as a Tamil. Runglall is not unique in bringing along his statuses as politician and husband of a Creole to the friendship context. The vaguer, less circumscribed a social relationship becomes, the more difficult it is to shelter it from influence from one's other social relationships.

Important dimensions of Mauritian social life cut across fields. Notably, this is the case with language and religion. Chapter 5 shows how religion and language function in the different fields.

Political bodies, boards of directors and other formally defined networks are founded with a specific purpose in mind; should the purpose disappear, so would these particular 'manifestations of fields' as such, even if some of the actors included therein should maintain links for different reasons. When Runglall invites colleagues and fellow politicians to his home and thus switches contexts (and fields) while still involving the same individuals, he attempts to justify and to reproduce bonds of non-contractual obligation, as opposed to certain contractual obligations, which are formally present in professional contexts and whose presence is necessary for them to continue to be defined as professional by the actors themselves.

Although the household and locality fields may be transformed in structure and meaning-content, depending on the performance of certain tasks defined in the set-up of statuses or changes in status set-ups, they will not disappear as instances of (abstract) fields because of failure to perform a single type of task.

This pertains to system complexity and to diversity of individual statuses involved in the reproduction of the field. If a large and diverse status inventory is activated by each individual in the reproduction of a field, it is less likely to disappear than otherwise. *Gemeinschaft* precedes *Gesellschaft*, as Tönnies would say – or, to put it more pointedly: a son need not be prime minister, but no male prime minister fails to be a son.

Notes

1. Most definitions emphasise political cohesion; more rarely, economic integration is mentioned. Both criteria would fit the Maurtian case.
2. The Mauritian rupee is roughly equivalent to 35p (mid-1990s).
3. The concept of the 'action-set' is taken from A. Mayer (1966) and is defined as 'the finite set of linkages initiated by an ego', as opposed to the entire '"unbounded" network of relationships between pairs of people, making up a field of activity' (*ibid.*:102). The term 'social network' originates in Barnes' (1954)

study of Bremnes, a West Norwegian parish, and was developed independently by Epstein in the 1950s (see Epstein 1992).

4. See Elster 1983.

5. The concept is Hegelian and should be contrasted to '*in*definite possibilities', that is, possibilities that are not considered at all.

6. Many of the studies associated with the Manchester School make the same point. In a review article, Mitchell (1966) characteristically notes: 'In following the same individual through several situations in an urban society, the observer is able to notice several inconsistencies in behaviour: the individual may behave as a tribesman in one situation but not in another. (. . .) This inconsistency is possible because all the values and beliefs in terms of which individuals interact in daily activities are not operative at the same time' (Mitchell 1966:58–9).

7. Christie's (1972) survey of former Nazi camp warders in northern Norway is one of numerous studies confirming this view. Christie finds that many of the Norwegian warders tended to treat the Yugoslav inmates very cruelly until the latter began to talk to them (asking for cigarettes in Norwegian, for instance), thus proving their humanity through the creation of intersubjective contexts.

8. This is a painful abstraction to make. Several of the other fields include 'working places' and links between colleagues. But, granted that most individuals do not participate in the fields I have defined as 'large-scale', the working place is a distinctive arena for interaction in that it denotes a context different from the home and the locality (cf. the conflicting allegiances of Veerasamy discussed above). It is chiefly an arena for encounters between structural equals acting on a small scale, whose tasks are explicitly and formally defined through the labour contract, as are their interrelations.

9. Yet the nodal persons in the political system are far from omnipotent, even if we disregard the power exerted by actors monitoring the economy. It is often said, for example, that communalism is an invention of the politicians (acting in the political system, communicating through national mass media). True, ethnic conflict is empirically being accentuated through participation in systems led by politicians, but it cannot be created *tout court* by politicians: rather, they are in a position to exploit sentiments, which necessarily are reproduced, potentially or manifestly, in the local fields. Naturally, the single actions performed in the nationwide fields have consequences for a greater number of persons than single actions in the three former fields, but the actual interdependence of the fields is, analytically, equally compelling for each.

10. Following the growing prosperity and the spread of video machines since the mid- to late 1980s, many cinemas have gone bankrupt. Some details regarding the media situation in Mauritius are doubtless obsolete at the time of reading, as this has been a turbulent field in the 1990s.

CHAPTER FOUR

Dimensions of Ethnicity

Ce pays cultive la canne à sucre et les préjugés. (. . .) Dans cet enfer tropical, personne ne rencontre personne – hors des castes, des franc-maçonneries du sang, tout est TABOU. Voici une Ligue des Nations où la guerre des préjugés est éndemique et atroce, surtout pour ce qui est du préjugé de couleur.[1]

— Malcolm de Chazal, *Petrusmok* (1979: vii)

Malbar res malbar (Once a Hindu, always a Hindu).

— Creole proverb

Malcolm de Chazal, poet, novelist and essayist, left for France as a young man. His works, some of them semi-classics, were written in Paris, and despite the bitterness he felt towards his insular home, they are cherished by cultured Francophone Mauritians. However, nobody wishing to participate in the public fields of Mauritian society can make statements like the one cited. It is doubtless true, as de Chazal states, that a number of topics are 'taboo' beyond the 'freemasonries of blood'. In this chapter and the next, I shall indicate in what sense and why this is so, eventually suggesting in which ways the social and cultural boundaries de Chazal so despised are being transformed.

• *Walking on eggs.* A few days after my first arrival in Mauritius, an intellectual explained to me that 'the way we maintain ethnic peace is through avoidance. We avoid discussing every controversial subject outside our inner circle.' This is a logical implication and a corollary of the policy of the lowest common denominator. The 'inner circle' alluded to may, according to context, consist of the family, the union members, the party, the religious congregation, the neighbours – or indeed any formal or informal group one might think of; and thus, the lowest common

47

denominator is dependent, as it were, on the overall content of the equation.

Very often and in crucial situations, nevertheless, the group in question is constituted on an ethnic basis. An expatriate, who had lived in the island over a decade, said, resignedly, that 'in this island, we walk on eggs all the time'. The policies where common denominators are actively sought are necessarily linked to policies of avoidance in an interethnic system of communication – which is, then, binary at least in this respect. Mauritius's first prime minister, Sir Seewoosagur Ramgoolam, repeatedly reminded the Mauritian people(s) that religion and (ethnic) politics ought not to be discussed in interethnic situations. So far de Chazal's despised *tabous*.

Differences That Make a Difference: Notions of Ethnicity

Ethnicity is a kind of relationship that amounts to *making cultural differences comparable*, and thus it presupposes a considerable degree of cross-ethnic cultural homogeneity; a shared cultural grammar and lexicon is required for talking about mutual differences.

Ethnicity, naturally, refers to a multitude of socio-cultural phenomena. It may appear at our doorstep any time and vanish in a matter of seconds: for instance, my relationship with foreign students at the university has ethnic connotations and can be viewed as an ethnic relationship. They enter my office and go away; the duration of such an ethnic relationship can be less than half an hour. Similarly, my Pakistani-Norwegian greengrocer enters my life to a very limited degree, and the ethnic aspect of our relationship is nearly negligible (although never entirely absent). On the other hand, the term ethnicity can also refer to large-scale, long-term political processes such as the relationship between African-Americans and the US nation-state; it can refer to intricate trade networks linking businesses in the United Kingdom with firms and families in India and Pakistan, or to the religious sentiments of individuals; sometimes ethnicity is transformed into nationalism through irreversible historical processes; in the perspective of *la longue durée* any particular ethnic relationship eventually vanishes altogether, and so on. In an important sense, ethnicity is created by the analyst through the questions he or she poses in research. What makes ethnicity an initially more relevant concept in the present analysis than say, class, is its empirically pervasive nature: ethnicity can be seen as an aspect of most of the social statuses of a Mauritian individual.

• *Ethnicity and modernity.* Some theorists regard ethnic identity and organisation as largely modern phenomena ultimately caused by social change in the form of modernisation and the increasingly important part played by forms of integration into nation-states (see, for example, Abner Cohen 1974b; Despres 1975, for two classic statements; see A. D. Smith 1991, Epstein 1978, and the contributions to Barth 1969, for other perspectives; see Eriksen 1993b, Banks 1996, and Vermeulen and Govers 1996 for critical overviews), thus making ethnicity analytically compatible with a conceptualisation of nationalism as the symbolic corollary of an industrial economy (Grillo 1980, Gellner 1983) or as a secular religious ideology (Anderson 1983).

Other writers on ethnicity do not consider modernisation as a crucial variable, but try to identify universal, substantial features of ethnicity, such as myths of common ancestry, shared language and religion, and so on (see Nash 1988 for a moderate version of this empiricist approach). The idea that ethnicity could be operationalised as a measurable property of social groups possessing certain identifiable cultural traits distinguishing them from other social groups, still common among non-specialists, has, as was noted above, been abandoned in social anthropology. For as one of the most subtle analysts of ethnicity insisted several times, ethnic groups are *self-defining entities*: 'Ethnicities demand to be viewed from the inside. They have no imperative relationship with particular "objective" criteria' (Ardener 1989:111).

• *Ethnicity defined.* In its most general sense, ethnicity should be taken to refer to the social reproduction of basic classificatory differences between self-defined categories of people and to aspects of gain and loss in social interaction involving such differences. Ethnicity is thus fundamentally dual, encompassing both aspects of meaning and of politics.

At the risk of repeating myself, let me nevertheless add that the relative importance of these phenomena varies immensely historically, geographically, contextually and situationally – both at the level of the individual and at the level of the political system. The mere fact that 'nationalism exists in country X' or 'ethnic minority groups live in state Y' does not necessarily imply that such ideologies play an important part in the lives and/or political processes encompassed by the system. The relative importance of nationalism and ethnicity is an empirical question.

• *Mauritian concepts of ethnicity.* Mauritian ethnicity is locally associated with family origins, language, religion, physical appearance (phenotype) and/or lifestyle or *habitus*. None of Mauritius' ethnic categories meet all these requirements; in fact, it can easily be argued that cultural differences are generally decreasing in the island as such (cf. Chaps. 7–9), although social ones may not be. Besides, there is no one-to-one relationship between cultural differences and ethnic differences, and, particularly in a society permeated by mass communication and a national educational system, cultural integration may well take place without social integration (Eriksen 1992b). Differences seen as primordial nevertheless tend to be spoken of as ethnic or racial ones.

Notwithstanding the general fourfold division described in Chapter 2, seven major ethnic categories are conventionally held to exist in matters relevant for individual lifespans, and this is widely assumed to be reflected in patterns of employment, in politics, education and the mass media. They are the Franco-Mauritians, the Creoles (excluding the Coloureds), the Hindus ('Hindi-speaking'), the Muslims, the Sino-Mauritians, the Tamils and the Coloureds.

Hindus form majorities in most rural constituencies, while the other ethnic categories together form political majorities in the towns. Over half the total Sino-Mauritian population live in Port-Louis, but the 'General Population' is the largest single ethnic category in all the five municipal areas.

Official and semi-official ethnic classifications are reified conceptually by actors and thus form part of their shared representations. Indeed, Mauritian Muslims have told me that 'until 1962, we were not an ethnic group', referring to the first census where they were granted a separate column.[2]

Had Mauritius not been integrated politically at the level of the state and economically in a very uniform capitalist system, ethnic conflict and competition could theoretically have been avoided altogether, since inter-group contact might then have been negligible. The actual situation, as defined and interpreted by the participants, entails potential ethnic conflict and ardent application of the policy of the lowest common denominator as well as policies of avoidance.

• *Taxonomies.* Every Mauritian possesses, consciously or not, a particular cognitive model of the ethnic set-up in the island. These socially reproduced mental constructs, linked with moral stereotypes of the other groups, have important bearings on action, and are in turn reinforced or modified by the accumulated outcome of actions, that is the social form or structure.

Figure 1 is a relatively exhaustive ethnic classification scheme, implicitly taking account of the various social fields on one hand, and the relevant levels of social integration on the other (from the endogamous group to the level of the nation-state). Smaller classificatory units exist with respect to certain contexts, and it should be stressed that many Mauritian categorisations do not depart from notions of ethnic differences. When the fourfold ethnic division was still in official use, Indo-Christians were sometimes regarded as Hindus, sometimes as members of the General Population. A former division, no longer applicable, obtained between Sino-Mauritian

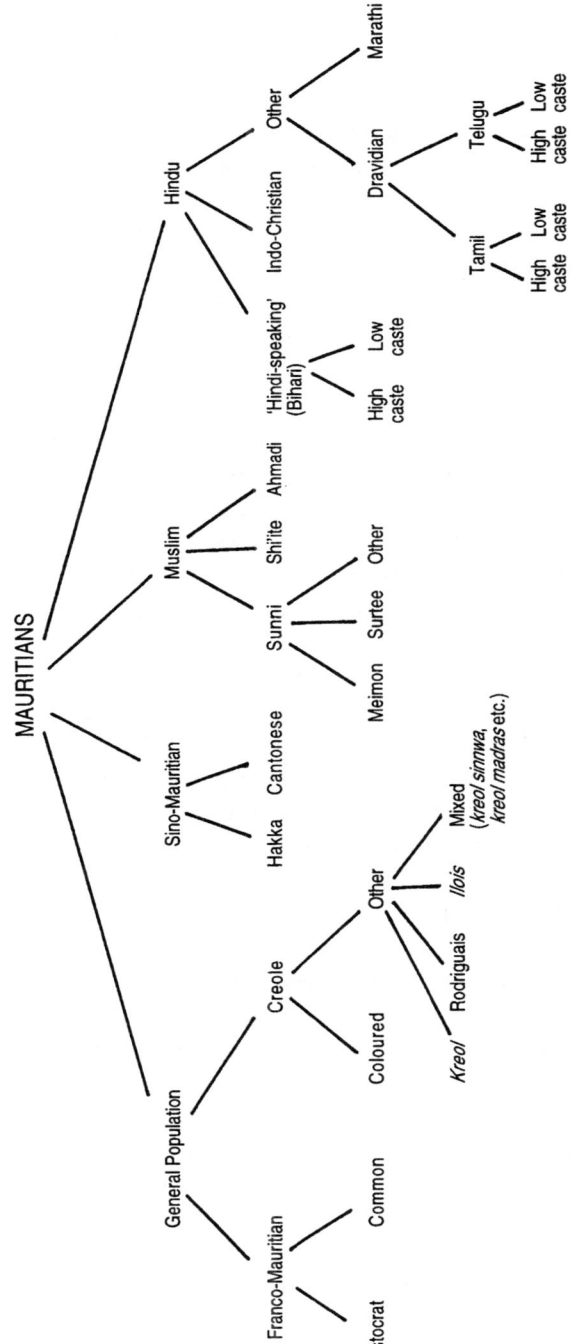

Figure 1. A possible taxonomy of ethnic identities in Mauritius (the author's invention).

speakers of Cantonese and of Hakka. The former are very few, and no longer form a distinctive entity in any relevant respect beyond the level of kinship. Further, it is noteworthy that Hindus and Muslims were lumped together as Indo-Mauritians in official censuses until 1962. Internal divisions among inhabitants of Indian origin, always present as a potentiality, became manifest in the late 1940s (Simmons 1982:108–9; Bowman 1991:33), to a great extent as a result of the extension of the franchise in Mauritius and Partition, which divided India into two states, an Indian and a Pakistani (both events took place in 1947). Tamils formed their own political party (now defunct) in the early 1960s, and it is believed that a majority of them voted against independence.[3]

The word 'White' (*blan*) is commonly used about Franco-Mauritians; the sub-category 'Aristocratic' is arguably an endangered one as numbers dwindle and categorical distinctions become blurred. *Kreol Sinwa* (Chinese Creole) refers to the offspring of mixed marriages between Sino-Mauritians and Creoles, relatively widespread in some parts of Port-Louis; *Kreol Madras* means 'Tamil Creole' (Christian Tamil, sometimes racially mixed) and *Malgas* or *Mazambik* refers, pejoratively, to the Creoles of most obvious African descent.

Figure 1 is both too simple and too complicated. It is simplistic because it neglects the existence of taxonomic anomalies – the Creole/Coloured category, in particular, contains many individuals of ambiguous ethnic membership – and because it emphasises ethnic categorisation while excluding other principles for differentiation (see Chap. 6). It is too complicated because Mauritians do not in general carry Figure 1 in their heads. They settle for the relevant part, meaning that their classifications become successively more detailed the more closely the categorisation approaches their own experienced life-world and the differences that make a difference to themselves. Thus, a typical urban Tamil taxonomy might be represented by Figure 2. A typical 'Aristocratic' Franco-Mauritian ethnic taxonomy, on the other hand, might be represented by Figure 3.

The differences between individual taxonomies correspond to differences between life-worlds or *Relevanzstrukturen* (Schütz and Luckmann 1979). In every society, culture is unequally distributed in comparable ways, and so these variations cannot be said to be 'caused' by ethnic variation.

Stereotypes as Shared Representations

Now turning to the moral stereotypes associated with taxonomies, they are to some extent interlocking and mutually defining, giving each ethnic

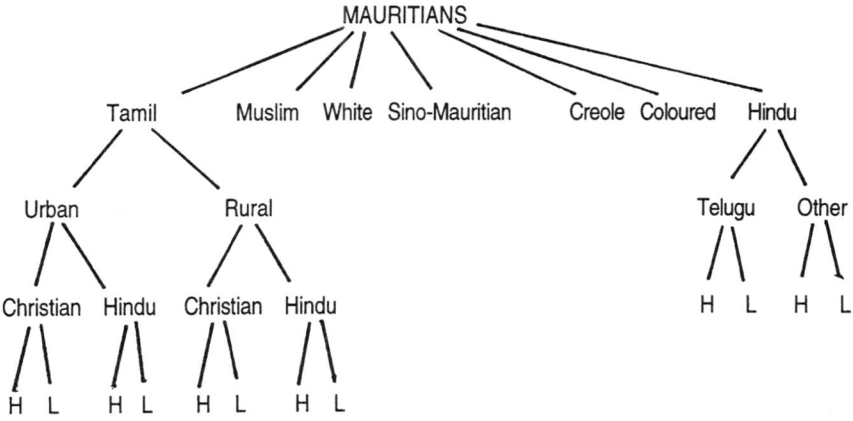

Figure 2. Tamil taxonomy

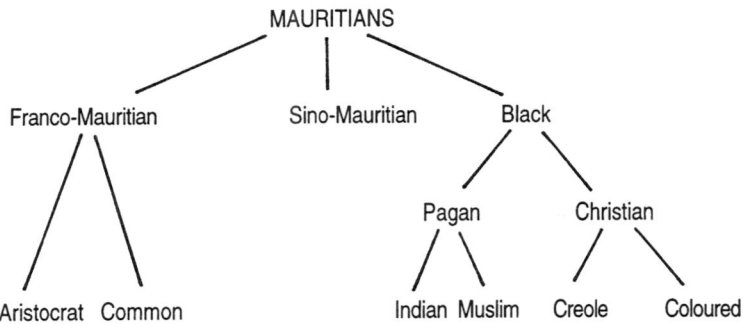

Figure 3. Aristocratic Franco-Mauritian taxonomy

category a particular destiny, as it were, through its contrasts with the others. Creoles and Hindus, in particular, contrast their respective lifestyles and outlooks in ways reminiscent of the moral dualism characteristic of Caribbean societies (P. Wilson 1978; Abrahams 1983). The stereotypes held by a particular individual, linked with their taxonomy, constitute a coherent symbolic system. These systems are being reified and reproduced in the local fields of household, locality and working place, chiefly intraethnically, and remain fairly constant. As part of the actor's early socialisation, taxonomies and stereotypes exist prior to action. They are necessary for the individual to act in a relevant way, even if they are not taken at their face value by the agent.

The lists given in Table 1 are simplified in that they do not take account of ethnically specific variations in stereotypes of others, nor in contextual differences relating to different fields. For instance, Creoles in general have

Table 1. Ethnic stereotypes

STEREOTYPES OF OTHERS	
Creoles	Lazy, merry, careless
Hindus	Stingy, dishonest, hardworking
Muslims	Religious fanatics, non-minglers
Sino-Mauritians	Greedy, industrious
Franco-Mauritians	Snobbish, decadent
Coloureds	Clever, conceited, overambitious

STEREOTYPES OF SELF	
Creoles	Sincere, humane
Hindus	Sensible, care for family
Muslims	Members of a proud, expanding culture
Sino-Mauritian	Clever, industrious
Franco-Mauritian	'True Mauritian', dignified
Coloureds	'True Mauritian', intelligent

a more positive view of the Franco-Mauritians than do the Muslims; Hindus and Muslims are sometimes socially close in rural areas, but rarely in towns, and so on. Nevertheless, although many Mauritians may disagree with the truth value of these stereotypes, they are reified as common knowledge, *shared meaning*, and must as such be reckoned with even by actors who do not agree with them. They do not, of course, prescribe action directly. Action is always underdetermined by norms.

• *Interlocking stereotypes.* Any one of the six major symbolic systems emerging from these standard perceptions, along with a particular version of the ethnic taxonomy, also incorporates knowledge of the ethnic others' stereotypes of self. This means, among other things, that the cognitive systems are not only similar, but that they, added together, constitute a seamless descriptive symbolic order at a higher level. The contradictions between the subsystems, then, originate not in differences in actual representations (although such minor differences are reproduced systematically) but in the cultural *values* attached to them in pragmatic interpretation of real-life situations. To a Creole, a Dionysian *séga* party may be an expression of positive values of friendship and joy; to a Hindu or Sino-Mauritian it may reflect the Creole's lack of foresight. When a Franco-Mauritian of 'Aristocratic' identity lifts his little finger along with his cup of tea, it sets him apart as more gracious, more of a gentleman than the dirty blacks – conversely, it also sets him apart as an empty snob. The interpretation depends on the perspective; and the perspective, incorporating judgements of value, is partly an aspect of cultural identity, but it is also partly modified

by social context. This is how our Tamil bus driver (Chap. 3) can dislike
and respect Creoles: he dislikes them when his conductor tells him about
his dirty neighbours, but respects them when they buy him a shot of cane
liquor.

Although there is no general agreement about the nature of the interrelations between the elements and their moral value, it seems perfectly
legitimate to talk of a *shared symbolic system* in this context, forming a basis
for compromises and movement of information across ethnic boundaries,
provided we distinguish representations from norms. The representative
models ('denotations') are perceived as being *really there*; only when linked
with values ('connotations') do interpretations differ. The Sino-Mauritian's
thrift becomes stinginess in the eyes of the Creole because their respective
normative systems differ. They are each mutually aware of the other's interpretation: there is apparently perfect intersubjectivity, although there is,
of course, also disagreement.

- *Flexibility in stereotypes*. In real-life situations, such value judgements,
naturally, invariably form part of the interpretation and cannot be separated
from the representation outside analysis. My point in distinguishing representations from values or norms here is simply to argue that a system of
representations, 'models-of', can be compatible with several systems of
norms, of 'models-for' (in Geertz' famous terms (1973); see also Holy and
Stuchlik 1983). An ethnic taxonomy has no means of reproduction unless
tied to a particular set of norms. And surely, for a particular normative
version of a shared system of representations to be officially established as
the universal one, its proponents will have to be those controlling the
nationwide social fields; that is, the Mauritian state apparatus (legal and
political institutions), the means of production (economic institutions), the
educational system and the private mass media (where modes of discourse
are being established and reproduced). No ethnic category is collectively
in such an omnipotent position in modern Mauritius, although there are
obvious asymmetries of power: Franco-Mauritians, Sino-Mauritians and
some Muslim families are economically powerful, Hindus are politically
powerful, and Coloureds dominate in mass media and 'cultural life'. At
the micro level, any particular interpretation may be regarded as *the* correct
one in a given situation. Conflict – in the form of violence or network
fissure – and avoidance are the two alternatives when there is sustained
disagreement, when compromise fails. The fundamental ambiguity of the
shared system of representations suggests that low-level conflict is often
inevitable.

In general, mutually defined stereotypes and partly overlapping taxonomies constitute *fields of shared meaning*, which can of course, like all shared

meaning, be contested. In so far as they normatively connote functional complementarity or indifference to the actors they remain unproblematic; otherwise they do not.

Stereotypes in Practice

The following examples, located in the working place and the locality, respectively, should indicate the significance of this point.

• *Stereotypes at work*. A Franco-Mauritian family in Curepipe, the husband employed by a shipping company in Port-Louis, the wife a housewife, employs two servants: a Muslim gardener, Mahmood, and a Creole domestic maid, Jacqueline (their relevant statuses: employees; type of relationship: uniplex). In this, there is already an inherent power hierarchy; the family's two employees, however, are of approximately equal rank (mutual statuses: colleagues; uniplex relation). The different genders of the two servants make their division of labour seem appropriate to themselves, as does cultural convention relating to ethnically specific career strategies. Their mutually exclusive tasks imply that they see little of each other; there is a functional complementarity. Jacqueline takes organic kitchen waste out daily to the garden dump, into Mahmood's domain; and he enters 'her' house daily to wash up and sometimes to drink a cup of tea in the kitchen. They tacitly accept each other's presence, but they are not on particularly friendly terms. They both regard the mistress of the house as a legitimate giver of orders, and turn to her rather than to her husband if they have a complaint or a request.

Jacqueline had been dissatisfied for a while with Mahmood's habit of entering the house without wiping his feet; during the rainy season this implied a not negligible amount of extra work for herself, and eventually she complained to Madame. 'These filthy Muslim men,' she said, 'they've got no idea of how to behave themselves in the house. At home, I bet he keeps his wife like a slave and has her kiss his feet whenever he returns from work.' Madame asked Jacqueline why she couldn't tell Mahmood herself, because, after all, it was a problem between them. But Jaqueline insisted that Madame tell him, because 'you'd think he would listen to me? *Ayo*, never, Madame!'

The mistress of the house reported the complaint to Mahmood, requesting him to take off his boots before entering the house. And so he did thereafter, for a while. Eventually, however, he returned to his old habit. He explained this to me in these terms: 'It is not good for a man to do what a woman tells him, it makes him weak.' I reminded him that he usually did what Madame told him, and he continued: 'That's different. It's not that woman, it's *that* one'; suggestively pointing towards the kitchen.

During the same period, Mahmood began to file complaints against Jacqueline as well. 'You should keep an eye on her,' he told Madame, 'I know that kind – very sweet and nice and all that, but how they steal! Besides, she's as careless as one'd expect from her kind. I've seen some of the things she throws out – good food, if you ask me.' When asked for evidence, he promised he would show her soon.

Apart from a further deterioration in the relationship between Mahmood and Jacqueline, nothing tangible happened after this demarcation.

In both instances, the protagonists applied ethnic stereotypes, presuming their Franco-Mauritian employer shared them, to strengthen their evidence. In the case of the dirty feet, the representational interpretation of the situation was naturally identical on both sides: Mahmood *did* enter the kitchen with dirty feet, and this *did* imply extra work on the part of Jacqueline. But the normative aspect of the situation differed. According to the Creole woman, a man should be kind and considerate, and besides, the woman rules in the house. According to the Muslim man, a woman should be acquiescent and respond sympathetically to any of the man's whims. Mahmood knew that Jacqueline was invoking stereotypical descriptions of Muslims against him, and for a while he did adapt to the meaning-context she and their mistress had defined, before deciding that it was unacceptable for a man to behave in this way. He fully understood their version of the facts, but rejected it as a false interpretation. His accusations against Jacqueline may have been fabricated, aimed at reinstalling his ethnic and masculine pride rather than at guarding his mistress's property. Had Mahmood been a less confident man, he would have complied with the two Catholic women's wishes, and thus contributed to the reproduction of a symbolic relationship between men and women that would have been unacceptable to him in other contexts.

• *Stereotypes in the local public arena.* The second example exemplifies the relativity of criteria for truth and relevance on a larger scale, with potential for ramifications into the national political system.

Somewhere in the Muslim heartlands of a Mauritian town, there is a Sino-Mauritian-owned café. Since the ethnic disturbances in the late 1960s, the proprietor had not sold alcoholic drinks nor food with pork in it, for fear of being ostracised, boycotted or perhaps even lynched by his neighbours.

Then, in a period of reduced public ethnic conflict, the café was purchased by a young Sino-Mauritian. The previous owner, an old man who left to spend his last years with his son's family a few blocks to the west, warned the purchaser that he should respect local custom. The new owner, Gérald, agreed with this.

Soon, some of Gérald's friends started to patronise his cafe, not mingling socially with the Muslim old-timers although sitting in the same room, a square room with a total of five tables. From the beginning, Gérald's friends complained that he did not sell alcohol and Chinese specialities like sausages and smoked pork's ears. He replied that he didn't want to offend his Muslim customers and neighbours – and besides, his profits would probably drop if he did so. Gérald's friends, concentrating on the economic aspect, retorted that his profits would clearly increase if he did what they suggested. Then, they claimed, he could attract more Sino-Mauritian customers and perhaps even people from Creole neighbourhoods nearby. After a few months of lousy profits, Gérald applied for a licence to sell liquor. While awaiting the reply, he took in supplies of beer (for which no licence was required) and included pork dishes on the menu. He kept the crates of beer out of view; but of course everybody quickly learned of his decision. His only employee apart from his wife, a young Muslim boy with cleaning duties, resigned shortly afterwards. But his customers did not disappear, and for a while, business went well. His small group of friends faithfully came to drink beer and eat pork, and sometimes they succeeded in bringing other Sino-Mauritians with them. No Creoles came, however.

After four months, Gérald had not yet received an answer to his application for a liquor licence, and he went to see the Mayor about it. He was then told that the Mayor had just received a petition urging the Municipal Council not to give Gérald his licence. The Mayor suggested that Gérald withdraw his application; the latter declined.

Then, eventually, his regular customers disappeared, all at once, possibly because of a collective decision at the level of the religious community. Gérald's Sino-Mauritian friends, sensing their responsibility, tried to mobilise their own, but with little success. A caricature of a Chinese with porcine features appeared on the external wall of the café. One day, a local imam entered the cafe and explained, diplomatically, that his congregation could not accept blatant and conspicuous breach of Allah's law in their midst, and urged Gérald to conform to local rules of decency. Gérald replied by referring to (universal) Mauritian law; the imam reminded him of the need to be tolerant in a multicultural society. Their views were incompatible, and compromise seemed impossible.

Gérald's friends were furious when they heard about this. 'Why, is this not a free society? Only three blocks from here, you can drown yourself in hard liquor if you like – why not here? Those Muslims are bloody fanatics!'

and so on. The truth was, however, that Gérald and (especially) his pregnant wife, were by now very worried about what was to happen next. *They* had to live here, after all.

More graffiti appeared on the walls; anti-Chinese and Islamic slogans (in the shared idioms of Kreol and French). Gérald's wife started to complain that she felt people staring at her when she went out. Apart from the imam, however, none of the locals talked to Gérald or his wife about this.

In the end, about a year after his takeover, Gérald announced that he would return to his predecessor's practice of no pork and no alcohol. His friends were, naturally, disappointed in him, but they understood. After all, the Sino-Mauritian key to success consisted in avoidance of open ethnic confrontation.

The graffiti were removed, and things returned to normal. The Muslim customers returned, and Gérald's friends now only came occasionally, usually during their lunch break, to 'see how things went'.

Gérald's participation in the local community was always limited to economic transactions: his locality, where he had kin, friends and was member of organisations, was in a different part of town (although very close). An outsider in a Muslim neighbourhood, he had to undercommunicate his discreteness. His status as a *commerçant* was acknowledged – that's how Sino-Mauritians are supposed to be, in the eyes of others; but in attempting to negotiate the meaning-content of this status, he lost. He tried to argue with reference to universalist values (the law of Mauritius); but his opponents interpreted him as a communalist, and claimed the primacy of their communal values over his in this local context.

• *Negotiation over values.* Both of the examples discussed involve negotiation over cultural – and in this case ethnically contingent – values. In none of the cases did the participants claim the universality of their own, ethnically specific values, only their validity in the actual relevant context. Jacqueline and Mahmood did not care what the other did at home, while Gérald did not mean to imply that Muslims, too, ought to drink alcohol; nor did the Muslims insist on universalising their value, that is try to force himself and his family not to consume pork and alcohol. What actually led to the conflicts seems to have been the necessity to interpret the situation according to values external to the definition of the social relation; in other words, by referring to a realm where no common denominators existed. Field-specific rules for conduct and compromise fail to function in such field-transcending relationships. At an abstract level, all of those involved could accept the presence of conflicting values in Mauritian society; their mutual links were defined according to an agreed version of the lowest common denominator. In the event, the situations required a redefinition of their context and thus of their own meaning. Truth was in other words being defined as something *local*. Finally, stereotypes were invoked in accounting for the ethnic other's presumably erroneous interpretation, and this reproduction of belief in one's own ethnically based moral superiority indeed seems to be a necessary cultural condition for ethnic boundaries not to dissolve in a multiethnic society.

Marriage and Taxonomic Distance

Taxonomic divisions are crucially relevant, and are reproduced, in practice, through customary marriage practices and household structure.

First, the choice of spouses always involves considerations of taxonomic distance. Ideally, ethnic categories are here activated at the very lowest level of abstraction. Hindus are ideally expected to be ethnically endogamous at the level of caste within each subgroup (Benedict 1961, 1967; see, however, Hollup 1994b on the diminishing importance of caste); Franco-Mauritians should not even marry Coloureds (otherwise considered taxonomically close); and Coloureds should not marry working-class Creoles. In practice, the ethnic categories are to varying degrees endogamous. The Creoles, notably, have no strong organisational devices for sanctioning their notions of ethnic endogamy; neither a strong kinship-based organisation nor stable corporate organisations.

A fundamental difference between the populations of Indian origin and the rest consists in the fact that within the former arranged marriage is still quite widespread. Among Sino-Mauritians, Franco-Mauritians and Creoles, both ethos and practice allow for a good measure of personal choice, although sanctions are applied if a child chooses an alliance that could be morally or economically disastrous.

Be this as it may, whenever intermarriage occurs, it is still usually disapproved by the family. One exception is when an ethnic category becomes so small that it cannot reproduce itself endogamously without literally degenerating. This has happened to the Telugu (after many years of *de facto* intermarriage with Tamils and North Indians and thus diminishing numbers); to the Cantonese (who are about to become totally assimilated into the Hakka-speaking majority of Sino-Mauritians); and to the Aristocratic Franco-Mauritians (after years of widespread intermarriage with 'Bourgeois' Franco-Mauritians and emigration to France and South Africa). A Telugu, himself exogamously married (to a Tamil), explains: 'Nowadays all the Telugus in Mauritius are cousins. We are poor people and cannot afford to go to India to find wives. So what does one do?'

• *Criteria for spouse selection.* When a couple decide to marry, or when their respective parents agree that they should, the most important single status is still that of ethnic membership. In some cases, however, the ethnic status is overruled by another. This could be financial or political position, or purely personal qualities. Parents usually emphasise kin alliances, where- as the young justify possible heterodox choices by referring to romantic love. Mauritius is full of sad stories, some of them confirmed, about young lovers who belonged to different castes or communities, and therefore committed double suicide, as it was impossible for them to marry. Indeed, when I revealed to a friend that I intended to look at interethnic marriages during my second stint of fieldwork, he suggested, with sad irony, that I should go to the *Pont Colville Deverell* – the highest bridge in the island, which has been a favoured spot for double suicides by young couples unhappily in love, unable to marry each other because of rules of ethnic endogamy or, more rarely, caste endogamy (see also Chap. 6).[4]

• *Endogamy and locality.* As a rule, ethnic categories (except Creoles) tend, or have until recently tended, to be endogamous at the lowest taxo- nomic level. The closer a spouse is in the taxonomic system, the less is an exogamous marriage considered a grave deviation. Marriages between Ilois from Diego Garcia and Mauritian Creoles are common (Walker 1986) and considered more 'natural' than marriages between, say, Creoles and Sino- Mauritians (which are also relatively common in some areas), not to mention Creole–Muslim or Creole–Hindu marital alliances (which are very rare). As regards the Hindus, it is much easier for them to get parental acceptance for marrying other Hindus, whether from different castes or even different subgroups, than for marrying into any other group. In other words, varying degrees of taxonomic distance are applied with respect to marriage strategies.

Further, the localisation of the new household is highly dependent on ethnic membership. Granted that it is to be neolocal (which is the most common variety nowadays), it should ideally be spatially close to the husband's parents' home. (This notion is weaker among Creoles than among others, but it exists there too.) If this option is not available, the household should at least be located in an area where one's own ethnic category is already numerous. Usually this presents no problem, since one's social action sets tend to be largely ethnically endogamous. In addition, the economic situation of a couple is strongly correlated with their ethnic membership. Thus, simplistically, one might say that Creoles are tenants in public housing estates (*cités ouvriers*), while Franco-Mauritians live in

Curepipe and on the south-western coast, and Hindus in concrete houses near the sugar estates. The point is not, of course, that taxonomies themselves reproduce a particular pattern of settlement, but that the practical application of taxonomies and kinship categories encourages reproduction of such a pattern, and along with other factors to be considered (notably division of labour and economic wealth), tends to inhibit the emergence of a less ethnically correlated pattern of settlement.

Many neighbourhoods in Mauritius are class-based rather than ethnically based, particularly in middle-class urban areas, and even rural and 'rurban' neighbourhoods are becoming increasingly mixed as the ethnic division of economic and political power gradually changes.

Ethnicity and the Labour Market

A few brief, general examples indicating the ethnic aspect of labour organisation will give a preliminary notion of the relationship between ethnicity and work.

• *The plantation.* Nineteen of the twenty sugar plantations traditionally constituting the backbone of the Mauritian economy are owned by Franco-Mauritian families.[5] A typical pyramid of authorisation within the plantation would place Franco-Mauritians on top, Sino-Mauritians and Coloureds in the middle administrative positions, Creoles in the factory, and Hindus and Muslims in the fields.

• *The industrial factory.* All ethnic groups have members possessing one or several EPZ factories, although Sino- and Franco-Mauritians are over-represented. Many are owned partly or wholly by foreigners.

If a factory (or a tourist hotel) is owned by a Hindu or a Muslim, it is likely that this ethnic category will be overrepresented among the employees. If it belongs to a Franco-Mauritian or a Sino-Mauritian, however, only the managerial positions are held by members of the owner's ethnic category, simply because these two élite ethnic categories have few or no members belonging to the working class. The changes in the Mauritian economy, from total dependence on sugar to a greater diversity, have led to a perceptible change in the principles of recruitment to the labour market; and, as will later be indicated, the consequences for ethnicity are profound.

• *The fishing boat.* Usually owned by a Hindu or Muslim *banyan* (middleman) along with the remaining equipment (nets, sails etc.). Most fishermen are Creoles (although this does not mean that most Creoles are fishermen), who thus are the employees of the *banyan* in practice; they are compelled to sell him the catch at his price.

Descending from the national economic system to the concrete working place, the situation is no different in the choice of patrons, of jobs and of friends at the working place. Perceptions of taxonomic distance are largely congruent in the household, locality, working place and economic system. This means that the agent's perceptions of ethnic closeness/distance are normally identical whether he considers marriage, buying a house, looking for a job or employing a subordinate.

Variations in size, position in the greater society and internal social resources suggest that the internal organisation of the ethnic categories follows discrete principles. Viewing the question from another angle, we may add that cultural differences and unequal distribution of property imply systematically divergent individual career strategies.

• *Occupational stereotypes as self-fulfilling prophecies*. Despite rapid social change, occupational stereotypes still cling to Mauritian ethnic categories. Every profession is in principle open to everybody, but the reproduction of social and cultural differences along ethnic lines is rooted in the traditional division of labour. This holds true, then, by and large on a practical level as well as on a representational level, just as the Indian caste system is by and large being reproduced in a period of fast social change.

An integral part of the normative taxonomies discussed above is the occupational stereotype of the ethnic other. Similarly, occupational stereotypes of self are widely justified with reference to one's own ethnically determined personal characteristics. Knowledge about one's own ethnic category's social and cultural resources in the competitive labour market is also applied to practices and thus plays an important role in the reproduction of the division of labour, although the process is naturally recursive, mediated through the duality of structure. A particular ethnic division of labour and property entails the predominance of the successful career strategies seeking to exploit it, and these strategies constitute its only means of reproduction.

Table 2 below is 'true' in the same respect as Table 1 and Figures 1, 2 and 3; that is, it exists as a coherent system of representations in the shared Mauritian culture – as implicit, and sometimes explicit, *préjugés*. The abstractions are mine.

The ideal stereotypes of occupations, confirmed in practice partly because of their existence (as self-fulfilling prophecies), are largely congruent with the actual distribution of power: Franco-Mauritian families control the most important means of production (the sugar estates); Sino-Mauritians have a virtual monopoly in retail trade and were the *de facto* founders of the EPZ; Hindus control the state apparatus (although most Hindus remain labourers and small planters); some Muslim families are

Table 2. Ethnically specific perceptions of resources in the labour market

	REPRESENTATIONS OF OWN RESOURCES	REPRESENTATIONS OF OWN OCCUPATION
Franco-Mauritians:	Property, knowhow	Managerial
Sino-Mauritians:	Intelligence, thrift	Wealth-generating activity
Hindus:	Kin solidarity, network	Agriculture (rural), politics, civil service
Muslims:	Corporate organisation	Professional, trade (urban), agriculture
Coloureds:	Education	Professional, civil service, artistic
Creoles:	Honesty, working ability	Manual, non-agricultural, police force

powerful in business; the Coloureds have, for historical reasons, a strong position in national communicational systems; and the working-class Creoles are collectively virtually powerless in greater society.

The individual examples that follow illustrate the direct relationship between occupational strategies and ethnic membership, and also reveals some of the hierarchical dimensions of ethnic organisation in Mauritius.

• *Billy* (49), a Creole, grew up in the village of Bel Air in eastern Mauritius. He received some schooling there; by the time he left school at twelve he could read and speak French and perform basic mathematics. Billy's father was a skilled worker at a sugar factory, with his mother periodically working as a domestic maid in Franco-Mauritian households. There were nine children. Billy was expected to join his father, who might be able to help him with a job, at the factory. But he wanted to go to town, and when he was fifteen, arrangements were finally made that he might stay for a period with an uncle in eastern Port-Louis. There, he found a job as a Creole carpenter's apprentice through the agency of his uncle, also an artisan. He remained in this man's service for five years, throughout which period he continued to stay with his uncle and paid him a little money at irregular intervals. He also went to see his parents 'as often as possible'. The job was not well paid, and he frequently applied for others. In his own opinion, the reason he didn't have luck was his ethnic membership. He comments: 'You know how people are – Chinese employ Chinese, and Hindus employ Hindus.' At the age of 21, a neighbour of his uncle managed to find him a job at the garage where he was working himself, and Billy was happy for a change, although this job was also badly paid. In 1963 he married a girl from the neighbourhood, and the ceremony and party were held, according to custom, in Bel Air. By now his father had been promoted, and claimed he could help Billy to find a better-paid job and housing at the sugar factory; Billy agreed to give it a try, although his wife disliked the idea. By 1964, they settled in Bel Air; this job was reasonably well paid and further, after a couple of months they got a flat in the sugar company's housing estate. Billy has worked at the factory to this date; he has never been offered another job, he claims, 'and besides, things are tough for us Creoles these days'.

• *Jean-Pierre* (53), a medical doctor who lives in Floréal, has his own private practice in addition to weekly visits to sugar estates.

Jean-Pierre grew up in a non-landowning family of higher public servants and professionals; his father was an attorney and his maternal uncle an officer in the British army (this was a matter of joke in the early days, but became serious during the war, when most of Jean-Pierre's family members supported the Vichy government. The man in question, by then a captain, was abroad throughout the war.) Jean-Pierre went to Mauritius' best secondary school at Curepipe, and was then sent to France for his higher studies. Naturally, his maternal language was French. Upon returning from France, he married a Frenchwoman who had accompanied him, and immediately had a house raised on the ample family plot in Floréal. There was no shortage of money. Reluctant to work as a hospital doctor, he quickly established himself as a general practitioner. A Franco-Mauritian friend of the family let him an office in his block in central Curepipe. In the mid-1970s, Jean-Pierre took the additional job at the north-western sugar estates; as a Franco-Mauritian, he was preferred to the other applicants, 'and in any case, I know all these people [directors] through my family; there's M. N–, M. de R– and . . .'. In addition to his houses (his parents are dead), Jean-Pierre has a *campement* at the seaside, where the family spends the winters (June–August) and weekends.

Jean-Pierre has three children (29, 31 and 32 years old), and has funded all their education abroad; two in France and one in Quebec. His daughter is married in France; his elder son has a managerial position with a sugar company; and his younger son has a similar job in a cargo-handling company. Both the companies are Franco-Mauritian-owned.

• *Robert* (27), a Sino-Mauritian and the younger son of a general retailer in Port-Louis, had no hope of taking over the family business because of primogeniture rules of inheritance. He took his School Certificate in 1978 with good marks, and applied for several scholarships in order to study commercial or related subjects abroad (in particular, he wanted to study computer science in Japan; the Chinese Chamber of Commerce had just founded this scholarship then). However, he received no scholarship, and decided to find a job instead of continuing his education at home. His patriclan was not a particularly big and powerful one; most of his uncles were in the retail business. He did not feel like working for his father. Eventually he got a clerical job at the Casino of Mauritius at Curepipe, owned by Sino-Mauritian non-relatives. Two years later he got a better-paid job at a seaside casino, not Sino-Mauritian-owned, and was quickly promoted further. At the age of 24, Robert wanted to set up his own business. He still lived with his parents, and had saved some money. He found a café for sale in central Rose-Hill, and borrowed more money from his father and yet more from two uncles (the former interest-free, but not the latter). The remaining money was raised through a bank loan. Later, Robert took over the café, including its living quarters, located in the high street of Rose-Hill and Sino-Mauritian-owned from the beginning. The same spring he married, and his wife came to work with him, as is the custom among Sino-Mauritians.

• *The significance of ethnicity.* In all the three examples, ethnic networks – often but not always simply kin networks – were activated in the pursuit of careers. This is hardly surprising, given the ethnic division of labour and the predominance of members of the subjects' own ethnic category in the personal action-sets of multiplex links.

The differences in the ethnic organisation of personal assets are obvious. In the last two cases, the preliminary conditions for individual career pursuits include property and education, whereas in the first case the actor's only assets were his working ability and personal action sets. The Sino-Mauritian could also activate his patriclan network. Creole genealogies are nearly always shallow, and Creoles lack kinship-based corporate groups. The average Creole has a large number of classificatory cousins, but rarely knows the descendants of his grandparents' siblings. Sino-Mauritian and Franco kin reckoning, on the contrary, tends to be deep and detailed, chiefly patrilineal, and recorded in writing.

Typical Hindu and Muslim careers would involve assets like geographic origins (in India), caste membership, education, kin corporations, and political acquaintances; while the main occupational capital of Coloureds has historically consisted in a higher than average education.

In this depiction, professional careers seem to be taken care of intra-ethnically. Employers claim they feel they can trust their own people and therefore tend to prefer them as employees; jobseekers, accordingly, turn to their own for help. Patronage in politics remains widespread – indeed to the extent that at one point, when the Minister of Finance was a Tamil, all the branch managers of the Bank of Mauritius were also Tamils. Systemic properties are reproduced in this way, but they can hardly be said simply to 'emerge' from aggregated action; properties of the greater society are already present before strategies are laid, and present as the structural conditions for action. Social structure does change, but enduring structural change is usually monitored in the large-scale fields;[6] it always involves a (gradual or sudden) new configuration of allocative and/or authorising power, and a new shared definition of relevant social reality. This kind of change will be dealt with later.

In the labour market, there is competition as well as complementarity. To some extent, ethnically based self-perceptions still imply systematically different strategies. In a coastal village of Hindu/Creole mixed population, there is a strong tendency to the effect that the Hindus work on the land, either as small planters or for an estate; while the majority of the Creoles have other occupations, the fishermen being the most visible ones. This is often perceived by the actors as a perfectly legitimate, if not natural form of occupational complementarity; indeed, this kind of division of labour may be seen as a functioning form of compromise so long as it does not contribute to a hierarchical system. When the division of labour involves great differences in wealth, on the other hand, there are inevitably murmurs about conspiracies and injustice. There is universal agreement over the value of individual economic wealth, and in this respect, the labour market is a field of constant competition over this scarce resource. But as I have shown, ethnically specific strategies to create personal wealth tend to differ in content and efficiency.

• *Ethnicity and kinship.* In the allocation of jobs and education, a taxonomic level lower than those included in Figure 4.1 has practical priority: that of kinship.[7] All other things being equal, one hires one's kin. Indeed, the dividing line between ethnicity and kinship is often a very thin one, particularly since classificatory kinship is sometimes invoked. Should one happen to be in the Ministry of Education and have to make a shortlist of candidates for a particular school, kin may well be favoured before other members of one's ethnic category. These practices are conventionally expected – by one's electorate and by the other politicians; but they are not explicitly seen as legitimate, and are often challenged publicly. In practical politics, the competition over scarce goods is usually understood as a zero-sum game between ethnic categories, one that frequently has to be solved through sequences of 'give-and-take' between politicians – a form of compromise that resembles booty-sharing more than a search for common denominators.

Politics

'Sak zako bizin protez so montayn,' said a prominent Hindu politician in 1983
('Each monkey has to protect his mountain'), and thus broke an unwritten
rule in Mauritian public life: 'Although you practice communalism, never
promote it explicitly in public!'

• *Ethnic division of power.* The Mauritian government has since independence been dominated by 'Hindi-speaking' Hindus, although they have
most of the time ruled with support from a small party representing
segments of the 'General Population'. The Hindus are also slightly overrepresented in the Civil Service and the parastatals, but not to the extent
that many non-Hindus believe (Eriksen 1988). The President is a Muslim.
The electoral system, based on the British Westminster system, ensures
the representation of minorities through a 'best loser' principle whereby
eight runners-up are secured seats. As for the legal system, the Chief Judge
is a Muslim, while three of the six judges of the Supreme Court are Franco-
Mauritians, one is Muslim, one Sino-Mauritian and one Hindu. Every major
ethnic category has its prominent lawyers. Mauritian law is an original mix
of the *Code Napoléon* and British judiciary principles.

• *A non-ethnic political party?* Most political parties in Mauritius have
overtly or covertly represented ethnic ('communal') interests, the classic
rivals of the 1960s being the Labour Party (Hindu) and the PSMD (Parti
Mauricien Social Démocrate), representing the 'General Population'. The
MMM (*Mouvement Militant Mauricien*) is often mentioned, by Mauritians
and foreign scholars, as an interesting exception. In the early days (before
the General Elections in 1976), the MMM would frequently put up Hindu
candidates in predominantly Creole constituencies, Muslims in Hindu
neighbourhoods, etc. This policy has been discontinued, as is evident from
any list of candidates from any general election after 1976. The ethnic
membership, and caste membership in the case of Hindus, of the candidates
is – in the case of the MMM as with the other large parties – closely
correlated with the geographical distribution of ethnic categories.

Having narrowly lost the 1976 election, the MMM Politburo, now
interpreting the situation in ethnic terms (admitting the pragmatic validity
of a model of society as divided along ethnic lines), realised the need for a
wider alliance before the 1982 election. They eventually decided to band
up with a small populist Hindu party with a sound rural base, PSM (*Parti
Socialiste Mauricien*). A formerly influential MMM faction, the Trotskyist
Lalit, left the party in disgust (LPT 1987). This alliance, uniting taxonomic
extremes, won the election.

Paul Bérenger, the founder of the party, was put up as the party's prime ministerial candidate for the first time in 1983, and then only as a *faute de mieux* option in the urgent situation that arose after the dramatic split of the party. In the early days, there was a shortage of Hindus in the party; when Anerood Jugnauth, a London-trained barrister, eventually joined, he rapidly acquired the status of the MMM's prime ministerial candidate. Despite Jugnauth's short career within the party, there was little internal opposition to this decision. Jugnauth was not only a Hindu; like Ramgoolam, he also belongs to the most numerous caste, the Vaish, considered neither a low nor a high caste.[8] This is probably no coincidence, as there were already low-caste, high-caste and minority Hindus of long-standing membership, who had also been active during the 'heroic era' of the party (1971–2), but who were discarded as potential leaders of the country. In other words, the lowest taxonomic level available was perceived as relevant. From 1976 to 1982, Jugnauth served as leader of the Opposition, and from 1982 he served as prime minister until the General Election of December 1995, when he was replaced by another Vaish, Seewosagur Ramgoolam's son Navin. When the ruling alliance split in 1983, MMM ideologists rapidly created an image of Jugnauth as a pawn in Bérenger's hands; a manipulated mascot with no independent will (cf. MMM 1985; Oodiah 1989).

The MMM, ostensibly working against ethnic divisions since its inception just after Independence, has thus consistently referred to ethnic taxonomies in its selection of political candidates at the highest level, that is in decisions taken by the party's Politburo before General Elections from 1976 to 1995.

• *Strange bedfellows.* In general, it should be noted that perceptions of taxonomic closeness/distance are not identical in politics with those in the other fields. Politics makes strange bedfellows, and Mauritian postwar politics has been a confusing sequence of shifting alliances, merging parties and changing strategies. The Mauritian two-bloc system is nonetheless stable as long as the blocs are roughly the same size. Muslims, Creoles, Tamils and Sino-Mauritians have during most of Mauritius' independent history been united in shifting strategic alliances against the Hindus, Coloureds and Franco-Mauritians; any alignment departing from notions of taxonomic distance would have looked fundamentally different. In other words, political ethnicity is not congruent with ethnicity in the household, in the locality and in the job market. The relatively short social distance between a rural Hindu and a rural Muslim is converted into a long distance in the Legislative Assembly; and because of the rivalry between the MMM and the PMSD – arguably the two parties with the least in common ideologically during the 1970s and 1980s, representing as they did the left and the right, respectively – the Creole/Coloured/Franco-Mauritian continuum is far from politically incorporated, the Franco-Mauritians, Coloureds and some

Creoles finding themselves periodically as the uncomfortable bedfellows of Hindu governments, while the majority of the Creoles have joined forces with Muslims and Tamils.

Education and the Mass Media

Primary education is nominally free and compulsory; in practice, it is neither. Parents must buy school uniforms, books and stationery for the pupils, and no sanctions are in practice applied to regular absentees. But the huge majority of Mauritian children do attend school, and more than a third proceed to secondary school. Some schools, on both the primary and secondary levels, are private (Catholic- and Hindu-supported schools, French *lycées*, an Islamic 'College', etc.); but most are public.

Perhaps surprisingly, the British presence from 1810 did not lead to a strong Anglicisation of educational institutions, which remained largely French in content and character – many of them private and linked with Catholicism (Ramdoyal 1977). Today's public secondary school curricula, nevertheless, are adapted from British ones, and lead to equivalents of 'O' and 'A' Levels. It is also noteworthy that some Indian children were already being taught in their vernacular by an Anglican missionary in the mid-nineteenth century.

Religious instruction is not a school subject in Mauritius, which has consciously confined religion to the field of mutual indifference or tolerance. Language instruction, on the other hand, is very important as well as being controversial, and it is discussed in detail in Chapter 5.

The educational system is directly linked to individual career development, is sanctioned in the political system, and is thus invested with power. Control over parts of the educational system entails not only definitional power, but also power to define which qualities of particular actors are to be seen as relevant in the later pursuit of careers – for example, when candidates for a particular higher educational programme are selected. Restricting ourselves to the national educational system here, we may state categorically that this process is carried out through the shortening of lists of applicants at several levels of decision, beginning at the school and ending in the ministerial office. The individuals acting on a high scale here are in nodal system positions, endowing them with much authoritative power.

• *Symbolic power.* Education is also a vehicle for the exertion of power in a more general and more elusive way, through the establishment of curricula and, more generally still, through the definitions of what is to count as relevant knowledge. In order for educational institutions and mass communication media to function as vehicles of power, they must necessarily be connected, in fact or potentially, with structures of allocation and/or authorisation in society – to which structures they do not strictly themselves belong.

In other words: control over educational institutions entails direct authorising power in the acceptance/rejection of applicants, but also implies power to provide *justified definitions of relevant reality*, that is power over symbols, sanctioned by the state apparatus in the case of public educational institutions, but by the ethnic leadership or some other relevant acting unit in private ones.

• *Ethnicity in the mass media.* The national broadcasting corporation (MBC) is government-controlled. During one week in 1971, roughly half the radio broadcasts were in French, a quarter in Hindustani/Bhojpuri,[9] a seventh in English and the rest in various minority languages (Baker 1972:25). The proportion of Kreol, absent in 1971, is now about 10 per cent (mid-1990s), while the proportions of French and Bhojpuri have decreased slightly. On television, Baker (1972) reports, 51 per cent of the broadcasts were in English, 41 per cent in French, 6 per cent in Hindustani and the remaining 2 per cent in other languages during the month of March, 1969. During March, 1986, the figures were: 21 per cent English, 62 per cent French, 12 per cent Hindustani, 3 per cent Kreol and 2 per cent in other languages, while the proportion of Kreol has risen slightly during the 1990s.[10] The stigma of Kreol, 'the unofficial national language', as a substandard form of French, is in other words still strong, although gradually decreasing. The replacement of English with French as the dominant language has its obvious practical reasons, while the increasing proportion of Hindustani (which is strictly speaking not a language spoken in Mauritius) was immediately caused by the introduction of two weekly Hindustani feature films.

• *The position of French and English.* The obvious interpretation of this policy is that French and English are retained as dominant languages in the state media as a symbolic justification of power on the part of the actors in decisive positions. French and English are exhibited as the natural linguistic codes of universal communication, and thus implicitly linked to the presumably universalist intentions of the men in power capable of using them. French and English are, for example, the only languages used in the Legislative Assembly, and are being reproduced symbolically as necessary knowledge in successful career development. On the other hand, the linguistic pluralism testified to by the presence of minority languages in the national media indicates the government's determination not to fuel discontent and unrest by 'muting' ethnic minorities. The programmatic pluralism implied can be described as a form of compromise, as symbolic power-sharing: as the antithesis of total hegemony.

Print media are owned by individuals, by political parties or by religious organisations. The great majority are published in French, but most of them print the occasional article in English or in an 'ancestral language'. The two leading dailies (*Le Mauricien* and *L'Express*), owned by non-corporate aggregates of individuals, have an overt policy of 'national responsibility', while the remaining press, to a greater or lesser extent, overtly or tacitly, addresses itself to chosen segments of the population, whether singled out on an ethnic/religious basis or not.

The power of the mass communication media can be described as an ability to *define fields and modes of discourse*, and their immediate importance is enormous in the ambiguous Mauritian minefield. As has been already argued, a particular alignment of interests is not the immediate result of a set of practices; rather, it is manufactured through interpretative mediations of practices, through the production of meaning. In this perspective, media, whether loyal to the relevant structures of power or not, play a part in generating the practices intended to maintain or change these structures; simultaneously they are themselves strongly influenced by the same structures (property and political power). This holds true whether taken on a national, an ethnic or a local scale.

Organisation and Meaning

Thus far, I have written comparatively much about ethnic *strategies* and little of ethnic *identity*. Indeed, if I had limited the analysis to the nationwide fields, where decisions that directly affect large numbers of people are taken, the common 'instrumentalist' idea of ethnicity as equating with certain forms of political organisation would have seemed accurate. At this level of scale, individual action-sets are wide and, to a great extent, single-stranded in character. Networks reproduced on this level are by definition problem-oriented in content; in other words, they would not have existed had their purpose not been defined from the outset. The dominant type of action at this level of scale is goal-rational (*zweckrational* in Weber's and Schütz's terminologies).

But these processes, often depicted as the strategic manipulation of symbols, maximisation and so on, presuppose both the reproduction of shared meaning cutting across ethnic boundaries *and* the reproduction of ethnic categorisation at the household and kinship levels. At its simplest the panethnic shared meaning denotes the need for agreement about what is to count as valuable. Common rules for conduct, codes of signification, and shared norms – in brief, what Schütz and Luckmann (1979) label social structures of relevance, *Relevanzstrukturen*, are essential for there to be any 'negotiation' or competition at all. Agreement is prior to disagreement, whether chronologically, logically or as a potential inherent in the concept of disagreement. Negotiation and competition take over where shared *Relevanzstrukturen* stop, but agreement over the constituting rules – in brief, common denominators – is necessary for there to be any game at all. In this way, it becomes clear that political ethnicity, far from being fundamental, is a secondary phenomenon dependent on the reproduction of ethnic categorisation at the local level.

In a more general vein, it may be noted that Tönnies (1912, § 10) argues that *Gemeinschaft* relations are prior to *Gesellschaft* relations. This suggests that action sets of vague mutual obligation ('generalised reciprocity', cf. Sahlins 1972) are ontologically more fundamental than those that are overtly contractual ('balanced reciprocity'), the former providing the cultural content and the social frame of intersubjectivity necessary for the latter to be possible. In the next chapter, the interrelationship between the meaningful dimension and the strategic dimension of ethnicity is illuminated by way of a discussion of the two main public markers of ethnic identity, which both cut across the social fields of the last two chapters: language and religion.

Notes

1. This country cultivates sugar-cane and prejudices. (. . .) In this tropical hell, nobody ever meets anybody – outside the castes, the freemasonries of blood, everything is TABOO. Here we have a League of Nations where the warring of prejudices is endemic and atrocious – above all that which is to do with colour prejudices.
2. Since the 1980s, ethnic membership has not been a census category. Ethnic membership is instead recorded in more oblique ways, through the categories of ancestral language and religion.
3. For a brief period in the latter half of the 1980s, a political movement professing to represent the Hindu minorities (Tamils, Telugus and Marathis) existed.
4. Nearly one attempted suicide a day is recorded in Mauritius, and there has been a sharp increase in the number of suicides in the 15–25 age group (Oodiah 1992:62).

5. In 1968, one of the sugar estates was purchased by the Mauritian state.

6. This is not always the case; consider, for example, caste climbing in India or any other type of successful 'grass roots' movement.

7. It is sometimes suggested that the real problem of communalism in Mauritius might actually be one of *nepotism*. Nepotism is largely activated in the labour market, in politics and in the national educational system – that is, on a high level of scale; and it may therefore be argued that nepotist practices, misinterpreted as communalism on lower levels of scale, determine ethnic relations generally. My material suggests that this hypothesis is only partly correct: non-kinship-based communalism is also widely practised on a high level of scale, although nepotism is preferred if available (and this is directly implied in the practical application of taxonomic levels).

8. The Mauritian term 'Vaish' lumps together what was originally a large number of clean castes in India, and only corresponds vaguely to the Indian Vaishya *varna*.

9. Baker lists this as 'Hindustani' *tout court*, but I believe most of the transmissions must have been in Bhojpuri. On TV, on the other hand, many programmes *are* in Hindustani: they are Indian feature films.

10. Since Mauritius now has two TV channels, the figures are not readily comparable.

CHAPTER FIVE

Contested Symbols: Language and Religion

Sakenn pe prie dan so fason. (Each prays in his/her own way.)

— Mauritian proverb

One of the most enduring debates in the literature on ethnicity concerns the relationship between its instrumental and its symbolic aspects – whether the main cause of the maintenance of ethnic distinctions is their political and strategic potential or their role as a repository of meaning. Since the Mauritian material has already suggested that ethnicity is dual in that it encompasses aspects of both strategy and meaning, the debate seems to rest on a false assumption, namely that we are talking about an 'either–or' kind of phenomenon. The distinction is nevertheless relevant, as it calls attention to the functional poles of ethnicity: if it is impossible to identify subjectively with an ethnic category, persons will by default not do it; and if ethnic distinctions have no social consequences, they are by definition non-existent.

• *Differences in ethnic incorporation.* The largest ethnic categories of Mauritius are organised along very different lines, and show the significance of the interrelationship between social organisation and meaning. As I have shown elsewhere (Eriksen 1986, 1988, 1991c; cf. also Mannick 1978), the social organisation and cultural values reproduced among Creoles effectively militate against the formation of a Creole corporate group. The emphasis placed on individual freedom, the shallowness and classificatory breadth of genealogies and kin reckoning, the 'crab antics' of friendship, obliging a male Creole to spend liberally on his friends,[1] and the suspicion of formal hierarchies – phenomena that form an important part of the dominant Creole self-identification – have prevented the Creoles from representing their interests strategically and collectively, as virtually all the other ethnic categories of Mauritius have done. Indeed, by climbing the social ladder and beginning to endorse middle-class values, Creoles may change ethnic membership and become Coloureds, no matter what their actual physical appearance.

This chapter will concentrate on two focal dimensions for ethnic and national identification in Mauritius, religion and language; and the interplay between aspects of strategy and aspects of meaning is apparent here. Language and religion are simultaneously instrumental and meaningful. They serve as political symbols and as structures of relevance; they can be held up as banners, and they provide personal experiences with a substantial, meaningful content.

Language Strategies in Ethnicity

The ways in which ethnic identity and organisation are linked to language are many and complex. As was noted earlier, the number of languages in Mauritius is high, but their respective uses differ greatly and crucially. Language can be invoked self-consciously as a marker of ethnicity, which is evident from the discrepancy between what many people *claim* they do, and what they actually *do* when it comes to speech acts in the widest sense (see also Eriksen 1990; Hookoomsing 1986). Language seen as linguistic practice can also bridge differences. All other things being equal, cultural differences in a complex society are naturally less marked when the constituent groups speak a common language than when they do not.

• *A typology of languages*. Mauritius has everything in this respect: community languages strengthening intra-ethnic cohesion, supra-ethnic languages bridging differences and serving as common denominators of both communication and identity symbolism, and languages that are not spoken but are invoked as ethnic symbols.

Henri Souchon, entitling his contribution to a conference on language and society[2] 'The Myth of Fifteen Languages for a Population of One Million' (Souchon 1982) aptly characterises the ambiguity of the situation. In his brief paper Souchon elaborates on former typologies of languages, and finally divides Mauritian languages into four categories (see Table 5.1).

Since Kreol is by far the most spoken language in Mauritius regardless of ethnic category, language is rarely used as an ethnic boundary marker in everyday situations. Interestingly, dialectal variations within Kreol are linked with age and region (see also Chap. 6), rather than with ethnic distinctions. Instead, connections with ancestral languages are stressed, sometimes to the extent of manipulating recorded facts. This discourse

Table 3. Languages in Mauritius

Language	Maternal		Ancestral		International	Ritual
Arabic	N	0.2%	N	7.0%	Y	Y
Bhojpuri	Y	20.4%	Y	19.0%	N	N
Cantonese	N		Y		N	N
English	N	0.2%	N	0.2%	Y	Y
French	Y	3.7%	Y	3.5%	Y	Y
Gujerati	N		Y	0.2%	N	N
Hakka	Y	0.6%	Y	2.0%	N	(Y)
Hindi	N	11.5%	N	23.0%	Y	Y
Hindustani	N		N		Y	N
Kreol	Y	54.0%	Y	29.0%	N	(Y)
Latin	N		N		N	Y
Mandarin	N		N		Y	Y
Marathi	Y	1.3%	Y	2.2%	N	(Y)
Sanskrit	N		N		N	Y
Tamil	Y	3.6%	Y	7.0%	N	Y
Telugu	Y	1.6%	Y	2.6%	N	(Y)
Urdu	N	2.5%	Y	5.8%	N	N*

Sources: Mauritius 1984, vol. II, tables 19 and 20 (percentages), Souchon (1982), Baker (1972), Stein (1983), Ramdoyal (1977), own field material.
*Urdu was used in Muslim ritual until the early 1970s, when its place was taken by Kreol. Today, Arabic gradually seems to be becoming the only language of the mosque, although Kreol is still widely used.

takes place in the national fields of politics, media and education, and ramifies into the local fields.

The percentages in Table 3 refer to figures from the population census of 1983. As the census was carried out as a questionnaire survey, the figures accumulate individual statements regarding which language they and their ancestors spoke, and these social facts are not necessarily coterminous with the historical facts.

The concept 'ancestral language' is an elusive one, and in practice it is held to replace the former census category 'ethnic membership'. Ethnic categories are now officially not included in Mauritian censuses, and to a great extent, statements about ancestral languages are to be understood as statements about ethnic membership.

Revelations from a Census

Read properly, which is to say between the lines, census figures reveal a great deal about both ethnic identification and ethnic organisation in Mauritius.

• *The place of Kreol.* In all likelihood, Kreol is casually spoken by much more than 54 per cent of the population. (At a later census (Mauritius 1991-2), 35.8 per cent stated that Kreol was their ancestral language, an increase of 6 per cent, whereas 61.7 per cent stated that it was the language they usually spoke at home.)

Perhaps the term 'mother tongue' is ill chosen, for indeed, many Indo-Mauritians speak Bhojpuri with their mother and Kreol with virtually everybody else. Be this as it may; the ideological linking of Kreol ('Creole') with the Creole ethnic category, and the historically correct assumption that Kreol began as a contact language used by African and Malagasy slaves, discourage non-Creoles from advertising the fact that Kreol is actually their maternal tongue. Before the census, further, religious and ethnic organis-ations ordered their followers to fill in the census forms in a way enhancing ethnic interests. Instructions were given from religious or otherwise ethnicist bodies through vertical religious and para-religious channels in order that information should be available in the local fields, outside mosques and temples, through *baitkas* and *madrassahs*, and in the mass media.

• *The 'non-Kreolised' Telugu.* An example of an ethnic minority organ-isation anxious that the cultural identity it embodies should continue to be recognised is the National Telugu Federation, which represents some 2.7 per cent of the total population, virtually all Kreolophones. Their newspaper advertisement reads as follows (in French!):

NATIONAL TELUGU FEDERATION

All Telugus of Mauritius are asked, as regards the new
population census,to write in the columns 11-12-13:
Telugu – Telugu – Telugu.

Thank you.

(Quoted from Hookoomsing 1986:124.)

The columns in question are those dealing with religion, ancestral language and language currently spoken.

Obviously, if all Telugus had in fact been casual speakers of Telugu, this advertisement would not have been necessary. Noting that only some 60 per cent of the Mauritians of Telugu ancestry actually did fill in the last column as asked, it is necessary to conclude that some interviewers did not take answers at face value,[3] and/or that many of the people in question followed values different from those of the organisation ostensibly repre-senting their interests: they allowed some identity different from their ancestral ethnic one to overrule it.

The second assumption is not inherently valid. Ethnic identity can be maintained despite the recognised disappearance of linguistic difference. The fact is that virtually all the Telugus of Mauritius stated that their *ancestral* language was Telugu. This means that even those of Telugu origin who admitted being Kreolophones remained self-ascribed carriers of Telugu cultural identity. For when does an ancestral language cease to be an ancestral language? Three generations after it was last spoken within the family? Five generations? Ten? A hundred? – It does when members of an ethnic category cease to regard themselves as such, which is to say when the ethnic category ceases to exist. When Mauritians whose ancestors were Telugus start to claim Kreol as their ancestral language, they will, it may seem, have acquired a Mauritian identity overruling the ethnic one. Why don't they?

The Telugu are a small minority (3 per cent of the Mauritian population) within the larger overarching Hindu category, and most of them are rural small planters and labourers, although Telegus, like other Mauritians, and most of all young women, are increasingly becoming industrial workers. Politically, the Telugus are, unlike the Tamils, generally believed to vote with the majority Hindus. Ritually, they share many practices with the Tamils and have a related ancestral language; but there has been no spectacular revival of Telugu traditions. The leadership of the Dravidian League of Mauritius is strongly dominated by Tamils, and there can be no comparison between the level of participation in the Dravidian festivals of Tamils and Telugus. The Tamils have a strong urban base and many wealthy members (notably merchants in Port-Louis), and several leading politicians. The Telugu have none of this. So why, then, was it so important to the Telugu leaders that their fellow Telegus stated that they spoke Telugu daily? The answer has both practical and symbolic aspects: one relating to utility, and one to meaning. First, the Telugu leaders would never have encouraged maintenance of their identity as discrepant unless they believed that this could endow them with greater power than they would have had, had they allowed their discreteness to disappear into greater Hinduness. This hypothesis is plausible enough in a wider context, where the rights of ethnic minority groups are unofficially recognised in the fields of politics (through strategic alliances and the best loser system), the mass media (through quotas of air time) and the educational system (through language instruction in 'ancestral languages'). A Mauritian interest group has an unspoken right to more power the larger the number of members it can credibly claim.

Secondly, it is in the utilitarian interest of the Telugu leaders to maintain genealogies and recognition of kinship as intact as possible. Nepotism is a major form of communalism. Should their mutual recognition of closeness disappear, it wouldn't follow that the individual Telugus approached any other ethnic category taxonomically, and they would as a result end up in a situation similar to that of the Creoles in the labour market: with no self-sustaining 'safety net', no networks facilitating social mobility and securing employment.

If this explains why the Telugu Federation encouraged people to over-communicate the cultural dimension of their ethnic identity, it cannot explain why over half the Telugus of Mauritius, most of them rural workers and their families, stated that their casual language was Telugu. Surely, from their own perspective, this could not improve their or their children's job opportunities? It thus seems much more likely that they did it in order to communicate their cultural identity (the symbolic aspect of ethnicity) to others and to themselves: to the interviewer they did not wish to admit to not being capable of speaking their ancestral language; for themselves, they felt ashamed about it. There is no reason to believe that they replied as they did for purely utilitarian reasons.

• *Arabic-speaking Indo-Muslims.* The Mauritian Muslims and their strategies in relation to the census also reveal the importance of unspoken languages for ethnic identity. In Emrith's *The Muslims of Mauritius* (1967), no mention whatsoever is made of Arabic as a language important to Mauritian Muslims. In the 1972 Census, *nobody* seems to have referred to Arabic as their ancestral language: the entire Islamic community still overtly recognised the Indian subcontinent as their ancestral country, and Urdu was still considered the ancestral language. By the 1980s, the Muslims, widely believed by Mauritian non-Muslims to act very corporatively in political matters, are split into several factions on the language issue. More than 40 per cent have redefined their own history, claiming that their ancestors spoke Arabic; a third stick to Urdu; and the remaining quarter are probably distributed over Kreol, Bhojpuri and Gujerati. (In fact, the majority of the ancestors of Mauritian Muslims spoke Bhojpuri, but Urdu would have been their literary language.) The turn towards Arabic during this period must be seen as an expression of (a) a wish to participate in the pan-Islamic movement, (b) part of a strategy to create employment for Mauritian Muslims in OPEC countries, and (c) a qualitative 'improvement' of one's own cultural identity. No social prestige is associated with links to Pakistan, while the Arab part of the world has been of increasing geo-political importance since the early 1970s (see also Hollup 1995).[4]

• *Undercommunicating Sino-Mauritians.* Among the Sino-Mauritians, a surprisingly high number state Kreol as their ancestral and currently spoken language alike. Mandarin is nonetheless widely read, and most Sino-

Mauritians are able to speak a Chinese language. Obviously, the Sino-Mauritian strategy is fundamentally different from that of the various Indo-Mauritian categories. Numerically weak but economically strong, the 'Jews of Mauritius' undercommunicate their ethnic identity in public, by claiming Kreol as a first language. In fact, this practice makes it difficult to identify the Sino-Mauritian ethnic category in the census. Altogether, about 21,000 Mauritians state a Chinese language as their ancestral one, which amounts to only two-thirds of the Sino-Mauritians. The rest cannot be identified with reference to religion either, since they are nominally Catholics, like the General Population. Clearly, the strategic option chosen by a growing number of Sino-Mauritians is Mauritian nationalism. As an economic élite, they have everything to lose in democratic communal competition. It is in their immediate interest that their ethnic identity is publicly under-communicated; as the 'Jews of Mauritius', the Sino-Mauritians further fear the very possible advent of anti-Chinese sentiment.

In a social context where national identity is more important than ethnic identity, the fact that many of the nation's important businessmen are of Chinese descent would diminish in importance. Simultaneously, the Sino-Mauritians efficiently reproduce their organisation and cultural traits *internally*, with a material base in the Chinatown of Port-Louis. This is where the various organisations with Chinese connotations (many of them with 'neutral' names) are based; it is where clans meet, where Sino-Mauritian newspapers are printed *and* distributed (I have hardly ever seen any of them outside this quarter), and where the signs of shops are in Chinese – many of the shops specialising in imported goods from Taiwan, Hong Kong and mainland China. Roughly half the Sino-Mauritians live in Port-Louis; the atmosphere of the Chinese quarter has a strong Chinese flavour, whereas the Chinese cultural element is virtually absent elsewhere in public Mauritius. The strategy has been to remain as invisible as possible externally, and to reproduce ancestral culture and forms of organisation intensely internally (Kouwenhoven 1988). The parallels to diaspora Jews are striking (cf. Epstein 1978:64, quoting a New York rabbi: 'For our own part, we are Israelites in the Synagogue, and Americans elsewhere.').

• *Non-African Creoles.* It should finally be noted that the Creoles do not collectively emphasise their African ancestry: virtually nobody in the census stated that their ancestral language was Malagasy, Kiswahili or Wolof, or even 'African' (the latter being, incredibly, an option in the census forms). Their history as an ethnic category begins with slavery. But the example of the Muslims shows that it need not be so, and changes in the Creole representation of their own history and thus their communal identity may be imminent (see Benoit 1985). A very low proportion of the Creoles state that French is their ancestral language, although many are of mixed phenotype.

• *Language and religion*. Hookoomsing (1986:126) finds a high correlation between ancestral language and religious inclination in the census figures. The Hindu categories display very nearly a one-to-one relationship; Kreol is slightly overrepresented *vis-à-vis* Christianity; the case of Islam has been accounted for above; finally, there are apparently many more descendants of speakers of Chinese languages than there are Buddhists. In fact, most of the Sino-Mauritians are today officially Catholics.

In sum, differences in the ethnic categories' mode of internal organisation are reflected in the strategies adopted in the population census. The Hindus tend to overcommunicate the Indianness of their culture, and the Hindu minorities overcommunicate linguistic markers of distinctiveness;[5] a substantial proportion of the Muslims are drifting from a Pakistano-Mauritian to an Arabo-Mauritian identity; and the Sino-Mauritians under-communicate their distinctiveness; whereas the Creoles, Coloureds and Franco-Mauritians have no corporate identity strategies in this respect.

Linguistic Diversity in Primary Education

The Mauritian system of education, initially designed by Europeans, has always been relatively uniform. Since Independence, there have been policies aiming to 'nationalise' it gradually, yet retaining its compatibility with European educational systems.

In November, 1984, the government appointed a committee of parliamentarians to 'consider and report on the circumstances in which registered school candidates sitting for the Certificate of Primary Education examination may opt for ranking purposes for an oriental language from among Hindi, Urdu, Tamil, Telegu, Marathi, Mandarin and Arabic in addition to the four compulsory subjects, namely: English, Mathematics, Geography and French' (Mauritius 1986:1). Instruction in Oriental languages had formerly been available in private institutions and as additional subjects in some schools. The novelty of the proposition was its suggestion that Oriental languages should now become important in ranking and thus have a direct effect on the admission to secondary school.

The committee was composed of 5 Hindus, 1 Muslim, 2 Creoles and 1 Coloured; two of the members belonged to the political opposition. Some of the members eventually resigned and were replaced, and the committee responsible for the report consisted of 5 Hindus, 2 Muslims, 1 Coloured and a Tamilo-Christian.

• *The hearings.* In two consecutive press releases during 1985, the public was invited to suggest solutions and discuss particular issues with the committee, and 109 actors responded to the communiques: 62 individuals and 47 organisations. Ethnically, they were distributed as is shown in Table 4:

The pressure groups were founded on different bases. Some were religious groups (most of these were Hindu sub-categories based on caste, ancestral language and/or denomination); and some represented formal language groups (such as the Mauritius Arabic Language Teachers and Students Association); while yet others were national or local parents' organisations, teachers' unions, humanitarian groups or youth organisations. The great majority of the individuals belonged to one or several élites.

The very time-consuming hearings took place within the national political system. While it is clearly true that the hitherto dominant position of French has been caused by power relations in the economic system and in public cultural life, the entire debate was this time undertaken with no reference to the local economy. The overt preoccupation was with fairness and compromise; and whereas it might have been legitimate and indeed desirable to display adherence to sectional interests in the political system, anyone wishing to participate in the national press, where the issue was discussed extensively, was obliged to emphasise his or her commitment to the common good.

• *A new common denominator.* The issue was extremely important in so far as Mauritians attach high – and increasing – value to education, and it

Table 4. Participation in public hearing on language instruction in public schools (*Source: Mauritius 1986*)

	Individuals	Organisations
Hindu	45	24
Tamil	5	2
Muslim	7	5
Sino-Mauritian	1	–
Creole/Coloured	2	5
Franco	2	–
Mixed Oriental		1*
Non-ethnic/unidentified	10	

* Basha Andolan is a loosely knit umbrella organisation comprising some 16 lesser collectivities: 14 of the member organisations represent segments of the Hindu population (divided by caste, denomination and language), 1 represents Tamils and 1 represents Muslims.

demanded a *redefinition of the lowest common denominator*. Formerly, the lowest common denominator had been colonially defined and sanctioned; this time, it had to be specified *nationally* according to democratic rules balancing the demands of compromise with the demands of national homogeneity.

In the event, a composite denominator resulted. I quote from the report:

(a) English being the official language and the most widely used international language should continue to be promoted and given due importance;

(b) it would be desirable and in the interests of all Mauritians to be encouraged to learn French, which is readily acquired in the Mauritian context;

(c) language, being also a vehicle of culture, must be given its importance in order to understand and preserve worthwhile ancestral values; and

(d) children who do not take an oriental language would be offered a course in Cultures and Civilisations in Mauritius (Mauritius 1986:11).

This means, in practice, that children belonging to the 'General Population' would be taught *Cultures and Civilisations in Mauritius*, a course aiming at 'making children aware of the rich cultural heritage of Mauritius' (ibid.), denoting a multiculturalist variety of nationhood (see Chap. 7). In this way, knowledge of Oriental languages did not give a disproportionate advantage to children of Oriental ancestry. Kreol was not considered to be a language worthy of systematic instruction, and, as far as I have been able to ascertain, none of the groups and individuals involved in the hearing of the Select Committee suggested that it should be (see further discussion below).

Questions concerning languages in the educational system continue to be among the paramount political issues in Mauritius (see also Kalla 1986; Bunwaree 1994; Nave n.d. 1). When Prime Minister Anerood Jugnauth supported, in 1995, a renewed suggestion to make Oriental languages an obligatory part of the CPE (Certificate of Primary Education), he was met with very strong objections from Creole spokesmen who argued that this move would deepen the *malaise créole*, the tendency among Creoles not to obtain higher education. This question became the main issue in the following electoral campaign, culminating in a massive defeat for Jugnauth's MSM/RMM government.

As the analysis has shown, language is a many-faceted symbol in Mauritius. It serves to symbolise ethnic identity in an essentially non-utilitarian way; but linguistic proficiency also directly impinges on a person's career opportunities. The two dimensions do not always coincide. For example, knowledge of Kreol is necessary in order to function in many fields in Mauritian society, but the language is scarcely valued positively. Proficiency in Hindi, conversely, has a strong positive significance among Mauritian Hindus, but has little practical importance.

Kreol and Mauritian Nationhood

> Comme de nombreuses bourgeoisies africaines qui affirment leur indépendance nationale et leur authenticité pour le retour aux sources, les riches Indiennes portent le *sari*. Mais celui-ci n'a rien à voir avec celui des femmes du peuple. Pour la bourgeoisie il a tout d'abord une fonction politique, celle d'affirmer sa spécificité nationale face aux autres nations de l'île, pour plus tard refuser le créole comme langue officielle, c'est-à-dire aussi refuser la nation mauricienne[6] (Durand and Durand 1978: 25).

Were it only this simple! According to this view, the Mauritian nation would by definition exclude culturally communicated Indianness from Mauritian nationhood. A main point in the forging of a Mauritian national identity has nevertheless been to accommodate the 'ethnic cultures', including locally adapted variants of Mauritian Indianness, within a wider national identity (see Chaps. 7 and 8).[7] Further, the 'political function' alluded to by the Durands cannot account for the enthusiasm and devotion encountered among Indo-Mauritians who strive to preserve, reinvent and revitalise aspects of their ancestral culture – language, ritual and beliefs, genealogies, pasts and localities – often at a considerable cost, without tangible political or material gains.

The Durands correctly identify one of the reasons that Kreol is not a respected language in the national fields of Mauritius; it is rarely written, never used in parliament, and is completely absent from school curricula and textbooks. While Kreol is of paramount importance in most households, in local networks and among colleagues, job advertisements and applications are always written in French or English, French and English are the only languages used in the Legislative Assembly, and Kreol is rarely heard on radio and television.

'Kreol is bad French. When you already know Kreol, why not take the extra effort to learn French? Kreol works fine orally, but it won't do in writing.' This kind of statement is very common, not least among people who do not master any other language properly. Replying to radical nationalists who rejected French on the grounds that it was the language of the colonisers, the chief editor of *Le Mauricien* once asked, rhetorically: 'Should one refuse Fidel Castro the right to speak the language of the coloniser of his country?' (Selvon 1984). When a Creole climbs socially and becomes a member of the Mauritian middle class, not only does he begin to exert influence in the national fields of Mauritian society, but he may also switch ethnic membership to Coloured and home language to French (Chaudenson 1979; Eriksen 1988:109–24). The case for Kreol as a national language, in other words, seems bleak. Or does it?

• *A national language is a dialect backed by an army*. At the time of the French revolution, about a dozen dialects, some of them distinctive enough to be considered separate languages, were spoken in France. The concept of the modern nation-state was developed during the same period; the peoples of France were to be integrated economically and politically at a state level. The demand for a common language as a practical instrument (in administration and the extraction of taxes) and as a vessel of national unity (in military and other matters) was strong. Two centuries later, most Frenchmen speak a variety of what was at the time the Île-de-France (Parisian) dialect.

Sometimes, but rarely, otherwise diverse peoples have been successfully integrated into national states owing to their common language (Germany is an obvious example). More commonly, linguistic homogeneity develops after the nation-state. Politico-economic units that cannot be homogenised linguistically are frequently either federations (Switzerland, Canada, Belgium, Yugoslavia until its break-up), or ruled politically and/or economically by a hegemonic ethnic/linguistic group (Ian Smith's Rhodesia, French DOM-TOMs (*Domaines d'Outre-Mer, Territoires d'Outre-Mer*), Ecuador) – or they are either not really integrated on a state level and/or unstable (which could be said of many African countries). A form of compromise between linguistic fragmentation and enforced homogenisation is the coexistence of several linguistic groups mediated by one or several *lingua francas*, as in countries such as India and Singapore. Processes of ethnic and linguistic change are continuous; structurally they may be perceived as systemic adjustments aiming for stability, individually as struggles for meaningful survival within a manageable opportunity structure.

In Mauritius, Kreol has over the last two centuries proved practically capable of uniting otherwise very diverse groups into a relatively homogeneous linguistic group. This does not imply that ethnic differences have been eradicated; moreover, the importance of language as a criterion of distinctiveness remains crucial in the continued reproduction, discussed above, of ancestral languages.

• *Languages and fields*. None of the languages spoken in Mauritius is strictly confined to a single social field. English is rarely spoken but frequently written; French is widely written and spoken in formal or semi-formal contexts; Kreol is normally used in informal situations, etc.

Generally, use of particular languages depends on social situation and status activated, not on field nor interactional partners. During the break, the university lecturer addresses his students in Kreol; the clerk addresses his subordinate in Kreol but his boss in French (and possibly his mother in Bhojpuri); the Franco-Mauritian housewife addresses the Sino-Mauritian shopkeeper in Kreol, but would speak French with the attendant in one of the posh shops of downtown Curepipe.

• *The stigma of Kreol.* Popular conceptions of Kreol are, despite its near-universal use in informal contexts, all but pejorative. This is partly because Kreol is associated with the Creoles. It is a language the Mauritians speak *malgré eux.* The language is still widely regarded as 'nothing but French badly pronounced and free from ordinary rules of grammar', as a colonial official would have it at the turn of the century. But Mauritians also fear further isolation from the international community if they were to replace French and English with the language spoken only locally: they feel their pride as *us*, the Mauritians seen under the gaze of the foreigners (see Chap. 7), threatened. Further, there are Mauritian intellectuals, sympathetically inclined towards Kreol, who doubt its ability to conceptualise the increasingly complex Mauritian socio-cultural reality. In their – and in many's – view, Kreol is a beautiful language in poetry and songs, an accurate one in the fields, a colourful one in the bar. But, they claim, its syntax and grammar cannot accommodate concepts of abstract and complex character, such as those necessary in, for example, sociological research, industrial design, or philosophical thought. This kind of argument was, incidentally, used against the European vernaculars after the introduction of Gutenberg's printing press, when they began to threaten the hegemony of Latin.

Some symbolic connotations of the 'linguistic division of labour' or diglossia between French and Kreol, can be represented symbolically as Table 5.

• *Power asymmetries.* Great efforts are made in order that the asymmetrical relationship between the two possibly most important languages in Mauritius should be maintained and justified *vis-à-vis* non-Francophones. Command of French is a prerequisite for and a tangible sign of high social status; the ruling class of *colons* have always been Francophone and have consciously used the French language as an important part of their ideological apparatus. In books and newspaper columns, Franco-Mauritians and Coloureds of respectable standing regularly link the decline of manners with the supposedly deteriorating position of French in Mauritius.[8] Arguing that making Kreol a national language would isolate Mauritius in the global community, they have, with a great measure of success, managed to shift attention towards the relationship between French and English rather than

Table 5. Normative connotations of French–Kreol diglossia

FRENCH	KREOL
power	impotence
abstract thought	practical tasks
steak & salad	*Kari masala*
wine & whisky	rum & beer
whiteness	blackness
refinement	vulgarity
responsibility	carelessness
religion	superstition
education	ignorance
literacy	illiteracy
seriousness	jocularity
bonne société	*milieu populaire*
(etc.)	

that between French and Kreol. The power of defining the relevant fields of discourse, alluded to elsewhere, is visibly exerted in the mass media field.

Representatives of France, the most important external power in the western Indian Ocean, are anxious to maintain a hegemonic position in the domain of 'culture'. The French cultural centre, *L'Alliance Française*, has a much higher level of activity than say, the British Council, and local dramatic groups staging plays in French receive financial support from France. Further, a powerful television transmitter broadcasting French programmes, aimed exclusively at Mauritius, has been installed on the eastern coast of the French DOM La Réunion. Quite unlike what occurs in many other societies (not least Quebec), French is perceived by the Mauritian nationalist left as the main language of domination, while English is seen as the more neutral language.

• *Cultural radicalism.* Since independence, the taken-for-granted asymmetry between Kreol and French has been challenged in a more serious manner in Mauritius than in the French DOM-TOMs (see Chaudenson 1979 for La Réunion, Bébel-Gisler 1975 for Guadeloupe and Martinique). From its foundation in 1969, the MMM used Kreol in its internal meetings, in press conferences and at public meetings. The discovery that their leader, an obviously educated and refined Franco-Mauritian, would rather speak Kreol than French, was a source of pride and wonder among the followers of the MMM.

The low symbolic rank of Kreol is thus not unambiguous. The radical postcolonial cultural movements seeking to justify a Mauritian nation in the decade following independence, some of them associated with the MMM, regarded the Kreol language and *séga* music[9] as important symbolic markers, and some of the more innovative activists introduced Oriental instruments and harmonies into the *séga*. While the MMM party was in power in 1982–3, a Kreol translation briefly replaced the English version of the national anthem played every evening at the end of TV transmissions. This caused a great uproar and contributed to the dissolution of the MMM government along largely ethnic lines (Oodiah 1989). Rather than unite the diverse populations in a nation, the decision awoke latent conflicts and accentuated the popular awareness of 'cultural differences'.

The strong hostility against making Kreol the national language was in part due to its being identified with the Creoles as an ethnic group, but there were also other factors (see Bowman 1991; Eriksen 1992a). In the early 1980s, the main slogan of the MMM was *Enn sel lepep; enn sel nasyon* (One single people; one single nation). A typical reaction among the sceptics was that this would imply that *'tu dimunn pu vini kreol'*; everybody would allegedly become a Creole in language and way of life. The *séga* music as a potential national symbol has faced similar obstacles, since it is still associated with the Creole ethnic group. The radical nationalists, most of whom were not ethnic Creoles, chose as their markers of nationhood symbols that were indeed uniquely Mauritian, but also happened to be symbols associated with the Creoles, who are the only Mauritians who cannot draw symbolic resources from an ancestral culture outside Mauritius. It is likely that if Mauritius had an ethnic composition similar to that in the Seychelles (with a modest Asian presence), Kreol could, in the early 1980s, have become a national language along with English and French.

Changes in attitudes to Kreol closely parallel political changes. From Independence to 1982, there was a period of increasing national sentiment and class consciousness, culminating in the general strike of 1979 and reaching an anticlimax of sorts following the 1982 election victory of the MMM-PSM alliance. Nationalist and class ideology were compatible with a higher evaluation of Kreol; indeed, it might be said that the latter follows logically from the former (or conversely). Thus the use of Kreol in unusual contexts came to be perceived as a sign that a unified, just nation was about to be built; at least, such was the hope of MMM strategists. These alternative dichotomies are represented in Table 6.

When attempting to replace folk classifications based on ethnicity with class-based ones, the cultural radicals alienated people seeing their own ethnically dependent strategies threatened and those fearing cultural uniformisation and further isolation of Mauritius, this syndrome being epitomised in the linguistic idiom of Kreol. Perhaps the dichotomies reproduced in Table 6 are acknowledged as 'true' by most Mauritians, but their personal experience and strategies in pursuit of their careers, and

Table 6. Alternative connotations of French–Kreol diglossia

FRENCH	KREOL
Oppression	Justice
Snobbery	Comradeship
Stratification	Equality
False consciousness	True consciousness

their perceptions of social rank (which are at least true as self-fulfilling prophecies), compel them, regardless of ethnic membership, to let the other model (Table 5), overrule them.

Kreol is correctly perceived as being in contradiction to social mobility. Within the Creole ethnic category, where no third language interferes with the French–Kreol diglossia, upward social mobility entails a switching of basic cultural codes. The switch to French language is crucial in this movement. As was noted above, literacy and seriousness are associated with French: 'One cannot live in a Western way and speak Creole.'[10] Thus the widely accepted division of labour between Kreol and French (sanctioned publicly in the media, politics and education) contributes to preserving Kreol as an oral language lacking vocabulary and structures to conceptualise crucial aspects of social life in modern Mauritius. The entanglement of social status and language is self-fulfilling, and remains valid until a new model of social reality, incorporating a model of Kreol as a perfectly adequate language, presents itself as a more compelling definition of what is to be perceived as relevant reality. Such a model is not viable at present, and Kreol continues to play a crucial role as a vehicle of unofficial, or informal, nationalism (cf. Eriksen 1993a) and as a cultural homogeniser, while it cannot, for political reasons, be used in formal, state-centred nation-building.

The Roles of Religion

Statistically, religious diversity in Mauritius is at a first glance even more kaleidoscopic and presents an image of an even more fragmented society than the statistics on linguistic diversity do. In the 1990 Census, about 90 different religions were recorded in a population of a little over a million (Mauritius 1991–2). As in the case of language, differences that make a difference are much less than 90 in this respect. In the main organisational contexts, only three major religions are relevant: Christianity, Islam and Hinduism. Besides, religious symbols are invested in politics in pretty much the same fashion by adherents of these three – although the *meaning-content* of the religions naturally varies.

• *Pragmatism in religion.* Before arriving in Mauritius for the first time, I had asked myself a naïve question: How could it be possible for a person to maintain sincere belief in a particular religious doctrine, granted that the surroundings offered a multitude of alternatives, visibly proven cognitively viable to their adherents. Of course, this way of posing the problem was quite beside the point and typical of a European intellectual. Agents do not conventionally subject their representations to systematic and critical scrutiny, nor do they endorse meta-views such as the one insinuated, unless they are 'cultural specialists'. Their representations are located in the 'body' as well as in the 'mind'; a 'culture' is as present in the mind of the fisherman as in the mind of the religious leader, and contradictions between representations and practices are significant aspects of social reality. Being 'Christian' does not imply that one regrets every act of adultery; it does not even necessarily mean that one relates to the Holy Trinity in any particular way. What makes a Hindu despicable to a Creole is not the fact that he attends ritual in the temple rather than the church, but the 'fact' that the former is a miser with no understanding of the 'real qualities of living', and the forms of competition in nationwide fields between the categories.

As a rule, Mauritians relate pragmatically to religious belief and practice – whether one's own or someone else's – in non-competitive contexts. Religious differences do not in themselves generate conflict and competition, but they can be situationally invoked. A few examples may indicate this.

• Historically and currently, an aspect of Franco-Mauritian cultural distinctiveness consists in their hierarchical relationship to the Creoles, who have historically worked for them as servants. However, Franco-Mauritians and Creoles belong to the same religion (Christianity) – even the same denomination (the Roman Catholic Church). In order to accentuate their superiority, many Franco-Mauritians have increasingly turned towards strongly traditionalist forms of Christian practice (performing Mass in Latin, for instance); forms of ritual perceived as élitist by the Mauritian population and, notably, perceived as snobbish by the average Creole. Among the Creoles themselves, on the other hand, the last decade has seen the development of a local form of 'liberation theology'. Young Creole priests have been important inspirational figures for the labour movement in the EPZ, and the organisation *Ligue Ouvrier d'Action Chrétienne*, led by Creole priests, has been perceived as belonging to the extreme left politically.

When political elections are approaching, however, the cultural unity of the different segments of the 'General Population' is stressed by campaign leaders, and the symbolic focus of the unity is, beside the French language and the common fear of Hindu dominance, Christianity.

• Tamils tend to stress the differences between their 'Dravidian' brand of Hinduism and 'Aryan' practices. The structural conditions for this overcommunication of cultural difference can be located in the labour market and politics, where Tamils and Hindus compete as different ethnic categories. Tamil temples are not generally perceived as Hindu temples in Mauritius.

• The split between traditional Sanatanism and reformist Arya Samajism has not led to the formation of separate political organisations, although the differences in *beliefs* are arguably more radical here than, for example, between Sanatanism and Tamil practices and beliefs.

• Large numbers of Tamils, and later Sino-Mauritians, have converted to Christianity because this seemed strategically useful during colonialism.[11]

Granted that we now consider religion as a social dimension and not primarily as a belief system, we may turn to the points of conjuncture between the religions practised in Mauritius: that is, the flow of information (embedded in practices) across the ethnic boundaries. This communication and modification of practices does not necessarily lead to the breakdown of boundaries, but it does – as stated earlier – change their meaning content.

The common attitude to religious diversity can be summarised in the 'ecumenical' proverb quoted as an epigraph to this chapter, *Sakenn pe prie dan so fason*. 'Syncretism' is fairly common, particularly in the towns – and is tacitly accepted by 'purists'. The flow of information across religious boundaries may take many visible forms, among which are the following:

• In later years, increasing numbers of Creoles have participated actively in the annual, spectacular Tamil *Cavadee* festival.

• Sino-Mauritians, most of them nominally Catholics, celebrate both the Christian and the Chinese New Year. They perform most of their rituals in church, but on certain occasions they solemnly enter the pagoda in Port-Louis.

• Hindu women observed at Christian Mass in a south-western village replied, when asked, that they certainly remained religious Hindus. They did not seem to understand my insistent questions about contradicting religious practices.

• Recently converted Tamil women, of whom there are quite a few in Stanley near Rose-Hill, always take their sandals off when entering church, sometimes even sacrificing bananas to Christian shrines. Both practices originate in Hindu ritual.

• An unknown, but probably enormous, number of Mauritians (mostly Hindus and Christians) turn to witchdoctors (*ban longanis*) when confronted with certain personal problems, although the witchdoctors represent a cosmology unacceptable within any 'Great Tradition'. Significantly, Hindu and Creole *longanis* share most of their practices and representations, which are partly of African origin (or so at least it is claimed), yet which contain discernible European occult, Christian, and Hindu elements.[12] The medical anthropologist Sussman, investigating the relationship between diverse medical traditions in Mauritius, found seven distinctive medical systems; but she also claimed that there was 'surprisingly little divergence between the [ethnic] groups' (Sussman 1983:364). She concluded her study by asserting that Mauritian society reproduces a *'unitary conceptual framework* that promotes the maintenance of several ideologically diverse therapeutic traditions' (ibid.:372–3, my italics). Sussman's findings indicate that the 'multiple cultural heritages' of this kind of society do not stand in a simple one-to-one relationship to the actual *Relevanzstrukturen* of the agents, nor does each 'culture' refer specifically to any fixed set of agents. Symbolic universes interact and merge; they cross boundaries even when the social boundaries may remain discrete.

Politicised Religion

Despite considerable interchange of symbolism and substance between religions, there is virtually no public discourse about the content of religious differences. Sir Seewosagur Ramgoolam's warning, to the effect that religion ought not to be a topic of interethnic and public discourse, seems to remain valid. Breach of this informal rule may have dramatic consequences. In 1984, the entire staff of the Libyan Embassy in Port-Louis were given 48 hours to leave Mauritius. The causes for the expulsion remain unclear, but it is known that the Libyans initiated a certain missionary activity among Christians in eastern Port-Louis in addition to subsidising infrastructural expenses and improvements in the city, a Muslim stronghold in Mauritius (as a tangible result, the main square in eastern Port-Louis was renamed Khadaffi Square). Further, it was rumoured that Christians were paid as much as Rs. 40,000 (then roughly £ 2,000) to convert to Islam. The strong official reaction to this indicates that religion remains a strong symbolic carrier of sectional interests; that it is seen as a political resource.

The government's reasoning was that if a sufficiently large number of Christians converted to Islam, the precarious ethnic equilibrium of Port-Louis (and of Mauritius as such) might have been upset, and the outcome would be unpredictable and possibly disastrous.

To attack others for adhering to a different religion is in virtually every case an expression of disagreement over a non-religious issue – generally competition over scarce resources. Had this not been so, it would have been meaningless for Hindu gangs to desecrate mosques and churches, which happened during the unrest of the late 1960s. The fact that Hinduism is a 'tolerant' religion does not necessarily make 'tolerant' people of Hindus.

The riots before and after Independence had, on the face of it, religious difference as their main premiss. The groups fighting in the streets of Port-Louis were mutually exclusive religious groups; Hindus, Muslims and Christians. They attacked each other's places of worship, and a number of people were killed 'because of their religion'. As most Mauritians are aware today, this description of these events is misleading (see Chap. 8).

There was strong disagreement in the Mauritian population over the issue of independence. Franco-Mauritians and Creoles, in particular, feared that independent Mauritius would rapidly be transformed into a 'Little India'; that cultural bonds with France would be severed, that Hindi would be the national language, and that the Franco-Mauritians and Coloureds would lose their privileges. Notably, Franco-Mauritians feared the national-isation of the sugar estates.

The 1960s saw a strong ethnic polarisation; among other things a short-lived Tamil party and a slightly more viable Muslim party emerged. There were social tension, heated political rhetoric, and, as mentioned, outbreaks of ethnic violence. The Coloured politician Gaëtan Duval made statements to the effect that every woman would be compelled to wear a sari in independent Mauritius. Muslim men grew beards to avoid being mistaken for Hindus. Throughout, *religion* seemed to be the criterion of allegiance.

However, religion, seen as a system of symbols and beliefs, has no direct relation to power, be it allocative or authorising. Around Independence, as during other dramatic periods in Mauritian political history, religion was exploited as a symbolic carrier of sectional interests. Religious symbols acquired new meanings directly connected with representations of power. This 'religious phenomenon' actually has nothing to do with the 'syncretist' women who took off their sandals before entering church, but with competition over power. Thus socially organised religion clearly is dual in the same way as ethnicity itself; it encompasses dimensions of meaning and of politics.

The Diard Affair

The following case story, famous in Mauritius, illustrates the instrumental and indexical character of religious identity, as well as indicating some of the interrelations between social fields.

Père Diard was a French Catholic priest who had worked in Mauritius for several years. In March 1986 his permit of work and residence expired, and it was not renewed by the authorities. This caused a great public scandal, lasting for more than two months, fading out in the press several weeks after Diard had left Mauritius.

The government's explanation was this: Diard had been preaching among the workers of the EPZ, encouraging them to organise in unions. He had associated with the radical Christian organisation LOAC (*Ligue Ouvrier d'Action Chrétienne*). This had been known for a while. Now, Diard had recently, it seemed, been instrumental in organising an illegal strike at several factories in Petite Rivière. This was a threat to the stability of the country and could not be accepted. 'If I had gone to France and done what Diard did here, I would have been evicted immediately,' said Prime Minister Jugnauth on television.

The diocese of Port-Louis quickly condemned the decision publicly, and thought it outrageous that Diard should be considered a communist (understating that had he indeed been a communist activist, it would have been correct to evict him).

It never became quite clear what Diard had actually done; contradictory versions from different factory owners, workers and politicians appeared in newspapers and periodicals. It is clear, however, that it had something to do with workers' rights, and that he claimed these rights on behalf of all workers, not merely the Christian ones.

• *From politics to religion.* From the beginning, there was a strong tendency to the effect that Diard was defended by Christians on an ethnic or religious basis. Reporters of the influential weekly *La Vie Catholique*, Catholic columnists in the best-selling weekly *Week-End* and other prominent journalists discussed the case without directly implying that the case was one of ethnic conflict. Some cried out about 'authoritarian measures' without specifying, but the implicit message was clear: a Hindu prime minister had expelled a Christian, pretending that he did so on 'national' and not on communal grounds. On government-controlled radio and TV, the case was regularly commented on, but from a perspective favouring national unity and stability, not defining the conflict as an ethnic one.

In the village where I was staying at the time, a fishing village heavily populated by Creoles, people nearly unanimously held that Diard was evicted 'because he was a Christian'. Many Hindus thought so, too. Only in one household of my acquaintance, a Hindu teacher's family, it was argued that Diard's being a Christian could hardly be a satisfactory reason to evict him. 'Probably he engaged in illegal activities,' the teacher said, 'and the same thing would have happened to an Indian pundit doing the same thing.'

• *Transcending field boundaries*. Linking the case to our social fields, we see that: Diard set about working in workplaces; his activities were then perceived as harmful within the national economic system; then the government applied authorising power to neutralise the effects, and the case was referred to and discussed in the national mass media; from these lay people received all their information about it; and this formed the premises for their discussions in the household and locality fields. The unity of interests between the economic and political systems is apparent. Notwithstanding the fact that many politicians have personal interests in the EPZ, they collectively support the interests of the capitalist economy sanctioning their power and justifying their policies.

The redefinition of the issue, from one of communism to one of communalism as it were, clearly took place in the local fields; but this could probably not have come about without the agency of journalists in the mass media field, without whose participation many people would never have learnt of the case at all. Virtually none of the articles dealing with the Diard case directly accuses the government of communalism, however. Some (particularly in *La Vie Catholique*) accuse it of being anti-Christian, but at the same time link Christianity with universal humanism, which is the form of socialism Diard was believed to support. In most of the written material circulating at the time, the conclusion that Diard was primarily a radical seems, to the outsider, just as likely as the conclusion that he was a Christian. The fact that most Mauritian Catholics perceived Diard primarily as a Catholic, rather than as a champion of social justice, exemplifies the pragmatic primacy of ethnic identity/membership, community overruling class in this case; and it is true that virtually any political issue is immediately interpreted (or re-interpreted) by ordinary people as dealing with ethnic conflict rather than with any other conflict in society. Yet there is no obvious link between such an interpretation of the situation in this par-ticular instance and people's perceptions of their own utilitarian interests.

• *Religion and ethnicity*. The large-scale social significance of religion in Mauritius today, viewed as a single polyethnic system of action, consists in its capacity as an unofficial mechanism for the distribution of certain scarce commodities, and religious organisations as well as sentiments may be exploited politically, although national politics was not initially one of their dimensions. It is by no means the only criterion; it forms part of a social 'package' that we may label 'ethnicity'. Since social relations in a society like Mauritius are pervaded by notions of 'us versus them', religion tends to be subsumed under the more encompassing heading of ethnicity. Incidentally, religions are not taught in public Mauritian schools; and hence *language* is a more relevant locus of competitive interethnic discourse.

Religious 'syncretism' has been dealt with above as a visible manifestation of the flow of information across ethnic boundaries. The socially most significant form of syncretism is not the 'mixing of religious beliefs and practices', but rather their replacement by a competing, more universalist symbolic system, namely supra-ethnic nationalism. Religion promotes cultural integration; but by contrast with the Medieval Church, operating in a religious universe that was largely homogeneous, the religions of Mauritius represent exclusive and mutually excluding forms of integration. When it is politicised, religion thus competes directly with nationhood in this kind of society. When it is not, religious diversity is compatible with Mauritian nationalism. Compromise in the form of common denominators implies, among other things, 'keeping silent about those things one cannot talk of' (Wittgenstein), such as cosmological differences, while playing a shared competitive game where religion is invoked like a flag or a banner.

Elements of Mauritian Ethnicity

Before moving to a consideration of non-ethnic alignments and identifications in the following chapters, it may be worthwhile to sum up the analysis so far.

• *The substantial content* of Mauritian ethnicity can in principle not be delineated, since ethnicity is relational and contextual, and therefore changes chameleon-like with the situation. The standard postwar official ethnic classification, which many Mauritians accept as a regulative idea, is inconsistent. Hindus and Muslims are defined according to religion. The Sino-Mauritians are defined according to their geographical origin. The General Population is a residual category; all or nearly all its members are nominally Catholics, but all the Catholics do not 'belong' to the General Population. If there is doubt about the actual origin of a person, he or she was classified there officially and known elsewhere as 'some kind of Creole'.

Ethnicity is locally associated with one or several among the factors of religion, language, geographical origin, phenotype, place of residence and class membership. Emphasis is placed situationally on one or several in a purely *ad hoc* manner, and all these 'ascribed characteristics' of groups or individuals have metonymical potential in the social creation of meaning.

• *Ethnic pressure groups* are organised along various dimensions: ancestral language, religion, caste, economic interests or political ambition. Ethnicity is invoked in public, overtly or covertly, as a uniting principle whenever somebody needs the support of a large number of people in a competitive context. Ethnicity has proved the most powerful unifying principle both cognitively and socially; deeper than class membership, more relevant in everyday life than nationality – and sufficiently vague regarding substantial content to be manipulated in potentially infinite ways. Yet 'it' remains an aspect of the social person that enters into the definition of most situations.

• Another important modality is the *ethnic network*. All ethnic categories are strongly integrated at the network level in the sense that information and resources flow through ethnically delineated channels, although there are important differences regarding other forms of incorporation. While the Creoles are generally integrated at the network level, Hindus, Tamils, Franco-Mauritians and Muslims also have functioning associations representing their corporate interests, while the Sino-Mauritians, concentrated in certain parts of Port-Louis, could be seen as an ethnic community (following Handelman's (1977) typology).

• Through the consistent application of ethnic *taxonomies and stereotypes* in accounting for interethnic situations (though not necessarily in the interaction itself; recall the exigencies of the dictum of the lowest common denominator), mutual ethnic identities are conventionally reproduced and reified during socialisation, as 'inert' properties of the individual. The intra-ethnic reproduction of stereotypes facilitates the task of understanding a world of immense complexity (not least because of the presence of other ethnic categories), and gives meaning and direction to one's own efforts (as a member of a superior ethnic category).

The application of stereotypes also indicates that the ethnically complex Mauritian society is not staggeringly complex on the level of the lay actor, whose conceptual schemata of the social world are simplistic.

• The sometimes slightly organised *collective consciousness about a shared life-world* and way of life (or *habitus*) within an ethnic category draws its persuasive power from notions relating to characteristics listed above. Few non-ethnic identities available in the shared cultural universe are conceptually and practically viable unless in some way linked with ethnicity (for example, as its negation).

The main theoretical point here is that ethnicity is, in practice, *not* an inert, categorical property of persons (although folk models tend to depict it as such), but a property of the relationship between agents acting in situations and contexts – and as such, its meaning changes with the context.

• Within the shared, but ambiguous, Mauritian system of symbolic ethnic representations, it is reasonable, for example, for a Creole to claim (to other Creoles) that they are poor because the Hindus have acquired a larger share than they deserve; Muslims may agree that non-Muslim decadence is a threat to the purity of their young; Franco-Mauritians may easily and programmatically blame the non-white populations for the 'state of the country' (which, according to many of them, is pitiful) – and they all know of each other's complaints. These ethnic skirmishes and quarrels are all important constituent parts of the *shared Mauritian culture*. Virtually everybody periodically feels discriminated against on an ethnic basis, which obviously encourages organisation along ethnic lines rather than any other option. *Notions of competition founded in (ascribed) ethnicity* constitute an important focal point in shared Mauritian culture.

• The ethnic category is organisationally united on principles of *us-hood* or dichotomisation. Any child knows that he or she is, say, a Tamil, and that this means, essentially, not being a Hindu, a Muslim or a Creole. The difficulties in propagating nationalism stem partly from this basic orientation, which is reified and confirmed in all the major social fields discussed.

• Identity is prior to organisation, although it may be reproduced (through socialisation) in a cultural realm largely defined by interethnic *relations* rather than by the substantial cultural *content* of the ethnic category in question. *Endogamy* is crucial in maintaining the sense of ethnic identity as primordial as well as reproducing it organisationally. This implies, among other things, that Barth (1969) is wrong in suggesting that if patterns of behaviour become identical, ethnicity vanishes. Differences that make a difference need not be ascribed to action alone: the physical appearance of middle-class North American blacks is sufficient to devalue the real estate market when they move into certain suburbs, and the lack of integration between Franco-Mauritians and Coloureds cannot be explained by referring to cultural differences or differences in *habitus* (cf. the debate between Bentley 1987 and Yelvington 1991).

The Significance of Identity

We have now viewed Mauritian ethnicity from a variety of angles, and it seems evident that ethnic identity is by and large perceived as primordial, although it is challenged from several directions – and there are important indications of change, which the following chapters will indicate. Ethnic *membership* (individual level) functions as an asset of varying importance in the labour market. It is also activated as a resource when collective action is required, while this agency in turn is monitored from the formal or informal leadership segment of the ethnic *organisation*. Although ethnicity is usually played out in competitive contexts, following rules of competition on the one hand and norms of compromise on the other, there is a non-competitive ('symbolic') aspect in every case considered. Sometimes the individual agents might, as the next chapter shows, have a greater perceived benefit through organising along non-ethnic lines than through using ethnicity as a basis for corporate action. However, ethnic *identity* (meaning) has empirically proved itself too pervasive, too fundamental in the individual's definition of self and others, for such organisations to persist and overrule the ethnically-based alternatives permanently.

In economic and political matters, there is interethnic agreement as to the desirability of the defined goals (property, power, security); this condition of shared meaning must be fulfilled *a priori* – as a common denominator – in order that competition may come about at all. The interethnic disagreements as to the use of authorising and allocating power[13] are due (a) to divergent interpretations of symbols, and (b) to systematic local variations of normative values within the shared system of representations – in other words, to the persistence and significance of distinctive ethnic identities. The issue of the place of Oriental languages in school curricula is an obvious case of a competitive issue (all agree that education is desirable) charged with ambiguous meaning. Thus, the competition goes on along two dimensions: (i) each actor attempts to win the supposed zero-sum game about the place of individual languages in school curricula, and (ii) each actor tries to present his interpretation of the actual situation as being more universally *true* than the others'.

Although it is certainly true that important aspects of Mauritian ethnicity can be revealed in studies of purely competitive contexts, such a procedure could never explain the *persistence* of organisation along ethnic lines where other, possibly more viable, alternatives are available (class and nation), nor the role played by non-strategic agency and representations in the production and reproduction of Mauritian multiethnic society. What makes Claude (pp. 33–34) dislike Hindus? Why do certain Muslims fear the legal sale of alcohol in their neighbourhood (pp. 57–59)? Why did Creoles emphasise *père* Diard's religion and not his political attitudes when he was evicted (pp. 95–96)? How do *baitkas* and *madrassahs* (Hindu and Muslim youth clubs, respectively), political parties and unions like the Hindu Teachers' Union recruit their members and ensure external support? Pure utility cannot account fully for these facts, even if it is tautologically true that a collective identity has to *pay off* in some way or another in order to be relevant.

Ultimately, it must be conceded that a person's socio-cultural identity, ascribed by self and others, reproduced in daily life, is the *raw material* necessary for ethnicity to be organised socially in competitive contexts. The reproduction of ethnic identity is a necessary condition for the formation of ethnic groups in the political sense, and is a more fundamental aspect of ethnicity than the latter. This is why the impact of globalisation and ideological individualism, considered in the next chapter, can prove so significant in future Mauritian identities and politics: such processes reshape the personal experiences of Mauritians and contribute to reconfiguring the structures of relevance they act within.

The common denominators informing and shaping interethnic relations may be redefined in any interethnic situation, and this happens frequently in independent Mauritius, where cultural differences between individuals diminish, sometimes transforming one or several ethnic categories, sometimes creating intermediate categories of people half-way between ethnic categories and half-way beyond the very logic of ethnic identity. Friendship and intermarriage are obvious examples of such a redefinition of relevant social reality, while the effect is less spectacular but no less significant in cases where an employer hires manpower from ethnic categories other than his own; or in the choice of dress, education, occupation, place of residence, written language or leisure club. These are the processes of change that will be looked into more closely in the following chapters, which indicate that ethnic organisation and identification, although at the moment strong in Mauritius, need not always be so.

Notes

1. The crabs try to climb out of the bowl. The edges are slippery, and they climb over each other's bodies. When one has reached the edge, he/she/it is dragged down by the others, which are also attempting to slip out. Peter Wilson's metaphor from Providencia (Wilson 1978) not only fits other Caribbean societies, but is also helpful in understanding social processes in Mauritius and The Seychelles (cf. Benedict and Benedict 1982).

2. Of 64 papers that were presented at the conference, 9 were in French (6 presented by members of the 'General Population', 3 by Indo-Mauritians), and the remaining 55 in English. The leftish organisation LPT wished to present

their contribution in Kreol, but were denied the right. Fifty-two of the papers were written by Indo-Mauritians (here comprising Hindus, Tamils and Muslims), 11 by members of the 'General Population' and 1 by two Sino-Mauritians.

3.   I have interviewed three census takers; all admitted manipulating with the answers given when they were 'obviously wrong'.

4.   (a) and (b) are the essence of conversations with two imams and a leading Muslim politician, while (c) captures the feelings of many ordinary Mauritian Muslims.

5.   This is considered legitimate in public; caste separatism is not.

6.   'Like many African bourgeoisies who advertise their national independence and their authenticity through a return to their "roots", rich Indian women wear the sari. But this has nothing to do with ordinary women. To the bourgeoisie, it first and foremost serves a political function, which consists in confirming one's national uniqueness *vis-à-vis* other nations in the island, only to reject Kreol as official language later; that is to say, to reject the Mauritian nation.'

7.   The complex relationship between utility and meaning, cultural change and adaptation, in Indo-Mauritian identity has been explored at some length in Eriksen (1992a).

8.   For examples, see Rauville (1967); Dinan (1983); Masson (1986).

9.   Vaguely reminiscent of the West Indian calypso, the *séga* blends French *chansons* and African rhythms. Nowadays, most *ségas* incorporate electric instruments, and the original *sega tipik* is becoming rare. An interesting recent innovation is the *seggae*, which blends *séga* with reggae – emerging in Mauritius ten years after reggae went out of fashion in Jamaica.

10. The quotation is from one of Bébel-Gisler's (1975) Guadeloupean informants, and it fits the Mauritian context perfectly.

11. Formerly, conversion to some variety of Christianity was a great asset in the development of individual careers. According to Tinker (1977:327) there is 'reason to suppose that Dr Laurent [leader of the early twentieth-century Coloured political group *Action Libérale*] was partially Indian by origin'.

12. A *longanis* of my acquaintance insisted that he was a devoted Christian, and explained the Eucharist as a 'ritual designed to purify the atmosphere and to exorcise the *mauvais air* ("bad air") from the participants' – an interpretation couched in entirely non-Christian terms and shared by many of the people in the village.

13. In stressing that power has local and global uses, I mean to emphasise that power does not only exist in the political, economic and communicational systems on a nationwide scale. The cases of the two servants in Floréal and the Sino-Mauritian restaurant (Chap. 4) exemplify the ethnic use of power on a smaller scale.

CHAPTER SIX

Cross-Cutting Ties: The Non-Ethnic

What I am saying is that these conflicting loyalties and divisions of
allegiance tend to inhibit the development of open quarrelling, and that
the greater the division in one area of society, the greater is likely to be
the cohesion in a wider range of relationships – provided that there is a
general need for peace, and recognition of a moral order in which this
peace can flourish.

— Max Gluckman (1982[1956]:25)

The preceding chapters have indicated the role of ethnicity in some of the
most important fields and levels of scale where Mauritian society is being
reproduced. Partly for this reason, alternatives to ethnic classification,
organisation and identity, which are considered in this and in the following
chapter, are to a great extent described *as opposed to* ethnic identity and
organisation. However, the 'bias' that this implies is ultimately justified in
the fact that most Mauritians themselves tend to think, act and classify in a
similar way: ethnicity is in many situations and in many fields seen as being
logically and ontologically prior to its alternatives, and thus it is an important
dimension of Mauritian social reality. Ethnic differences tend to make a
difference, even in social contexts based on other differences.

In most of Mauritian history from the eighteenth century onwards,
different kinds of resources have been bundled together in social networks
and organisations based on kinship and ethnicity. Of course, a great number
of situations incorporating members of different ethnic categories have
throughout this period been accounted for in ways with no exclusive or
even important bearing on ethnic differences. Personal acquaintances are
frequently excepted from stereotypically founded prejudice, and many
networks in all the main social fields are based on a variety of non-ethnic
criteria (although the ethnic element is usually also present there). This
chapter shows ways in which group cleavages and relevant social boundaries

can be conceptualised along non-ethnic lines, and also indicates in which way the compass of these classifications is increasing in scope and social importance. However, since the next chapter discusses Mauritian nationalism at length, this 'alternative to communalism' is not considered here.

Class Organisation

• *Trade unions and ethnicity.* Since the formation of trade unions during the first decades of the century, and later through political parties, there have periodically been successful attempts to redefine the pervasive conflicts of Mauritian society as being based on class rather than community (see Oodiah 1986; R. Virahsawmy 1979, 1986; Simmons 1982: 52–70; Bowman 1991:33). In her political history of Mauritius, Simmons writes: 'The ethnic divisions between the French, the Creoles, the Hindus, and the Muslims shaped Mauritian society. But just as important were the class distinctions between the elite and the laborers and small planters. (. . .) Divisions in Mauritius in 1937 were based primarily on class rather than ethnic community, and so was the violence' (1982:52, 54).

Repercussions from the economic depression of the 1930s struck heavily on countries like Mauritius, little cogs in the great imperial machine. The year 1936, a year of island-wide riots, also saw the foundation of the Mauritian Labour Party/Parti Travailliste Mauricien by the Coloured medical doctor Maurice Curé. Remarkably, Curé's two successors to the leadership were both Coloureds/Creoles like himself, although the majority of the party's voters were eventually Hindus. After the Second World War Curé, worried about the increasing influence of educated Hindus in the upper echelons of the party, changed his position several times *vis-à-vis* the party he had founded. 'Curé did not like the rise of the workers of Indian origin under the leadership of Dr. Ramgoolam', notes Varma (1981), implicitly referring to the constitutional reform of 1948, virtually introducing the one man–one vote system and thus enfranchising thousands of Hindus and Muslims, 'suddenly alter[ing] . . . the political balance on the island' (Simmons 1982: 103). Curé's concern was shared by his successor Emmanuel Anquetil, who, in the aftermath of the 1948 election 'complained of the tendency of rural voters to select candidates from their own community': '[This tendency] is due to the non-political education of the Indian labourers or to their desire, after all legitimate, to elect Indian representatives instead of candidates of the coloured population or any other community. Even some of the Indian candidates are more conservative than the white Franco-Mauritian conservatives' (Anquetil, quoted in Simmons 1982:107). Simmons' own comment on the 1948 elections is that '[t]he real victors were the Hindus' (ibid.:109). Eleven of the nineteen elected candidates were Hindus, but the Hindu rise to political power was temporarily hampered by colonial nominations to important political positions (Bowman 1991:34).

Dr Curé, for his part, remained an on-and-off member of the Labour Party until the mid-1960s, a period of accentuated communalism presaging the 1967 General Elections (in practice a referendum over independence). At this point he took an open stance against Labour, aligning himself with conservative non-Hindu politicians on an ethnic basis. When the Labour weekly *Mauritius Times* celebrated the 50th anniversary of the Labour Party in 1986, the newspaper thus conceded that the party's founder (who died in 1977) had become a 'national disgrace' towards the end of his life, and that it was 'difficult to understand' his change in attitude towards the 'labour movement'.

Curé's political development actually related situationally to the two major principles of social division being reproduced in Mauritius; class and community. During the economic crisis of the 1930s, the main conflict was perceived as being class-based. Curé's class rhetoric was politically successful across communities; he, an educated Creole, represented the stereotypical *gen de couleur* intellectual: the go-between, the man who, by virtue of being an ethnic anomaly, could also be an entrepreneur. After the constitutional reform of 1947, Curé, worried about the increased Indian influence, oscillated to and fro, uncertain of which conflict to emphasise. Then, during the independence struggle of the 1960s, the basic conflict was persuasively presented as communal. The Creole politician Gaëtan Duval now threatened that if Mauritius were to be independent, all women would be compelled to wear saris; he launched the slogan *Malbar nu pa ule* ('We don't want Coolies'), and generally exploited communal sentiments to an extreme degree. Curé went along with this rhetoric, despite the profound political differences between himself and Duval's *Parti Mauricien* (later renamed, arguably misleadingly, *Parti Mauricien Social Démocrate*).

Let us now turn to the activation of potential class divisions in independent Mauritius. Despite the short time-span involved, the political tenor has since Independence swung, simplistically put, from predominantly ethnic politics, to class politics represented in the MMM and militant trade unionism, and back to ethnicity from 1976 to the mid-1990s, when, following the elections of December 1995, a broadly based government with a very heterogeneous ethnic base replaced Anerood Jugnauth's MSM. Jugnauth, who began his political career in the MMM, had then served as Prime Minister for 13 years.

• *The MMM and class.* The riots around Independence were expressed in discourse and action as a problem concerning the ethnic division of power, allocative and authorising – politics and the economy. In other words, the riots were ethnically based, drawing on the logic of the zero-sum game, and no ethnic category remained collectively neutral. Then, from 1969, the anti-ethnic MMM emerged as a major political force, forging strong links with trade unions, particularly in Port-Louis (see MMM 1985; Oodiah 1989; cf. LPT 1987). MMM leaders argued that the Creole dockers and the Hindu labourers had common interests against the Franco-Mauritian 'sugar barons' and the growing Hindu state bourgeoisie – and thus they presented virtually a verbatim repetition of the labour movement rhetoric of the 1930s. To support the MMM apparently signified a wish to replace communal divisions with class struggle. The new party represented an alternative to the model of communal conflict; a replacement of the old division with a new division signifying a new social order and a juster society. Can this explain the phenomenal success of the early MMM? Probably not. Class divisions are perceived as important by Mauritians, but they also tend to stress their correlations with ethnic ones (Keng 1991). In the local social fields, people conventionally point to links between economy, political power and ethnic injustice. '*Azordi, tu pu malbar*' is a common expression among Creoles and Muslims alike ('Today, everything belongs to the Hindus') – and they justify their statements by selecting events from the nationwide fields that support them. The MMM, far from promising the demise of ethnicity, promised a just system of compromise between the ethnic groups.

• *Ethnicity overruling class.* One Creole informant, a factory mechanic in eastern Mauritius, showing me around his village, pointed to a large canefield. 'This belongs to a so-called small planter,' he said. 'The government has done everything to help small planters, they don't pay any taxes or anything. You reckon this *malbar* is a small, poor guy who needs help? *Bonom*, he's the richest bugger in the village!'

In this, he implicitly refers to the government's late-1980s programme to aid small planters; furnishing bank loans, relieving them of taxes, etc. And he went on: 'What have those people done for us Creoles? Phew! *Naryen!* Nothing!' As a matter of fact, the village had many poor small planters as well (one of them my informant's closest neighbour). The one example selected for me was a rare case and besides, this man employed many fellow-Hindus, kinsmen and non-kin, at very low wages.

The macro facts are the following: there are 33,000 small planters in Mauritius, who among them possess 66,000 arpents of caneland (1 arpent is about 1 acre); 70 per cent of them have plots of less than 2 arpents. My informant must have known this; in the *cité* where he lived, there were numerous poor, small planter Hindu families. This did not change his argument. Further, due to the ethnic division of labour in the sugar industry, Creoles have traditionally been better off than the Hindus in plantation areas – and to a great extent they still are. My informant himself earned about 20 per cent more than his Hindu neighbours. In other words: rather than join forces with his Hindu neighbours, against the capitalist structure of ownership, he indirectly supported the Franco-Mauritian 'sugar barons' against increasing rights for small planters, since small planters were seen as largely Hindu. Competition was interpreted as an ethnic zero-sum game, not as an individual one.

Later in our conversation, I asked him about the MMM. He replied: 'It's a good party. I like Paul. He's one of us. He can tackle the *malbar*. Not like Duval, the bloody traitor.' (He refers to Paul Bérenger, the MMM leader, and to Gaëtan Duval, who had at an earlier stage gone into a coalition with the winning Hindu party. Duval's 'treachery', then, consisted in collaborating with the traditional enemy. Incidentally: Bérenger has later held important posts in Hindu-led governments, and, at the time of writing he is Minister of Foreign Affairs in Navin Ramgoolam's government. Duval died in 1996.)

I said: 'But there's plenty of Hindus in the MMM?' My informant retorted: 'They belong to the *ti-nasyon* (low castes), so they're not really Hindus, see? Besides, they don't have much of a say with Paul around.' Although the conflict between Bérenger's MMM and Duval's PMSD was in the 1980s fairly consistently presented (in the media) as a conflict between socialism and liberalism or, more generally, as 'Left' versus 'Right', this lay voter (and he is far from being the only one) chose his party on a communal basis. Through emphasising Duval's 'treachery', he magnifies the glory of Bérenger. (Other working-class Creoles would have done exactly the opposite.)

• *Class overruling ethnicity.* Mauritius has no umbrella organisation for its trade unions. On rare occasions, notably during the MMM-led 'general strikes' of 1970 and 1979, unions of diverse ethnic composition have briefly collaborated against government policies and social injustice, and in these particular situations, social class was obviously perceived, situationally, as a more important variable than ethnicity. 'It was fantastic,' says a Hindu from Belle-Rose (now a clerk in Quatre-Bornes, then a transport worker) who had participated in 1979. 'It was as if the words *malbar, laskar* and Creole had no meaning any more. We were all united, supporting each other, we knew our unity was founded on a deeper truth than communalism.'

Other informants who also professed to have participated in the strike, less philosophically inclined than this man, stressed the material gain of the panethnic 'general strike'. 'It was necessary; we were miserable. We badly needed better wages,' explained an elderly Creole from eastern Port-Louis. Whatever the 'true nature of class struggle', the latter statement is probably more representative of the Mauritian working class than the former. For once, union leaders and opposition politicians had succeeded in persuading people that the potential material gain would be greater if workers from all communities collaborated in fighting the rich and powerful, regardless of community, than if they put the blame on each other. The fact that the strike was only moderately successful in terms of real material gain helps to explain why no similar collective action has taken place since. There is little indication that changes in popular representations of political oppositions derive from models of society different from the ethnically based zero-sum game, although many Mauritians claim to oppose this logic. The values involved are nearly invariably individual prosperity, security and education for one's children, and the institutionalisation of one's own cultural pride, that is, symbolic power.

As has already been noted on several occasions, definitions of truth, conceptual and normative, are always relative to a particular experiential and situational context. Granted that the improvement of one's material conditions is already defined (by the lay actor) as hinging on a zero-sum game, any specific model for action must argue that it somehow *plays the game better than* a different model. In other words, during these polyethnic strikes, class conflict seemed more relevant than ethnic conflict. Why is it not usually so?

• *Ethnicity in the job market.* A tautological (deductive) way of answering this question might be to say that this is because the taxonomies and stereotypes discussed in Chapter 4 are more frequently and more persuasively reproduced in people's minds, than the model of class divisions depicted in Table 7 below. This, obviously, is perfectly true; but how and why? The Mauritian Left has customarily blamed the mass media and government propaganda. But with a few striking exceptions, none of the leading Mauritian mass media can be said to promote communalism – on the contrary, the large newspapers *L'Express*, *Le Mauricien* and *Week-End* take great pains to remain neutral. Indeed, newspaper articles and editorials criticising social injustice with no primary communal connotations are much more common than articles criticising communal policies.

The continuous reproduction of the ethnic division of labour is doubtless important. In order to acquire a job, it is a crucial asset to know someone in a position to help, whether employer or employee. In so far as the individual project consists in acquiring and retaining a satisfactory job, it is empirically true that intra-ethnic acquaintances on a vertical axis are much more useful than interethnic ones on a horizontal axis.

• *The importance of cultural identity.* The primacy of ethnicity over class is also being reproduced as *cultural continuity* within any ethnic category, across social classes. Despite social differences, the members of the same ethnic group have, in general, a common mythology and a common ancestral language, common dietary taboos and a common religion. An important symbolic dimension of ethnic boundary maintenance consists in comparisons between one's own lifestyle and the presumed lifestyle of the others. Ordinary people tend to identify with successful people *from their own community* and aspire to share their lifestyle. They find it reasonable that there are rich and poor people, for after all, do they not themselves harbour a secret dream that they might themselves become rich one day? Simultaneously, they do not approve of the way of living of wealthy members of other ethnic groups. 'That silly P– [a successful Hindu],' said an elderly Franco-Mauritian lady during a rather sumptuous dinner party, 'he could have had anything he'd like for supper, and there he is – in the kitchen with his fat wife, eating *dal puri* and *paratha* with his disgusting greasy fingers . . .'. In other words, she thought this Hindu's high standard of living a waste of resources; he lacked the good sense to know how money should be spent. The attitude is commonplace among poor Mauritians too: wealthy people ought to conform to their own lifestyle ideals.

The political success of the late Gaëtan Duval, the uncrowned 'King Creole', politically active from the early 1960s until his death in 1996, can largely be understood along these lines. During election campaigns, he frequently threw lavish parties, presenting his working-class Creole electorate with generous amounts of rum and food. 'That's a good Creole,' was the expected response: 'Even if he's rich, he's one of us.' Whatever the contents of his politics, Duval expertly contrasted ('Dionysan') Creole and ('Apollonian') Hindu lifestyle ideals in his campaigning, accentuating ethnic conflict without a word.

A common saying goes: 'If a Creole has ten rupees he spends fifteen, but if a Hindu has ten rupees, he spends seven.' Creoles and Hindus alike may quote this as an argument for the superiority of their own cultural values.

Social differentiation on an ethnic basis in this way becomes less palatable than class differentiation, because the differences are represented as differences in *values* rather than as based on competition within a shared value system. Since Independence, political groups ideologically close to the European Left and to the Indian Left-leaning party Janata Dal have attempted to redefine society as class-based rather than ethnically based. Their model can be represented approximately like Table 7.

The failure of this class model of Mauritian society largely results from an underestimation of the importance of cultural identity as meaning first and foremost ethnic ('communal') identity.

- *The political Left.* Since 1982, the neo-Trotskyist party *Lalit*, with its educational organisation *Ledikasyon pu Travayer* (LPT, 'Education for the Worker'), has been the most vocal advocate of class struggle in the island. The LPT/Lalit have, during its existence, 'done everything its members could to reinforce and even create non-communal societies, such as trade unions, health societies, cooperative schools, funerary societies, local councils, workers' education, parent–teacher committees, women's movement, students' groups, saving schemes, etc.' (*Revi Lalit* 1985:6–7, my translation). Most people know something about LPT/Lalit, but few support it. The organisation's lack of popularity is, certainly, in part due to its rhetorical form, invoking a large number of concepts alien to the potential electorate (classic Marxist jargon). But, at the same time, very few of my informants are willing to agree with Lalit's postulate of the 'ontological' primacy of a class analysis of Mauritian society. 'In a way, Lalit may be right,' a typical statement goes, 'but it's impossible to go along with this, as we rural Hindus would lose in any case.' In brief, the existence of social classes is widely acknowledged, but class as such is abstractly *unthinkable* removed from community: The informant quoted regards himself as being more basically a Hindu than a worker, and whenever he has to choose between the two statuses he tends to choose the former – which is due to his perception of his ethnic identity as an aspect of his interpretation of the current zero-sum games. In the discussion of lifestyles and social differentiation above, we noted that the normative aspect of the zero-sum

Table 7. Classes according to the Mauritian Left

EXPLOITERS	AMBIGUOUS	EXPLOITED
Foreign capitalists	Lower white-collar	Canecutters (H,M)
Higher white-collar (Fr, H, M)	Petty bourgeoisie	Dockers (Cr)
Sugar barons (Fr) (Cr,H,M)	Academics	Misc.workers
Rich traders (All but bl.Cr) (Cr,H,M)	Journalists, teachers	Unemployed
Industrialists (All but bl. Cr)	Doctors, lawyers, priests	

game over material gain was ethnically determined. So long as there is no shared and stable working-class identity in Mauritius, uniting Creole and Hindu, rural and urban workers, etc., in a shared and acknowledged habitus, a way of life, the popular socio-cultural basis necessary for the Lalit/LPT ideology to spread is absent, be it as 'sensible' (in agents' eyes) as it may.

• *The lumpenproletariat.* Among the very poorest people in Mauritius,[1] ethnic differences seem to have little importance in everyday life. Intermarriage is frequent, and the quest for daily survival encourages cooperation rather than competition. Besides, the poverty of the people in question sets them apart as a distinctive group; different from moderately wealthy people regardless of ethnic membership. The stigma of utter poverty, then, is an ascribed status stronger than the ethnic status.

Conversely, it is to some extent true that class transcends community among the very rich as well. It is widely known that certain rich Muslim families of Port-Louis, for example, entertain links of courtesy and formal friendship with some of the wealthiest Franco-Mauritian families of Curepipe.

This account of class and ethnicity depicts the situation during the economic take-off of Mauritian manufacturing and tourism from about 1986 until the early 1990s. In the following chapter, it will be shown in which ways economic changes encourage changes at the level of local organisation and social perceptions of difference.

Region and Locality

Theories of neo-colonialism contrasting town and countryside are not easily applicable to the Mauritian context. Distances are short and the system of public transport excellent for a 'Third World' country, and most Mauritians move from village to town and back with ease. Nevertheless, there is a cultural discontinuity between rural and urban Mauritius that cannot be accounted for as ultimately ethnic. When I was about to leave my village in the south-west in order to do urban fieldwork, the local Creoles warned me against living in a particular Creole quarter in Port-Louis: 'Many of those townsmen are smart crooks', 'There are so many pickpockets in Port-Louis', and so on. Not a word was said about the ethnic membership of the 'crooks', and the villagers were quite aware that the population of north-eastern Port-Louis were largely Creole like themselves. Within the Hindu ethnic category, a more dramatic division obtains: in the countryside, particularly in the north-east, there are people (mostly women) who cannot go alone to town because they are unable to speak Kreol. Although virtually everybody under 50 speaks Kreol, Bhojpuri is widely used in this part of the island – even, in some cases, in communication between Hindus and Creoles (Stein 1983; Hollup 1994a). The ethnic unrest of the late 1960s was largely an urban phenomenon, centred on eastern Port-Louis and, to a lesser extent, the Plaines Wilhems.[2] Most villages have a mono-ethnic majority, but there are always minorities. Visible ethnic differences are as marked in the country as in town (dress, religion, pattern of consumption); yet fellow villagers are united in seeing such differences as peripheral. The unity becomes visible when they are confronted with urban ways.

• *Situational rural identity.* While doing fieldwork in a coastal village, I once took the bus to Quatre-Bornes with two villagers (one Hindu, one Creole) – our going together was due to my being acquainted with both; they were not mutual friends. On several occasions in town, they would discuss features of urban life; the shops, the cinemas, the market, the traffic – and they agreed that life was better in the village (more quiet and safer). They behaved as friends, paying for each other's drinks, which is a token of friendship in Mauritius, as in many other societies. Back in the village, however, there was no sign that a permanent multiplex bond had been forged: the Hindu went to his family and the Creole to his peer group, and they did not subsequently meet independently of my agency (and, under four eyes, each expressed suspicion towards the other). In other words: in town, their common status as villagers overruled their discrepant ethnic statuses; whereas it is likely, given the experience of others, that had they remained in town for a period, with kin or otherwise, the significance of common origin would gradually have faded as they would have acquired urban cultural competence and new, ethnically specific networks. Conjectures and divergences in this domain are analogous to those of class, discussed above. The rural identity sometimes overrules the ethnic one, but actors usually perceive the cultural continuity with members of their own ethnic category in town as being stronger than that with ethnic others in the village. This is, *inter alia*, reflected in election results.

• *Rural political rhetoric.* Hindus are the majority in most rural areas, while non-Hindus form the urban majorities. When the Hindu politician Harish Boodhoo launched his party, the PSM (*Parti Socialiste Mauricien*) around 1980, his virulently communalist campaigning was directed almost exclusively towards Hindu villagers. In his rhetoric, Boodhoo denounced the decadence of town life and the dishonesty of (urban Hindu) civil servants and Labour Party leaders, and praised the virtues of the hard-working, deeply moral and prudent village life, and the Bhojpuri language.

His campaigning succeeded in briefly segregating the Hindu community into an urban and a rural faction.[3] Boodhoo's representation of rural–urban differences could be summarised in a list of opposites such as Table 8.

The first four 'rural diacritica', held to be true by most urban Mauritians, would also incorporate rural Muslims, Tamils and Creoles. The fifth and sixth dichotomies exclude the Creoles, who are, in this perspective, seen as just as decadent as the townsmen, while it is likely that Boodhoo received a fair number of rural Tamil and Muslim votes. Boodhoo's emphasis on traditional Indian values (through his dress and manner, he tried to trigger local notions about what Gandhi might have been like) was met with applause from the Creole leader Gaëtan Duval, who stated (in a newspaper interview in 1982) that Boodhoo's frank communalism suited himself perfectly, because it would encourage Creoles, feeling their communal rights threatened in the MMM/PSM coalition, to vote for his plainly communalist PMSD party.

In sum, Boodhoo's move aggravated rather than alleviate ethnic tension, strengthening its symmetrical opposite number, the PMSD. And we have seen examples suggesting that, as in the case of social class, the rural/urban opposition does not normally operate without being informed and dominated by ethnicity either.

• *Localist politics.* In village politics, the ethnic aspect of competition is conventionally undercommunicated. The chairman of a village council in south-western Mauritius[4] stated, during a structured interview: 'Here, in the village hall, we do not want people to come and talk politics. I want to develop my village, and those who want to accompany me are welcome to join, regardless of their community. Politics divides; we need unity for our village to develop.' Note that, when saying 'politics', he means 'ethnically biased politics'. In his opinion, the popular divisions that this entails constitute an obstacle to (normatively positive) change. The council chairman thus contrasts 'politics' with 'development', politics being conceived of as a zero-sum competition, development as beneficial to all. His council is composed of nine elected and three nominated members (the latter are

Table 8. Rural–urban dichotomies

RURAL	URBAN
Poor	Rich
Illiterate	Sophisticated
Peripheral	Central
Traditional	Modern
Moral	Decadent
Bhojpuri-speaking	Kreol-speaking
Exploited	Exploiter

chosen by the District Council); there are nine Hindus and three Creoles (two of the Creoles are women, while all the Hindus are men). In this village council area, comprising three villages, about 60 per cent of the inhabitants are Creoles, while the rest are mainly low-caste Hindus (except the Chinese shopkeepers and their families). However, there has not in recent years been more than one list of candidates. The chairman's own village has a Hindu majority, and since the early 1970s it has taken on the role of the local centre: it has grown rapidly in size and prosperity, whereas the two Creole villages have remained virtually unchanged for decades. When asked how this development could be explained, the council chairman replied: 'In La Gaulette, we have a spirit of cooperation and faith. Note that the Creoles, too, are better off here than their fellows in Case Noyale and Petite Rivière Noire [neighbouring villages with substantial Creole majorities]. We are also closer to the hotels, a fact that ensures employment and encourages discipline.' Asked about the role of the village council in this process of change, he says:

> There isn't a lot we can do. We have very little money, and so we depend on the Village Development Officer and his ministry for funds. What we do when we need to have something done, is to send petitions to him and to the minister in question. The new dispensary was funded by the Ministry of Health after a long campaign involving petitions and so on. Many people come to see me every week, and I help them as far as I can, writing letters to the bank for personal loans, giving advice, et cetera.

Why are Case Noyale and Petite Rivière Noire being left behind in the economic development of the area? 'It is their own responsibility. The Village Council is theirs, too. If they're not interested, that is their own problem.' A nodal person in many contexts of the local field, notably those relating to local development, he largely depends on people's own initiative in order to act on their behalf. Most of those who came to see him were kinsmen or at least fellow Hindus: during a fortnight in 1986, 16 individuals came to his house for advice or direct help with a task relating to their personal prosperity and thus, in his eyes, village development. All were from La Gaulette, his own village: 8 were close or distant kin, 6 other Hindus and 2 Creoles.

• *Region and ethnicity.* Case Noyale, a village of some 700 inhabitants, is about 2 km. north of La Gaulette (which had about 1,200 inhabitants in the mid-1990s, following growth in the 1970s and 1980s). Put together, the two villages constitute a single locality in some respects: between them, they have only one church, one temple, one post office, one café, one welfare centre and one village hall. The shop in Case Noyale has a poor selection of goods, and villagers tend to buy much of their food in one of the two shops in La Gaulette. There is much informal interaction between Hindus of the two villages, but relatively little between non-related Creoles. When there is a social event at the governmental Welfare Centre in Case Noyale, youth from La Gaulette attend – but they can frequently be discriminated from the locals by their looks. The young Creoles of La Gaulette tend to dress in a fancier, more European way; the girls tone their skin, and many of the boys have Rastafarian dreadlocks. There is a joking relationship between these two categories of local Creole youth, but those from La Gaulette tend to communicate superiority. The latter are being talked about behind their backs: 'Hey, what does this guy think he is, bloody snob! Thinks he's a white man just because he works at the hotel. It's like my father says, the Creoles of La Gaulette ain't real Creoles no more. More like the *bann malbar* [Hindus].' In this context, there are strong indications that locality overrules community, although intermarriage is virtually unheard of. In the *baitka*, the Hindu youth club of La Gaulette, there is actually a Creole member (a rather unusual case). The Creole-founded sports club (a branch of the nationwide Creole NGO *L'Organisation Fraternelle*) has an increasing number of Hindu members. In La Gaulette, further, the division of labour is less ethnically based than in Case Noyale. There are, for example, seven Hindu fishermen and many Creole field labourers; members of both communities work at the hotels.

Mixed groups of youngsters can often be observed in front of the shop. The Creole minority has publicly adopted many typical 'Hindu' values (thrift, planning, soberness); but privately they tend to demarcate their distinctiveness, like engulfed ethnic minorities in many other societies (see Eidheim 1971).

'It's a good thing that the village develops,' says a middle-aged Creole mechanic, 'and we've got nothing against the Hindus here in La Gaulette. We may be different from the Creoles in Case Noyale, but they are still our brothers. Come the General Elections, and our vote is for the MMM.'

• *Competition and progress.* Under what circumstances, then, can we say that locality overrules ethnicity? In this particular case, the perceived context is obviously one of rapid local progress distinguishing the local field from the backward surroundings; the spirit is very much, as the council chairman says, one of 'pulling together for the common good'. Competition follows regional rather than communal lines, and the prerequisite in the form of shared culture and lifestyle (which was found not to exist in the case of Lalit's class model) is that of *modernity*. Modern ideals of consumption have reached La Gaulette through links with the five-star hotels nearby, and working for the French-owned hotels has instructed villagers in modern 'bureaucratic' or 'industrial' forms of discipline. In other words, the common denominator functioning in the public arenas of the village has been successfully shifted from agreement concerning the rules for political competition to shared notions of progress.

• *Territory and ethnicity.* A different process, but displaying the same crucial characteristic of collectively organised competition along regional, not communal lines, took place in an ethnically mixed village of about 1,500 inhabitants in eastern Mauritius. The issue was this: a pipeline through the village was projected by the State. The course of the pipeline was already decided; it was to follow the coast along the shortest possible line. Many villagers were discontented; over half of them lived a considerable distance from the closest point where one might install a public tap. Through their representatives in the village council, they organised a petition and put pressure on their fellow villagers for a 'solution that might benefit the majority of the villagers'. Nothing eventually came out of it – the decision had already been taken on a higher level. But this *ad hoc* action is interesting in that it cut across ethnic and even kin ties: the self-appointed leader of the action was a male Creole, and the largest ethnic category of the upper section of the village was Hindu; while Creole families were in majority in the lower section. The leader's brother-in-law, also a member of the Village Council, opposed the motion.

I visited the village about fifteen years after this event, and found no indication that any permanent fissure along spatial lines had developed. Marriage was largely regulated by intra-ethnic practices, and the informal social groups were more or less mono-ethnic, composed of men from different parts of the village.

The shared cultural orientation necessary for collective action is here narrower and more of an *ad hoc* character than in our first example. Thus it was not to be expected that the conflict should lead to a permanent social reconfiguration. Once the issue was decided and the statuses of petitioner/anti-petitioner made obsolete, the ongoing interaction based on those socio-cultural statuses relating to kinship, work and religion served to reinstate the status quo.[5]

On a general note, it should be kept in mind that the people in question are far from exclusively integrated locally, but also maintain important links at different systemic levels. The village is in important respects being reproduced as a part of a nationwide system, and connections with the global economic system are important as well – both at the level of social reproduction and at the level of representations. This exemplifies A. P. Cohen's general point (1985) about the shortcomings of the simplistic dichotomy between 'anonymous' urban society and 'face-to-face-based' village society. Case Noyale is a village that in important respects is integrated on an anonymous basis, through links with the outside world. Regarding Mauritian localities in general, be they rural or urban, interethnic interaction is in principle not necessary for cultural integration to take place on a nationwide scale, since this integration is mediated by mass media and the anonymous structures of the state and market. In a tribal village, people may produce their own food on a household basis, and/or may obtain it through barter. In Case Noyale, villagers buy food in the shop; in this way, their patterns of consumption become similar as a result of causes other than interaction. The nation is not constituted through interaction; it is defined from above, and offers opportunities to those who support it. A certain degree of cultural integration is necessary for interaction to take place, but the inverse does not hold true in this kind of society. Local identity can therefore never be as fundamental there as in societies integrated at a lower level of scale.

Gender

Little (1978) has written about feminism, or rather community feeling between women, as a 'countervailing force' in African ethnicity. Meaning shared by women from different ethnic categories is, Little argues, sometimes of greater situational importance than the meaning shared between men and women of the same ethnic category. This can doubtless be true in many cases in Mauritius, and gender as a principle for social differentiation, already overwhelmingly important (as in any society), could aspire to significance in the nationwide fields.

• *Feminism.* There were in the late 1980s three feminist organisations in Mauritius. The *Mauritius Alliance of Women* stresses complementarity with men and agrees basically with the traditional sexual division of labour. It is dominated by the Hindu middle class, and has generally projected housewife ideals. More radical groups exist as well. During the 1980s, several small feminist groups, including the *Muvman Liberasyon Fam,* a modern marxist feminist group connected with LPT/Lalit, and the *Ligue Feministe,* a tiny radical group of university-educated women from all communities, ran petitions, held courses and promoted a European-inspired feminism with little popular support in Mauritius, where patriarchal values remain hegemonic.

• *Informal ties.* Informal contacts between women are socially more important. During my fieldwork on the south-western coast, there was an

International Women's Day meeting at the *Centre Social*. Creole women were well represented at the meeting, where a female Member of the Legislative Assembly gave a speech – but there were virtually no Hindu women present. The next day, I asked two young Hindu women of my acquaintance why they had not been present at the event. Both admitted that they would have liked to, but their husbands would not let them. This is one of numerous instances confirming ethnically specific differences in the position of women. While some Hindu and Muslim women envy the Creoles' greater personal freedom, they tend to reject the latter's presumed loose sexual morality. Creole girls, conversely, frown at the thought of arranged marriage (which is still common among Indo-Mauritians).

In the local space, there are extensive female interethnic contacts at the grocer's and at the public standpipes, but similar encounters in the private fields are uncommon. Granted that women of all the large communities (including Creoles, if to a slighter degree) are by and large confined to the household in their daily activities, the unity of women is not currently an operative force in social change in this kind of village.

• *New careers for women.* Economic changes may lead to a dramatically new situation in this respect. The industrial revolution in Mauritius largely affects young women, and it potentially creates unity along the dimensions of class *and* gender. More than 70 per cent of the employees in the EPZ are women, most of them young. In the beginning, Creole girls were overrepresented; as the sector has grown, so has the proportion of Hindu, Tamil and Muslim girls. Some of the smaller factories are family businesses and thus mono-ethnic. But in the larger industrial estates, women from all the three largest ethnic categories work together. Here, groups of Creole and Indo-Mauritian girls can regularly be seen taking their lunch breaks together, and in this, they arguably represent a new modality of inter-ethnic contact, in many cases transcending ethnic boundaries (see also Chapter 7).

Age

Youth connotes honesty, purity and *espoir* – hope – in Mauritian public discourse. The success of the MMM is perhaps linked to the fact that its candidates in the 1970s were young and reputedly honest (by contrast to Ramgoolam's middle-aged politicians, who were frequently wealthy men with dubious reputations). The 1976 General Elections could be seen, partly, as a competition between the young and the old: while the average age of Labour's candidates was 50, the MMM's candidates were on average 32

(Simmons 1982:195). Later elections fail to present a similarly clear distinction between the blocs.

Generation gaps are almost a universal phenomenon in human society, and they become particularly dramatic in situations of swift change. The statuses linked with young age in modern societies often connote political radicalism and sometimes naïve optimism. This holds true for most Mauritian fields of discourse, too. Widespread programmatic anti-communalist statements, such as can be heard much more frequently among those under 25 than among their elders, should perhaps therefore not be accorded great importance as signs of social change. In so far as there are significant changes in socialisation patterns, nevertheless, one may informedly guess that certain changes may come about in society as such, later on.

• *Post-independence youth.* Four important factors relating to secondary socialisation have changed since the 1960s. First, the educational system has increasingly been universalised – a larger proportion of children take the CPE (Certificate of Primary Education) annually, implying that today's young have wider areas of shared meaning than their parents did. Second, the exposure to global youth culture is now, in prospering Mauritius, more universal and more pervasive than before. Third, only those under 25 have grown up wholly in an independent nation-state where the importance of national unity is repeatedly stressed in public discourse. Fourth, the period since 1960 has seen the rise of nominally non-ethnic youth organisations, notably the Boy Scouts and Girl Guides; but there has also been a revitalisation of ethnically-based youth clubs – actually boys' clubs (Hindu *baitkas*, Muslim *madrassahs*, and Creole *clubs fraternels*, the last founded in 1969). In the towns, only non-ethnic youth clubs are now recognised by the municipal councils. In the case history that follows, the issue is whether this legislation is likely to promote non-ethnic unity among the young.

• *Ethnicity in youth clubs.* This concerns one of the many youth clubs in western Rose-Hill.[6] Nominally, the club is non-ethnic and is therefore allowed to use public sports arenas, in addition to receiving some support and legitimation from municipal authorities. In fact, the club has a single non-Hindu member, a Creole who joined ostensibly in order to be the goalkeeper on the football team. This young man rarely patronises the clubhouse (a modest house where cards and dominoes are played in the afternoons). Other Creole youngsters in the neighbourhood claim that he must have been paid a bribe to join the club, which would otherwise not have been recognised by the authorities as a legitimate youth club.

Dev (Hindu, 18), the son of a tailor, is the most outspoken anti-communalist of the approximately 18 members of the club. Having failed his SC (School Certificate, equivalent to 'O' Levels) once, he is now making a second attempt. He has had a brief fling with a Coloured girl, and ardently defends intermarriage as a nationalist idea. Initially, it was due to his initiative that the Creole boy joined. Dev's negotiating with him was applauded by his friends in the club, who saw in this a strategic move to gain them support from the Municipal Council. According to the unwritten rules of 'non-ethnic' youth clubs like this one, people from outside the ethnic group don't usually apply for membership.

But Dev would like the club to be truly multiethnic, 'a model for Mauritian youth'. Once, he brought a Tamil to a club meeting, presenting him as a *mam* (mate) who considered becoming a member. The President of the club, clearly not keen on accepting the young Tamil, was not impressed. The situation was embarrassing to him and the other members, as it seemed to compel them to make the implicit rule explicit, and in a wider context, to break a Mauritian 'taboo' ('Never make communalist statements when there are ethnic others present'). Upon my first visit to the club, the President had explained that 'anyone can become a member, sure, we don't have communalist policies here'. In this situation, he rapidly found a solution, stating in a matter-of-fact way that this would have to wait until the General Assembly at the end of the year, when the young Tamil's application would be considered. The statement seemed ridiculous to myself (the club was in fact a very informal organisation), but none of the nine boys present smiled. Dev, torn between conflicting loyalties, was in a rage. 'How come you invented this rule just now?' he shouted. 'Now come on,' said someone, 'look at this place, d'you think there would be space for everybody here? We can't have everybody as a member.' Sensing he had lost, Dev walked out, shouting that he would never set his feet in this *lakaz krapo malbar* (house of Hindu toads) again.

• *Informal networks.* Months later, I met Dev on Rose-Hill's *Route Royale*, and asked him about the club. He said he didn't go there any more, adding in an apologetic tone that 'Mauritians are like this, you see, stupid people.' A survey of young men's personal networks in the area proves him partly right: the youth clubs and street gangs are largely mono-ethnic, but there are also pluri-ethnic venues for voluntary encounters, such as the cinemas, religious centres, dancing schools, cafés and evening classes. These venues are growing in importance as consumerism and 'Western' youth culture are becoming more important for personal identities, and there has been a marked shift towards multi-ethnic, urban-looking youth gangs influenced by global fashions since the mid-1980s. In Rose-Hill, a favourite hang-out for such groups is the new shopping mall, which opened its doors in 1990.

Beyond Compromise: Intermarriage

The nationalist slogan 'unity in diversity' denotes a sharp distinction between public and private fields,[7] implying that interethnic compromises or non-ethnic modes of organisation are required in every context perceived as *public*, that is conceptually linked with the interests of the Mauritian people as a whole. This is where the principle of the lowest common denominator is necessary, granted that different ethnic categories continue to represent rivalling interests, for the system to be integrated at the societal level. 'Unity' (universalist representations and practices) is the legal and ideological ideal of the public service, the political and educational systems, and the economy (our national fields). Seen from the perspective of action (as opposed to structure), the official ideal for Mauritian society is the *meritocracy*. On the other hand, the officially acknowledged 'diversity' is ideally to be confined to 'private life', that is, the fields of family and locality. 'Diversity', which is locally understood as ethnic differences, is generally positively sanctioned in religious practices (which are, incidentally, a 'public' type of activity), as well as in ideologies and practices relating to language, marriage and informal networks generally.

• *The significance of intermarriage.* It is widely held by Mauritians that ethnic conflict is fostered by strategies practised by politicians or, more generally, in public zero-sum games. Most of the material discussed in the present work lends itself fairly easily to such an interpretation, although I have emphasised that even zero-sum games are culturally constituted and draw on non-utilitarian symbolic universes of meaning in order to function in mobilising ways. The preservation of Oriental languages in education, for example, can hardly be conceptualised as a zero-sum game, while the ratios of different languages on national radio can. Religious meaning is not a scarce commodity, but the power inherent in religious organisations is, and so on. The case of interethnic, or 'mixed' marriages, which will be analysed in some detail below, is interesting for two reasons. Unless we try to explain Mauritian ethnicity in sociobiological terms, which would be extremely far-fetched considering the facts on the ground, what is at stake in most interethnic marriages is meaning to a greater extent than utility. Further, intermarriage belongs to the private context, to the household field. No major political movement has encouraged intermarriage, which, if sufficiently widespread, would imply the end of ethnicity as we know it in Mauritius, replacing the digitally bounded categories with an analogic continuum akin, perhaps, to the black–white continuum found in Brazil. In other words, intermarriage articulates both with the private–public distinction, with the instrumental–symbolic dimension, and with the very logic of ethnic classification. It can therefore be a privileged site for studying social and cultural dynamics in Mauritius.[8]

• *The issue.* Many, if not most, important resources have traditionally been channelled through ethnic and kinship organisation in Mauritius: employment, material and social security, group belongings, 'old age insurance', marriage and political influence. There are indicators that the main foci for indentification may be changing for a substantial part of the population, which will be discussed in the next chapter. For now, I will concentrate on the current changes in marriage strategies and criteria for spouse selection. In 1960, the number of interethnic marriages seems to have been nearly negligible; in 1982, the number was 497; while in 1987, the number had risen to 989 cases, being 8.8 per cent of the total number of marriages contracted on the island (Oodiah 1992:59). The number of divorces is also increasing significantly, and doubled from about 300 in 1982 to about 600 in 1992, which also may indicate that the social significance of marriage and the family institution is undergoing a transformation in parts of Mauritian society. Although it is clearly indefensible to extrapolate from developments over such a limited period, which do not necessarily indicate a long-term trend (cf. Nave n.d. 2), Mauritian society is undergoing changes that make a scenario of increase in divorce rates and interethnic marriages likely, as will now be argued.

As previous chapters have made clear, in most of Mauritian history from the eighteenth century on, different kinds of resources have been bundled together in social networks and organisations based on kinship and ethnicity. The family remains very important, and when asked, many young Mauritians will say that they cannot marry outside their ethnic group 'even if I wouldn't mind myself', because the family would reject it. In a society where employment opportunities and financial support are channelled through kinship and metaphoric kinship organisation (that is, ethnic organisation), it can be a very serious thing indeed to disobey parental orders. Although the marriage pattern is changing and individually based 'love marriages' (as opposed to arranged marriages) are now widespread, even among Hindus and Muslims, parental authority remains generally strong.

How do interethnic marriages function in a society where ethnicity is the most important criterion for ordering the social world? There is no simple answer, but through discussing a few selected cases, I will indicate the circumstances under which mixed marriages can be viable, as well as some variations, and finally I shall suggest some possible consequences for Mauritian ethnicity in the twenty-first century. Since endogamy is crucial for both ethnic identification and organisation, interethnic marriages are a grave threat indeed to Mauritian ethnicity.

• *Engulfed by an ethnic logic: Marie-Claude (*née *Gita) and Jean.* The couple lives in a coastal village dominated by Creoles, but with a sizeable Hindu minority. They were married in 1976 and have three children. She runs a *tabagie* (sweetshop), and Jean works at the small coffee factory nearby. When she was baptised as Marie-Claude at the local church in order to marry Jean, her widowed mother did not attend the ceremony, and she has since remained adamant that 'her daughter is no longer her daughter', meaning that Marie-Claude is not allowed into her home and has little contact with her family. Her younger brother Ram explains that he has nothing against Creoles, but that Marie-Claude is responsible for her social alienation herself, since she can no longer be a member of a Hindu family after converting to Christianity. Jean's family, who are Creoles, were only mildly opposed to the marriage, and are on reasonably good terms with their son and daughter-in-law.

This 'openness' of the Creole ethnic category requires some comment here. Creoles may describe themselves as a 'mixed' people, since they have no single shared tribal or geographic origin, speak a 'mixed' language (sometimes described as a language composed of French words and East African syntax), and have few if any ancient folk traditions exploited in ethnic boundary processes. In addition, it should be kept in mind that the Creoles do not form corporate groups at the lineage, family or ethnic level. Compared to the other ethnic groups in Mauritius, the Creoles command few corporate resources. This suggests that there are few strong reasons for Creoles to be endogamous, and as a matter of fact, they have no strong rule of endogamy. On the other hand, Creoles tend to stress their cultural values, including Christianity, and for a non-Creole affine to be fully accepted into the loosely knit kin group, he or she must usually convert to Catholicism (or another variant of Christianity). Relatively speaking, the Creoles are more open at the social level than at the cultural level.[9]

The case of Jean and Marie-Claude is interesting in at least two respects. First, Jean was a nonconformist already as a teenager, and he had few close friends. In other words, he did not have to worry about losing his primary peer network, which is usually an important source of recognition and personal identity to a Creole, through marrying a Hindu girl. Second, Marie-Claude quickly became economically independent through setting up her *tabagie* immediately after marrying. Had their personal circumstances been different, the marriage might never have succeeded. It should also be noted that mixed marriages have always occurred in Mauritian villages, and that this one had little connection with the ongoing changes in Mauritian society. It was locally perceived as an anomaly, perhaps even as an aberration; and the couple itself did not challenge the ethnic logic of the village organisation as such. They admitted having broken the rules.

• *Ethnicity or class: Françoise and Abdul.* This is a very different case. Françoise was an upper-middle-class Franco-Mauritian girl who fell in love with a lower-middle-class Muslim boy. When her family found out, she was sent to live with relatives in France for a year so that she might change her mind; but upon her return, she immediately re-established clandestine contact with Abdul, and with the help of friends they arranged to spend two weeks together in La Réunion. Despite very strong warnings from Françoise's family, they married five years before I met them. They live in a flat in central Plaines Wilhems.

Abdul's family were critical of the marriage, but eventually accepted it and, Abdul admits, were 'both ashamed and proud' that their son should marry a white girl from a posh family. She converted to Islam, but they both describe themselves as 'indifferent Muslims'. They have one child, who has a Muslim name and who will be brought up as a Muslim, although they admit he will not be a 'complete Muslim'. For Abdul, the cost of marrying Françoise was minimal; and since she has converted to Islam, she is accepted as a member of his family. He has a clerical job in his uncle's firm in Port-Louis.

To Françoise, the choice was a more consequential one. She lost her birthright to a secure and predictable life surrounded by material wealth and a tight network of Franco-Mauritian friends and relatives. She says she has very few, but very loyal friends left, and that she is often spoken of in Franco-Mauritian circles as a tragic example of a woman gone astray. At one of the last family gatherings she attended, she wore a sari, and her mother commented, 'You are dirtying the blood of your family.' Later, her mother said, as an argument against the marriage, that Françoise apparently 'did not want any friends'. She retorted that she did indeed have some friends, whereupon the mother remarked that they were either not from *ta societé* ('your society', referring to both class and race) or nonconformists (single, gay or professionally idiosyncratic). At the final quarrel, Françoise says, the mother said that she would rather see her daughter as a drug addict than as the wife of a Muslim. Most of the Mauritian Muslims are descendants of indentured labourers, who were servants and labourers working for the Franco-Mauritians, and many Mauritian Christians, like many European Christians, regard Islam as a threat and as an inferior religion.

Since Abdul and Françoise do not live with his parents, her personal freedom is greater than it would have been otherwise, but she admits that she cannot smoke cigarettes or drink alcohol at home even if she would have liked to. (Being 'indifferent Muslims', they serve alcohol to guests.)

The case of Françoise and Abdul exemplifies a number of general points pertaining to the viability of interethnic marriages.

First, the question of religion can be crucial. She herself remarks that if she had been strongly religious (Christian), the marriage would not have been possible. (This is not a question of gender. A Christian man would also normally have been obliged to convert.)

Second, if she had regarded herself as socially, psychologically and economically dependent on her family and *sa société*, she would not have been able to marry Abdul. Her practical and reflexive ability to sever her ties with her family (which she was on basically good terms with until the dramatic events) was a necessary condition for the marriage.

Third, the most difficult aspect of mixed marriages in this kind of setting – the self-defined plural society with no hegemonic group – may be the identity of the children. As Françoise and Abdul admit, they are worried about their children, who will grow up as anomalies in a society where ethnic distinctions are seen as nearly as fundamental for a person's identity as gender distinctions.

Fourth, this example may remind us that to 'marry down', classwise, is socially much more problematic than to 'marry up', and this pertains to men as well as to women. This variable does not have a strong bearing on interethnic marriages as such, and is just as relevant in mono-ethnic mixed marriages between bourgeois and proletarians. In Mauritius, where the correlation between class and ethnicity is traditionally strong, the two kinds of variables are often difficult to distinguish. Consider, for example, the elderly Franco-Mauritian who can frequently be seen roaming the streets of Beau-Bassin on his old moped. He carries a revered aristocratic name and belongs to one of the island's most powerful lineages. When, in his youth, it became known that he had fallen in love with a Coloured girl, he was disinherited and literally thrown out of his family, and has since then made his living as a junk merchant. Regarded as an anomaly by everyone, he has no primary network.

Finally, it should be noted that there is no convincing sociological explanation for the fact of Françoise and Abdul falling in love. Neither of them were 'misfits' or 'radicals' in their respective social environments. The act of falling in love seems to be an independent variable in this regard, but the realisation of their marriage was, as we have seen, dependent on other factors that might not have been present.

• *Beyond the ethnic logic: Vishnu and Shalini.* This third example brings out further dimensions of the issue. Vishnu, who is classified as a Tamil, has petit-bourgeois and proletarian family origins. He grew up in the cosmopolitan town of Rose-Hill, and owing to a combination of family efforts and his personal grant-winning abilities, he was able to pursue university studies in France. Upon returning, he was an underemployed intellectual for several years until, in the early 1990s, he became a successful consultant for private enterprises. Shalini, who is a Hindu of high-caste origin, comes from a wealthy merchant family. She and Vishnu had been sweethearts since their teens, had studied together in France, and were married shortly afterwards. What is striking about their case is, that it is entirely unspectacular in the Mauritian context. Neither of the two families was opposed to the marriage, although Shalini's parents were for a long time slightly suspicious of Vishnu – more or less in the same way as an upper-middle-class European family would have felt ambivalent towards the long-haired, but obviously kind and intelligent radical courting their daughter. Vishnu explains, 'I have never thought of us as a mixed couple. We have grown up in the same town, been to university together, shared the same experiences and so on.' In certain periods, they have depended on Shalini's family financially, and there is no indication that their marriage has weakened kinship bonds.

This example adds several further points to the discussion of mixed marriages.

First, and most obviously, the very notion of 'mixed marriage' presupposes an ethnically informed epistemology. When I interviewed a married couple of political activists, asking them a naïve question about their mixed marriage, they quickly retorted: 'What do you mean, "mixed marriage"? We have the same class background, the same kind of education and the same political views. What do you see as "mixed" about our marriage?'

Second, the case of Vishnu and Shalini exemplifies that Mauritian ethnicity can in practice be a matter of degree in the sense that the perceived taxonomic distance between groups varies (see Mitchell 1974 on taxonomic distance in general). There is no doubt that some groups perceive themselves as closer than others, and that a Hindu–Tamil alliance is less controversial than a Hindu–Creole or Creole–Muslim alliance would have been. Had Vishnu been a Creole, Shalini's family would probably, despite their liberal attitudes, have been much more unenthusiastic about the alliance.

Third, the case indirectly brings out some of the complexity of Mauritian society and the ensuing difficulties in generalising about Mauritian ethnicity. Within the life-worlds of Vishnu and Shalini, the Mauritian white-collar world of university academics, writers, journalists and business people, 'primordial identities' do not necessarily make up an important dimension of social organisation. Such identities can be activated symbolically, and they are in some cases: hardly anywhere in Mauritius does one see more young women in saris than at the Mahatma Gandhi Institute. However, and that is the point here, in this kind of environment, ethnic identity is not perceived as 'second nature' as it still is in most of village Mauritius and in ethnically segregated Port-Louis; it has to be chosen self-consciously.

Fourth, the very question of ethnic identity as opposed to other forms of identification is made explicit by Vishnu, Shalini and many others in a similar kind of situation – not just urban intellectuals living in mixed marriages, but also others with comparable experiences and outlooks. Vishnu says that when asked what his ancestral language is, he replies that it is Kreol. The next question is, 'But aren't you a Tamil?'. His answer would be: 'My mother-tongue is Kreol. My parents' mother-tongue was Kreol. My grandparents may have known Tamil, but I always heard them speak Kreol. Why do you think I should go further back than that in order to find my ancestral language?' This exchange brings out the main contradiction in current Mauritian identity politics – which can be described as a tension, sometimes a contradiction, between an orientation towards the past and an orientation towards the present and the future. Unlike Françoise and Abdul, Vishnu and Shalini do not worry about the ethnic identity of their children. Rather, their main concern is that the children should have a good education.

• *Plurality and post-plurality*. These three examples reveal great variations between interethnic marriages. In relation to the role of identity politics in contemporary Mauritian society, they could perhaps be graded on a scale from the bounded to the unbounded network.

Jean and Marie-Claude are trapped inside an ethnic system of signification and organisation, and have improvised considerably to carve out an anomalous existence outside it – at a significant cost. The system of ethnic distinctions is able to absorb a great many marriages of this kind, bringing light-skinned Creole children (who nevertheless remain Creole children), into Mauritian society without changing its structure and modes of legitimation.

Abdul and Françoise are actively rejecting and opposing practices of ethnic segregation, but are nevertheless faced with subjectively perceived dilemmas of belongingness, personal sacrifices and the children's social identity. They recognise the continued importance of ethnicity and willingly pay a price for deviating from it.

Vishnu and Shalini, for their part, do not see themselves as being 'up against' anything. To them, marriage appears as a voluntary contract between two individuals, which does not necessarily involve families or other groups. Their professional networks, informal social life and perspectives

on the future do not necessitate collective organisation based on shared
ancestry or ideologies of shared culture.

It is important to note here that the differences between the three
marriages cannot be reduced merely to 'personality differences', but must
be seen in relation to differences in life experiences and structural positions,
generating different structures of relevance and different perceived possibilities of choice. In a sense, the outcome is identical in the three examples
– an interethnic marriage; but both the social consequences and the very
meaning of the term 'interethnic marriage' (*mariaz miks*) vary with the
context. Among patrilineal groups, the gender of the 'outmarrying' person
may be important. It seems, for example, that Sino-Mauritian parents are
more tolerant of allowing their daughters to marry non-Chinese than they
would be of their sons.

• *Mixing as 'creolisation'?*[10] Let us pursue the topic of intermarriage
further still. As remarked earlier, many of the children of interethnic
marriages are classified as 'a kind of Creoles'. However, within the Creole
ethnic category, there are many views as to what a mixed marriage amounts
to. Some of the middle-class Coloureds would, as a matter of principle, not
consider a marriage to a white Catholic a mixed marriage, but they might
consider a marriage to a dark-skinned working-class person mixed. What
is class, what is ethnicity and what is aesthetic judgement is sometimes
hard to extricate, and in these cases, the interrelationship between ethnicity
and the other criteria for social alignments and differentiation discussed
in this chapter becomes very close indeed.

Marie-Josée, a young woman from a light-skinned but working-class Creole
family living in a *cité* near Rose-Hill, has two elder brothers. One of them
is married to a very dark Creole, the other is engaged to a low-caste Hindu
girl. Marie-Josée resents both about equally for their respective choices –
although only the second case is one of interethnic alliance. 'I don't like
very black people,' she says, and adds, 'and I don't like *bann malbar* either.'
Her mother, on the contrary, is only hostile against the Hindu girl. Her
other daughter-in-law, the dark-skinned Creole, is, after all, *nasyon* (fellow
Creole) and therefore acceptable, while the poor *malbar* girl, although about
to be baptised, remains polluting, as it were: *Malbar res malbar*, the mother
explains; 'Once a Hindu, always a Hindu.'

As far as Marie-Josée is concerned, her cultural ideals, to be confirmed
in choice of spouse, are European: the more European, the better. Since
her elder brother's wife looks like an African, she cannot be any good.
According to her, the perfect husband (for herself) would be a foreign white,
with for second choice a liberal Franco-Mauritian, and third a *gen de couleur*
or any light-skinned Creole. With regard to the prospect of marrying

somebody not included in these categories, she equates physically black Creoles with *bann madras*, Tamils, as a last option. She is favourably inclined towards anything she considers upwards conversions through intermarriage. Her mother, on the other hand, represents Mauritian Creole identity: anything non-Creole is suspect. Thus, when I visited the family for the first time, her mother, at first suspecting me of being her daughter's lover, was friendly in a very sarcastic way. This intra-ethnic value conflict is frequently activated in issues to do with marriage, and, like similar conflicts in the more endogamous ethnic groups in Mauritius, it can be seen as a confrontation between commitment to cultural values and indiviual choice. In fact, what both Marie-Josée and her mother are up to amounts to *saving the symbolic capital* of their respective scarce values. Intermarriage represents dilution and irretrievable loss of ethnically specific meaning, which is – from their point of view – limited and bounded. If culture is reified thus as an object, then bits can be sliced off from it. Intermarriage in the immediate family is, then, the ultimate loss of true Creoleness. It is not, unlike what occurs in several other communities, associated with the loss of other forms of capital, as few material resources are channelled through the Creole family.

Marie-Josée's brothers also have similar representations of their culture, but the normative interpretation is different in this respect. To the elder, it is no deviation from Creole custom to marry a dark-skinned Creole; to the younger, marrying a Hindu girl is a manifestation of shared Mauritianness. To Marie-Josée, I (a pale-skinned foreigner) was no outsider; to her mother, I was. As always in Mauritian ethnicity, the system of representations is shared by the antagonists (which means that the communication of distinctiveness, paradoxically, is a shared cultural trait), but the normatively charged interpretations differ.

  • *The varying significance of intermarriage.* The differences in the social organisation of the marriage institution should finally be noted. Indo-Mauritian traditions advise that the parents should monitor the marriages; this custom remains strong, notably in the countryside, and explains why Marie-Claude's mother's reaction was so much stronger than that of Jean's parents.

In other words, the meaning of a term like 'interethnic marriage', although apparently clear enough, greatly changes with the cultural and structural context. The cases and further notes above thus further confirm that (a) ethnicity only has (shifting) meaning in ongoing social processes, and (b) the ethnic category takes its substantial content from the contexts in which it is being reproduced – in other words the ethnic category itself depends on a particular frame of relevance in order to 'exist'. These situational frames of relevance (or language-games, if one prefers) are enormous in number, even intra-ethnically, because social and cultural boundaries are not objectively fixed but ambiguous. Thus Marie-Josée may credibly argue the relevance of a representation of endogamous Creole subgroups based on colour but not class – a model that her mother rejects.

Intermarriage presupposes intramarriage, and in so far as it is correctly perceived as a deviation, it may serve to strengthen the respective group identities in a Durkheimian fashion. But the practice must also be considered as applications of a variety of 'bridging principles' between cultural differences. After all, Marie-Josée still sees her brothers; her Hindu sister-in-law comes to their house on Sundays, and so on. In this way, intermarriage does contribute to breaking down ethnic boundaries, although it also confirms them as long as it is seen as something exceptional.

Individualism and Globalisation

Interethnic marriages are justified in terms of individualism, and the idea of individual uniqueness contradicts ideologies of ethnic loyalty and tight ethnic incorporation. There are many current tendencies working against ethnic incorporation in contemporary Mauritius, favouring individualism and abstract loyalty to the state instead, and most of them are associated with industrial capitalism (replacing plantation capitalism), uniform education and mass media.

• *Modes of participation.* Important bridgeheads of global culture include tourism, pop music, travel, TV and cinema films, and printed media, as well as all kinds of consumer goods. These systemic aspects are culturally homogenising at the national level; they could also be seen as resulting in an ever-increasing differentiation. If, following the increasing commodification of culture and concomitant processes of homogenisation in other fields, virtually everybody in Mauritius will celebrate Divali (the Hindu feast of lights) in fifteen years' time, this will not necessarily entail that all, Hindus and non-Hindus alike, participate in identical ways. As Baumann (1996) has shown in a recent analysis of a polyethnic setting in South London, there are different modes of participation available in the contexts delineated by identical rituals. Like successful ideologies, the rituals are ambiguous and open to different interpretations – and this is also an important property of the potential white noise of mass communication.

The Creole preference for black pop artists and actors, and the popularity of Indian feature films among people of Indian origin exemplify the idiosyncratic reinterpretations, and to some degree reinventions, of the metropolitan messages that are so important in the constitution of modern identities in the context of 'the global ecumene' (Hannerz 1992). On a domestic scale, religious as well as culinary syncretism is widespread – and to label this 'plural acculturation' would only make matters worse, since such a term indicates the existence of discrete 'cultures'. The point is that identical objects (cars, bottles of Coca-Cola, TV sets . . .), which are familiar in many societies, may take on different meanings in different societies and in different social contexts in the same society (see Miller 1994). Even if all or nearly all components of local symbolic universes were derived from 'the West', their actual forms are entirely different because of the peculiar internal organisation of the signifiers, and the diverging symbolic values (meaning) invested in objects and cultural institutions with identical names and external forms. Two examples from the same part of urban Mauritius may indicate the impact of globalisation on personal identity, showing additionally that global culture does not create global persons, but rather contributes to changing the meaning of the local.

• *'Westernising consumption': The Rioux household.* The quarter of Roches-Brunes, located on the western outskirts of Rose-Hill, is dominated by a municipal housing estate (*cité ouvrière/site uvrie*), and most of the approximately 1,500 people living in the area are working-class Creoles. The more imposing dwellings belonging to a few affluent families are located at a distance from the relatively monotonous *cité ouvrière*. Apart from the Creoles, some Coloureds (light-skinned Creoles with middle-class aspirations) and Chinese live in the area, as well as a few Hindus and a single Muslim household.

In describing the relationship between the global and the local in personal and social identification, I shall focus on the Rioux household. It is what is commonly described as a matrifocal household, consisting of Mme Rioux, her daughter Aline (20), her two sons, François and Jean, both in their mid-twenties, Aline's baby daughter and a tenant, a young student from Rodrigues. Their income is average by local standards. Aline works as a shopgirl in the town centre, her elder brother François is a carpenter's apprentice, and her younger brother Jean is unemployed. The household sometimes receives remittances from other relatives, notably a married daughter who lives in La Réunion, and the student from Rodrigues pays a moderate sum in monthly rent.

The living-room in the Rioux' home contains several objects signifying connections with distant places. Two posters depicting pop stars (one English, one American) are prominently displayed; so is a cupboard with glass doors, behind which are souvenirs from Paris, Bombay and London. There is a cassette player and a black-and-white TV set. On the floor next to the TV set, there is a small heap of foreign magazines, some of them in English, which is a language none of the household members is able to read.

The mass media consumed in the household confirm the common stereotype of life in 'the Western world' as an easy, glamorous life. Local knowledge of Europe generally suggests it is a continent of affluence and excitement. Many Mauritians have emigrated, the majority to France and Britain. Aline Rioux says she wouldn't emigrate; she has heard too many ugly stories of girls who were forced into prostitution, or who were married to old men living in some remote rural part of France. There has, in other words, been a certain feedback from other parts of the global system. She reads *romans-photo*, 'photo-novels' of French origin, and occasionally a local magazine. She is very fond of sentimental French pop music.

François Rioux plays soccer and follows world politics in the local newspapers; he frequently discusses global issues with his friends. The whole family watches American soap operas on TV; the younger generation go to the cinema to see largely American films dubbed in French about twice a month. They are devout Catholics and go to Mass every Sunday (Aline goes more rarely).

The members of the household agree that education is important for a person's opportunities, unless he or she has relatives in high places. François, Jean and Aline are all prepared to compete for jobs and promotion. None of them has completed secondary school.

• *How global?* Seen superficially and in a fragmented way, as I have looked at them now, the world-structures and patterns of consumption of the Rioux household seem comparable to, similar to, those of working classes in many other countries. The globalisation of culture seems predominant in Roches-Brunes, which to an untrained observer like the Lévi-Strauss of *Tristes Tropiques* (1955) must seem a squalid backyard of civilisation. Scrutinised more closely, however, the lives and world-structures of the Rioux and the others in the *cité* have a distinctively local character, and cannot at all be understood outside their local context. Ethnicity is a component, but not the main ingredient, in this emerging aspect of everyday life in Mauritius, where the main relationship invested with meaning is the local/global dimension.

Soccer and pop music may be seen as quintessential embodiments of global culture. The anthropologist Eduardo Archetti (personal communication) tells this anecdote about an incident in Burkina Faso, which may illustrate the global nature of soccer as channelled through mass media. Arriving at the airport in Ouagadougou with his Argentinian passport at a time of political instability, just after Thomas Sankara's assassination, he expected difficulties. At first, the passport official seemed suspicious, glancing through his passport. He then left the room with the passport, re-emerged, opened it on a blank page and stamped it, smiling, while uttering the magic word: 'Maradona'.

Unlike cricket in the Trobriands, soccer in Roches-Brunes follows the same rules as in Britain. Unlike World Cup soccer, however, it is entirely local in character. François Rioux owes much of his reputation in the neighbourhood to his skills as a soccer player. As a result, he is popular with the girls and makes friends with the boys; and in fact he got his present job at least partly because of his personal popularity. Concerning pop music, a similar local context applies. It is played at local parties and in rumshops, and may evoke sentiments and stimulate social relations quite different from its effects in other environments. In the black Jamaican working class, for example, the world-famous pop singer Michael Jackson was unpopular already in the late 1980s because he was considered 'not sufficiently black' (following his gradual 'whitening', his popularity must have diminished further); in the black Mauritian working-class, he is second only to God, not least because he *is* black.

When watching dubbed American TV shows, the Rioux comment on them incessantly. Very often, they compare the characters with people they know; when commenting on rich and miserly men, they might make remarks to the effect that 'Hey, that's just like L– used to treat my friend,' referring to a neighbourhood Chinese merchant. They always compare the plots and social milieux on the screen with contexts they are familiar with. It should also be noted, significantly, that for a Mauritian Creole European culture is attractive partly because it is reflexively being contrasted locally with Mauritian Hindu culture. Films and magazines describing middle-class life in Europe or North America, for example, thus make sense and are popular partly because they can be interpreted into a local dichotomous schema depicting Indian culture as inferior. Overcommunicating what is locally perceived as Europeanness indicates a culturally valued air of superiority *vis-à-vis* the local Indians. In their selective interpretations of aspects of global culture, the inhabitants of Roches-Brunes appropriate them and transform the global into something local.

• *Roger's aesthetics.* A few kilometres to the north, in Beau-Bassin, a young man named Roger is busy negotiating his identity in the intersections between global modernity, Creole ethnic identity, Mauritianness, gender, age and class. Roger is a light-skinned urban Creole with a French surname; most of his distant ancestors were Indian and African, but he definitely does not dream of an Indian or African name for his own part. Roger's vernacular is Kreol, but he prefers to speak French or even English with foreigners. He thinks little of the local panethnic national movement that tries to win official recognition for Kreol: according to Roger, French is superior as a written language not only because it is an international language, but also because it is, in his view, richer, more beautiful and more nuanced than Kreol. Concerning music, which has an important place in his life, Roger is fond of sentimental French *chansons* as well as some British and North American pop and rock'n'roll. He does not like contemporary rap, dub and house, which, he contends, lack melody and feel; nor does he particularly enjoy so-called 'roots' music, such as reggae, rhythm'n'blues and traditional jazz. When confronted with North American, African and Caribbean notions about 'black culture' and the black consciousness movement, Roger tends to shrug and say that this movement has little appeal to him; he does not believe in its politics and does not like its aesthetic expressions. Similarly, he has no time for those Mauritian cultural movements that try to replace metropolitan expressions – music, literature, language, food, clothing – with local ones. Concerning local *séga* music, which is very self-consciously local and rooted in local experiences, Roger likes very little of it, because, as he says, the quality of the songs is really quite poor if one compares them with European music.

Roger and his brothers frequently rent video films: many of them are low-budget Hong Kong kung-fu films; others are American films dubbed in French. He says that the criterion for a good film is its ability to stir the sentiments of the audience, and both violent and romantic films are in his view capable of that.

• *False consciousness?* Someone infused with a traditional view of culture as a fixed, rooted or semi-metaphysical entity shared by a population would have no other choice than concluding a study of Roger's views and priorities by stating that he suffers from a serious attack of cultural dependency and false consciousness; that he is alienated from his roots and probably despises himself. My conclusion is nearly the opposite. It is easy to see that Roger's selection and consumption of symbols in intercultural space are consciously undertaken in order to help him make sense of, and enrich, his life experiences. He has relatively little education and works as a junior clerk; his immediate chances for promotion are slim. He does not see Europe as a land of milk and honey, and, unlike many Mauritians, he does not dream of professional success in France, Canada or Australia. His life-projects are modest and local: he wants to marry his girlfriend and to improve his social standing a little; and he wants to continue to be able to enjoy himself through a lifetime of work and married life. He does not see black people as being either superior or inferior to white people, but, as he accurately puts it, 'your skin colour is important for your career opportunities worldwide'. Not a politically oriented man, Roger does not think this will change easily or in the near future. There is, in a word, no reason for him to attach himself to what middle-class intellectuals may think of as national culture on the one hand, and black culture on the other hand. His life-projects and his interpretation of his own experiences are congruent with – and informed by – the cultural commodities he transforms into expressions of his own individual identity. Although traditional identity tags (ethnicity, nationality, gender, age, class . . .) would be applicable to Roger, they would not account fully for him as a person, nor would they help in predicting his actions. Mediated by his reflexive positioning in Mauritian society, his personal taste and his consumer habits, his identity is in relevant respects individual and unique, and he strives to keep it unique.

In a word, the final non-ethnic dimension discussed in this chapter is the individual one, which should not be underestimated in a society where wage work is becoming universalised, meritocracy is becoming an increasingly important principle for recruitment to the labour market, the flow of cultural signification is increasingly being disembedded from ethnic distinctions, and the relationship with the outside world is becoming a defining dimension of a growing number of situations, thus replacing interethnic relationships as decisive.

Notes

1. My material is chiefly on squatters on the southern outskirts of Port-Louis. In this neighbourhood, there are Creoles, Rodriguans, Tamils and Hindus. Many families are ethnically mixed, but the configuration Creole–'Hindi speaker' was only encountered once.
2. The concept 'locality as a social field' clearly does not have the same significance in town and village. Generally, local networks are denser in the countryside, meaning that social relationships involve a larger average number of statuses.
3. In the 1982 election, Boodhoo's PSM were in a 'tactical alliance' with the MMM. The next year, the MMM went into the general election alone, Boodhoo having joined forces with the Hindu-dominated MSM. In the town constituencies, the MMM vote remained virtually unchanged; in the countryside it declined drastically. The MMM/PSM alliance also, of course, divided the *rural* Hindu vote.
4. This example is essentially based on material from 1986.

5. This second example further indicates the importance of the *spatial* aspects of social life, a dimension emphasised in the concept of social fields. On the macro level, the spatial set-up of the island – its size, position and the actual distribution of ethnic groups – are important non-sociological background variables when we try to account for the practical necessity of policies of common denominators.

6. Vinesh Hookoomsing, who has carried out sociolinguistic research in the area, describes the youth clubs as 'beads on a necklace' (personal communication): they are next to each other, they look pretty much the same, but they have different colours (i.e., recruit from different ethnic groups).

7. I do not propose a definition of the 'real' nature of public and private spheres. Here I follow the conceptualisations currently used in Mauritius.

8. For a fuller treatment of intermarriage, see Eriksen (1997a). An American anthropologist, Ari Nave, carried out fieldwork on marriage strategies and ethnicity in Mauritius during the mid-1990s. While his empirical findings, based on a quantitative survey as well as many qualitative interviews, seem to confirm mine, he questions my assumption to the effect that interethnic marriages are currently becoming more common in Mauritius because of (i) processes of cultural homogenisation and (ii) the decreasing importance of kinship and religion in certain, especially urban, Mauritian milieux. At the time of writing, Nave has published little of his work, but it will doubtless be generally available soon (cf. Nave n.d. 1, n.d. 2).

9. In a study of ethnicity in Trinidad, Klass (1991) argues that Afro-Trinidadians are socially open and culturally closed, whereas Indo-Trinidadians are culturally open (they assimilate black culture) but socially endogamous. The Mauritian situation is somewhat different (cf. Eriksen 1991c, 1992a for comparisons with Trinidad), since the size of the Indian population is larger and the gravitational pull of India itself makes itself felt much more strongly than in Trinidad. It might be remarked, though, that while Mauritian Hindus often hold racist stereotypes about Creoles, Creoles tend to hold culturalist stereotypes about Hindus.

10. The pun here lies in the dual, but related, meanings of creolisation. In the social science literature, creolisation (especially in Hannerz 1992, 1996; also in Eriksen 1994b) refers to the development of new cultural forms due to the mixing of existing cultural forms (terms such as 'hybridisation' are, admittedly, often used to similar effect). In Mauritius, it would mean *tu dimunn pu vinn kreol* – everybody becomes a Creole. However, as the Creole ethnic category is defined by others and sees itself as inherently mixed, phenotypically and culturally, the two meanings are actually quite closely related.

CHAPTER SEVEN

Mauritian Nationhoods

– But do you know what a nation means? says John Wyse.
– Yes, says Bloom.
– What is it? says John Wyse.
– A nation? says Bloom. A nation is the same people living in the same place.
– By God, then, says Ned, laughing, if that's so I'm a nation for I'm living in the same place for the past five years.
So of course everyone had a laugh at Bloom and says he, trying to muck out of it:
– Or also living in different places.
– That covers my case, says Joe.
– What is your nation if I may ask, says the citizen.
– Ireland, says Bloom. I was born here. Ireland.

James Joyce, *Ulysses* (1984 [1922]: 329–30)

Nationalism is a kind of ideology (or secular religion) that holds that there should be congruence between cultural boundaries and political ones. Most of the nationalisms that have so far been studied systematically by anthropologists have been ethnic in character: they are nationalisms that justify their state-building projects by postulating a shared past and a shared culture on behalf of the citizens or potential citizens encompassed by their conceptualised nation. A fair number of studies deal with the relationship between minorities and hegemonic ethnic groups in states, and some of them analyse minority movements as nationalisms (such as Heiberg 1989; Handler 1988; McDonald 1989). However, few of the world's 180-plus states are nation-states proper if by that term we mean countries where the bulk of the population is locally conceived of as a single ethnic group with shared culture and a shared past (a point famously hammered home by Connor 1974). For example, only a very few African countries are founded on an ethnic principle (and among these, only Lesotho, Swaziland and Somalia are virtually ethnically homogeneous; which is something of an irony in a world where it is still common to believe that ethnic homogeneity is a condition for successful nation-building, now that Somalia has been on the verge of complete breakdown for years); in Central and South America, the Caribbean, the Pacific and Asia, there are also many states where the official national ideology does not openly represent one of the ethnic categories or groups that make up the population – India, with nearly twice the population of the European Union, being the largest – but rather claims to represent all citizens, regardless of their ethnic identity. Since these states were not founded as ethnopolitical projects, many of them would be threatened by fission or civil war if the state were to become too closely identified with the corporate interests of a single ethnic group, as has indeed happened in a number of cases in recent years, from Sri Lanka to Rwanda, Burundi and the Soviet Union.

• *Solutions to multiethnicity*. Three main strategies have been pursued by modern states in order that this may be avoided. First, the state can be strongly dominated by one group, which also controls the military force (this is the classic 'plural society' solution of colonialism, cf. Furnivall 1948); secondly, ethnicity can be underplayed systematically and the state ideology can focus on civil rights instead of ethnic commonalities – it can promote a *political* nationalism rather than a *cultural* one, to use Hutchinson's (1994) terms (this is the case, among other places, in Tanzania and post-apartheid South Africa); and thirdly, the state may represent itself as an agent of compromise between ethnic groups through openly acknowledging that distinctive, endogamous groups based on self-ascription co-exist in the state, and by guaranteeing their rights as culture-bearing groups. This is the kind of model nowadays often spoken of as 'multiculturalist'. These three options are not mutually exclusive.

Because of its European bias, the recent outburst of theory and research on nationalism has largely failed to account for such cases.[1] It would probably be fair to say that French and German nationalisms have been the 'classic cases' for the theory of nationalism (often seen as 'civic' and 'ethnic' nationalisms, respectively), and the late Ernest Gellner's seminal book *Nations and Nationalism* (Gellner 1983) was heavily biased, as was admitted by the author himself, towards nation-building in nineteenth-century Central Europe. Contemporary nationalisms may turn out to be very different in character from these ones. The Wilsonian–Leninist doctrine of the right to self-determination of nations no longer holds sway globally, and new models of nationhood are being tried out not only in countries such as Mauritius, which could never model themselves as mono-ethnic even at

the level of state ideology (see Chatterjee 1993 on India), but also in states
hitherto dominated by single ethnic groups. Members of many minority
groups refuse to become assimilated into a majority or dominant ethnic
group, and 'cultures' as well as 'ethnic histories' have become objects of
pride rather than shame, acquiring legitimacy both internationally through
the UN system, in global political discourse through NGO networks and,
in a great number of cases from Norway to New Zealand, in domestic
politics.

• *Non-ethnic nationalisms.* Nationalisms that fail to fit the Franco-German
paradigm of nationalism are sometimes regarded as something different
from nationalism – A. D. Smith (1983) suggests 'nationism' as a descriptive
term for African state ideologies – while the more conventional notion of
'plural societies' used in connection with polyethnic polities in general tends
to stress asymmetrical power relations or competitive relationships between
groups, and disregards the possibility of successful compromise or shared
ideologies (such as a supra-ethnic nationalism) in polyethnic societies.

Conversely, although Gellner (1983), Hobsbawm (1992) and others correctly argue that state policies in modern societies must encourage some
form of cultural homogeneity, this does not rule out the possibility that
they may also, simultaneously, encourage cultural diversity, albeit in clearly
delineated social fields, as I have indicated in the earlier chapters of this
book. Although education, the media and the labour market will tend to
create some forms of cultural homogenisation affecting 'the same people
living in the same place', self-conscious minority identity movements may
also emerge from processes of modernisation (see, for example, Roosens
1989; Friedman 1990; Eriksen 1991b, 1992c). These movements of ethnic
awareness and ethnopolitics need not be secessionist in character and are
therefore not necessarily nationalist in the commonly agreed-upon sense
of the word. Instead, they may coexist with a nationalism, which to a greater
or lesser extent acknowledges their existence. Extreme cases of non-
acknowledgement in recent history are represented by Japan and Turkey:
the Ainu of Hokkaido were not acknowledged as a minority at all until
1987, and the Kurds of eastern Turkey are still, in the late 1990s, spoken of
in official discourse as 'mountain Turks'. An extreme case of acknowledgement, as has become clear through this study, is represented in
Mauritius and its official dealings with ethnic variation. The Mauritian
example shows that nations may emerge from very diverse 'cultural
materials', which apparently do not need to postulate shared origins and
which need therefore not, perhaps, be ideologies of metaphoric kinship.
The study of nationalisms such as the Mauritian one can also serve as a
reminder that although the origin of nationalism may be European or nearly

European (but see Handler and Segal 1992), this kind of ideology has, after having been globalised, taken on a great number of local forms. As Joyce, Gellner, Smith and many others – who otherwise differ in their views on nationalism – would agree, nationalism is essentially a political doctrine about 'the same people living in the same place' and their relationship to the state, but the terms 'the same people' and 'the same place' are highly problematic and contestable – in Mauritius as well as elsewhere.[2]

Local Concepts of the Nation

Compared to other postcolonial polyethnic states, such as Nigeria, Sri Lanka or even Malaysia, the case for a civic, or political, nationalism seems strong in Mauritius. No mono-ethnic hegemony could possibly establish itself officially without a devastating civil war (which would not be a zero-sum game but a below-zero-sum game), and political separatism is not an option for anybody. Yet we have seen many examples of the practical reproduction of ethnicity as providing ultimate frames of relevance (both as organisation and as identity) in civil society. Let us therefore look more closely at the attempts to establish unitary nationalist ideology, briefly dealt with in previous chapters, and the conditions for its emergence as a symbolic system capable of overruling the 'particularistic' ideologies.

• *'Nasyon' as a Kreol concept.* When, in the 1970s, the MMM launched its nationalist slogan *Enn sel lepep, enn sel nasyon* ('A single people; a single nation'), there was much confusion. 'What else can you expect,' comments a Mauritian journalist retrospectively, 'considering *nasyon* in Kreol means *jati* [sub-caste] and not nation like in French . . .'. During fieldwork, I once asked a middle-class Creole whether he conventionally tipped waiters. '*Selman bann nasyon*' ('Only nation people'), was his rather confusing reply. Later I was to learn that this meant he only tipped waiters who were fellow Creoles. At another occasion, I introduced two African friends to a group of urban Creoles. '*Mo kontan zot parski zot nasyon*', said one of the Creoles, addressing himself to the uncomprehending Africans ('I like you, since you belong to my *nasyon*'). During a political discussion with a group of Hindus, somebody mentioned *bann ti-nasyon* ('the small *nasyons*'), referring to the low castes. Again, when my brother came to visit me in Mauritius and we would exchange the odd phrase in Norwegian with others present, people might tell each other that '*Zot pe koze so langaz, anfen, zot mem nasyon*' ('They're speaking their language; you know, they are the same *nasyon*').

Mauritius, on the contrary, is rarely talked about as a *nasyon*. If asked 'What is Mauritius?', a native might reply that it's *enn lil* (an island) or *enn peyi* (a country). Only people speaking a Kreol heavily influenced by the French language and corresponding concepts could conceivably describe Mauritius as *enn nasyon*. The word is used normatively in political rhetoric; the MMM has been mentioned, and in addition, the word is listed in LPT's Kreol–English dictionary (LPT 1985) as meaning simply 'nation'.[3] Other politicians tend to avoid using the word altogether, and would rather talk of *le peuple mauricien* or *tous les Mauriciens* when invoking the concept of national unity: they are less likely to be misunderstood.

The Kreol word *nasyon* has, in other words, several meanings. An examination of the different concepts of nationhood in use in Mauritius calls attention to the different, if sometimes overlapping, criteria, that criss-cross and differentiate Mauritian society. The criteria discussed in the previous chapter add further to the complexity indicated below. It is, in other words, difficult to speak of Mauritians as 'a people'.

The academic concept of the nation as a self-defined people, either aspiring to statehood or already in a dominant position in a state, is recent and unusual in Mauritius. Nevertheless, the term 'nation' (*nasyon*) is still used in at least five different meanings in the island: (i) *Jati* or caste, (ii) ethnic community, (iii) race, (iv) language community, and (v) political community of citizens with a shared state. All these meanings denote communities of people with a shared identity in some respect; but each of them would divide the Mauritian population into segments along different lines.

Nation (i), the caste concept, notably distinguishes between *bann gran-nasyon* (high castes) and *bann ti-nasyon* (low castes) within the Hindu population; of the former, there are two (Babojee and Maraz), of the latter two (Rajput[4] and Ravi Ved); all of them are relatively small groups, and the majority of Mauritian Hindus belong to the middle caste, the Vaish (*vaishya*). This principle of social differentiation has not only separated high castes from low ones, but it has also contributed to accentuating the differences between Mauritians of North Indian and South Indian origins, since the Biharis tend to regard Tamils and Telugus (South Indians, Dravidians) as low-caste people regardless of their actual caste origins. The 'Hindi-speaking' are the politically dominant group, and the non-Bihari Hindus as well as the *bann ti-nasyon* are in general not followers of the Hindu-dominated parties. There are also sanctions against intermarriage between all groups, practised with varying degrees of rigour.

One sometimes talks of *bann gran-nasyon* with reference to the Muslim, White, Creole and Chinese ethnic groups as well. They contain endogamous élites with cultural markers distinguishing themselves from other members of their ethnic group, and sometimes with different voting patterns. In such a context, this concept of nation seems to be used metaphorically – but on the other hand, the Mauritian Hindu castes do not have a much wider field of relevance than other endogamous groups.

Nation (ii), meaning ethnic community, is still commonly used in Mauritian discourse. According to this concept of nationhood, the Mauritian population is divided into a certain number of ethnic categories, dealt with earlier in this study. This concept of nation overlaps strongly with nation (i), but fails to distinguish between endogamous élites and 'commoners' within each category.

Nation (iii), which refers to race, is less important socially and politically than nation (i) and (ii). It is largely invoked in discourse relating people to their 'ancestral cultures', so that the Franco-Mauritians can consider themselves as members of the same 'nation' as Frenchmen, Indo-Mauritians as the same 'nation' as people living in Bihar or Uttar Pradesh, and so on.

Nation (iv), referring to language community, is potentially more encompassing than the three others. Since a growing majority of Mauritians speak Kreol as their mother-tongue, this concept potentially includes the bulk of the population. As was noted earlier, the Kreol language was the main symbol of national unity used by the anti-communalist Mauritian Left, notably the MMM, during the 1970s and early 1980s (Oodiah 1989). However, even this concept of nationhood is potentially divisive, since a sizeable minority (roughly 15–20 per cent) are bilingual in Bhojpuri and Kreol, and many of these regard Bhojpuri as their mother-tongue; and further, Mauritians sometimes refer to their ancestral language rather than the language customarily spoken when asked about their language community.

Nation (v), finally, refers to the community of citizens. Although this concept of nationhood is more frequently encountered in political speeches than in everyday language, its implications are readily understood by Mauritians. They associate it with the official campaigns against communalism and nepotism, and some fear the loss of privilege or even cultural identity in a future Mauritius where unity rather than diversity is emphasised.

The word nation, it should be noted, is not used to describe religious communities in Mauritius. A reason for this may be that there is no simple one-to-one relationship between religion and ethnic membership, and therefore such a concept of nationhood would contradict several of the others, notably nation (i), (ii) and (iii). There are Catholics who belong to the Chinese, Franco-Mauritian, Coloured and Creole ethnic categories, as well as Christian Tamils and a few thousand 'Indo-Catholics' who may define themselves as Hindus in an ethnic sense, emphasising origins.

In Search of National Symbols

Unlike European and many Asian nationalisms, Mauritian nationalism cannot, apparently, draw upon either a shared mythical past or ethnic unity in its ideological self-justification. It therefore seems to be an instance of what A. D. Smith (1991) has labelled 'territorial nationalism' as opposed to 'ethnic nationalism': being an island, Mauritius can easily be construed as a naturally bounded territory. On the other hand, Smith's distinction seems to confuse matters somewhat in so far as it seems to presume that territorial nationalisms do not require an ethnic or cultural element to be successful in their legitimation. On the contrary, the territorial battle has been won decades ago by the political rulers of the Mauritian state, while the project of nation-building remains a major issue in identity politics as well as economic strategies, and most Mauritians would agree that it has only just begun. As I shall argue, Mauritian nationalism has a strong *cultural* element without being *ethnically* justified.

• *Colonial symbols.* Symbols of nationhood must be multivocal, like the ritual symbols famously analysed by Turner (Turner 1969, 1974), and they must simultaneously legitimise a political structure *and* be meaningful; they must, in other words, help to reproduce both the formal and the informal dimension of nationalism (Eriksen 1993a) – both the functional nationalism of the state and the expressive nationalism of civil society. It goes without saying that symbols of national unity are difficult to construct and justify in independent Mauritius. The public symbols of 'Mauritianness' current today are largely inherited from colonial times. This continued use of colonial symbols and history as national ones is much less controversial in Mauritius than in most African countries. In Mauritius, there was no violent discontinuity from colonialism to independence. Conflicts over indepen- dence were internal and did not involve the colonial power directly. The white settlers did not generally flee after the referendum (which the pro- independence factions won by a slight margin). If it hadn't been for the French and the British, there would have been no Mauritius – and people know this.

The national coat of arms depicted on bank notes, coins, postage stamps and official publications was introduced in French times: it consists of a key, a star, a ship and a small cluster of palms. The meaning of its Latin legend, *Stella et Claviscus Maris Indici* ('The Star and the Key of the Indian Ocean') is widely known. Until 1986, Queen Elizabeth I of Mauritius (Britain's Elizabeth II) was represented on all Mauritian currency. She is now gradually being replaced by the first prime minister of independent

Mauritius, Sir Seewoosagur Ramgoolam, who also served as First Minister of Mauritius during the last seven years of British rule.

Statues of the nineteenth-century governor Sir William Newton, Mahé de Labourdonnais and Queen Victoria have been erected in front of the parliament (and even the MMM has to my knowledge never suggested removing them). The French missionary Jacques Désiré Laval, working in the mid-nineteenth century and beatified in 1978, is also recognised as a great Mauritian by Christians and non-Christians alike. Crucial events in Mauritian history – the French–British battle of Grand-Port (1810); the abolition of slavery and the arrival of the first Indian indentured labourers (1835); and Independence (1968) – are frequently invoked as justifications of Mauritian nationhood: shared meaning in its most encompassing sense (to do with identity) is held to lie in shared history.[5] The interest in local history is not confined to academic circles: for instance, there is a regular monthly magazine devoted exclusively to the history of Mauritius and the neighbouring islands (*Gazette des Iles de l'Océan Indien*). Despite attempts to break with the tradition (such as Allen 1983; Selvon 1985), Mauritian historiography remains largely the history of men (and remarkably few women) in positions of power.[6]

• *Two nationalisms.* In order to avoid the symbolic identification of the Mauritian state with one ethnic group, Mauritian nation-builders have followed two strategies: a multiculturalist one depicting the nation as identical with its cultural 'mosaic', and a universalist one depicting the nation as supra-ethnic. The first of the two examples presented below is an attempted application of a form of 'multiculturalism' as a national ethos. The second case, on the other hand, represents an attempt to transcend ethnic identities altogether, replacing ethnic symbols with non-ethnic, national ones.

Independence Celebrations in the Plural Society

During Independence celebrations on and around 12 March, a number of 'composite cultural shows' are performed in local community centres. One typical such show took place in 1986, in the village hall of a large, ethnically diverse village. The show included two Sino-Mauritian entries, two Tamil contributions and one Telegu, one European song, three performances representative of the Creoles, three each by Muslims and Marathis, and four entries in Hindi or Bhojpuri. The programme was printed in English, and the opening and ending speeches were given in Kreol.

The aim was to display and encourage 'unity in diversity': among other things, the object was to accustom spectators to the traditions of ethnic categories other than their own. In a word, these shows (and similar events taking place from time to time) strive to give significance to metaphors of 'organic wholes' composed of incongruous elements but fused in the common destiny of the Mauritian people: that is to say, the whole (the show) signifies something qualitatively different from its parts (the separate performances). In the terminology of system theory, we might say that a composite cultural show propagates subjective perceptions of being integrated on a higher systemic level – of a transition from communal to national identity. Now, Mauritians are already – and have been for some time – participants in the same economic system, although their positions and degree of participation to a great extent have been ethnically determined. Independence celebrations, like Ramgoolam's funeral (below), but unlike the trade union militancy of the 1970s, are intended chiefly as *redefinitions of cultural reality*. If such events are successful along these lines, people will accordingly redefine their cultural universes and modify their models for action (although patterns of social action itself are more inert than their models, and thus may remain unchanged for a while). An individual defining himself or herself as being a member of a nation rather than of an ethnic category in a particular context, will then modify his or her representations relating to politics, economical relationships, marriage strategies, friendship, etc. – and then proceed to modify his or her patterns of action (see D. Virahsawmy 1983).

It cannot be taken for granted that this strategy will be successful, even on the abstract level of folk representations. For one thing, the concept 'unity in diversity' represents a contradiction in terms for many Mauritians. National unity can be taken to imply loss of distinctiveness (ethnic identity), whereas remaining distinctive precludes national unity. Furthermore, the practical reproduction of ethnic personal networks (in matters of say, work, marriage and friendship) is still believed to 'pay off' as long as the wider social context (offering 'incentives and restraints') remains unchanged. These two phenomena, ethnic identity and ethnic action, cannot, therefore, be done away with by means of certain cultural policies. When the channels for – and the meaning of – successful career paths are changed, however, new representational and actional patterns necessarily result.

Ramgoolam's Funeral

Sir Seewosagur Ramgoolam (1900–85) was Mauritius' prime minister during the first fifteen years of independence. A Hindu from the Vaish caste, he led the Mauritian delegation during independence negotiations in London in the mid-1960s. During the election campaign in 1967 he led the pro-independence parties to a relatively narrow victory, and he is popularly considered as the man to whom Mauritians owe their political independence. Ramgoolam was a clever politician, cunning in the art of compromise and surrounded by an aura of wisdom and fairness. He earned the respect of many non-Hindus when persuading the leader of the anti-independence bloc, the eloquent Creole Gaëtan Duval, to join his first government.

In 1982, his Labour Party lost the general election to the MMM–PSM alliance, and Ramgoolam, disappointed, reluctantly accepted the post of Governor General (an occupation independent Mauritius retained until it became a republic in 1992). Now he, the political loser, received the pity of his opponents and was simultaneously in a position to stay aloof from petty quarrels. Although bitter with the electorate, Ramgoolam thus spent his last years consolidating his reputation as the wise man of the *nation* Mauritius.

In December 1985 Ramgoolam died. He was by then acknowledged by virtually every Mauritian as the founding father of their nation – indeed, he had become a 'myth' in his own lifetime in the sense that his unpopular or mistaken judgements were rarely mentioned publicly; until Sydney Selvon's biography (Selvon 1986) even non-commissioned biographies of Ramgoolam were testimonies to his unfailing glory. Not all of them were written by Hindus.

The ceremony accompanying the cremation of Ramgoolam's body, therefore, had to be one relevant for every Mauritian. I shall go through it in some detail.

The news of Ramgoolam's death was broadcast on radio and television on 15 December and appeared in the newspapers the following day. In advertisements, citizens were urged to do their 'Chacha' (Hindi for teacher) one final honour by attending the procession leading to the garden where the ceremonial cremation of his corpse was already scheduled to take place on the following day (17 December 1985).

The procession started from Ramgoolam's home, a colonial mansion at Réduit that was also used as the residence of the Governor General before Independence. *Une queue interminable* of people filled the courtyard. At noon, the yard was considered full, and newcomers were denied access by the police. A Hindu religious ceremony was next conducted, following immediately upon the arrival of Ramgoolam's son. At least two of the pundits performing came from Ramgoolam's native district in the north of Mauritius. The *tatri* (a stretcher decorated with flowers) was brought outside and the corpse was placed on it by close relatives of the deceased.

The journey towards Pamplemousses began towards 1.30 p.m. Heading the procession, the police corps played Chopin's *Marche funèbre* at the departure from Réduit. The *tatri* was placed in an open military vehicle, accompanied by policemen on motorcycles and followed by local luminaries in cars. Those not possessing their own means of transport would have to travel by bus to Pamplemousses if they wished to witness the incineration of the body.

Huge crowds of onlookers had gathered on pavements and balconies as the cortège passed through the urban centres of Rose-Hill and Beau-Bassin, the industrial estate Coromandel and the capital, Port-Louis. Throughout, the audience threw flower petals on to the *tatri*. Notably, churches on the itinerary rang their bells in approval of what was principally a Hindu ceremony.

In front of Ramgoolam's former residence in Port-Louis, the procession made a brief halt while the orchestra played Handel's *Funeral March from Saul* and repeated the performance of Chopin's *Funeral March*. Upon reaching the Gardens of Pamplemousses at 5.30 p.m., the *tatri* was placed on the funeral pyre. Members of the police and paramilitary forces paid their last respects, as did high officials and foreign guests, while flower petals rained down from helicopters. There was still a huge audience present.

Ramgoolam's son was dressed entirely in white, whereas most of the others in the front row (the Interim Governor General, the Speaker of Parliament, the Chief Judge, the Doyen of the Diplomatic Corps and certain foreign guests) wore Western clothes.

Finally, Ramgoolam's son (who is today Mauritius' Prime Minister) went through the last motions strictly according to Sanatanist Hindu tradition, eventually setting alight the funeral pyre.

The religious parts of the ceremony, then, did not at a single point deviate from tradition nor from the rules laid out in authoritative Sanatanist texts. Orthodox Sanatanism is still the largest Hindu denomination in Mauritius, but it is by no means a majority religion. And unlike the situation in the former socialist countries of Eastern Europe, there is no panethnic, nationalist or humanist alternative to religious burial available in Mauritius. (And in any case, resentment towards Hindus has little or nothing to do with Hindu religious practices.)

• *Supra-ethnic symbolism*. Important elements in the ceremony seen as a whole nevertheless transcend ethnic boundaries. Most striking, perhaps, was the choice of music to accompany the procession. In choosing the music of two European composers rather than having the police band play

Indian funerary music (which is not as impossible as it may sound: similar things have happened before),[7] the administrators lifted, as it were, Ramgoolam's person above the Mauritian everyday reality of petty skirmishes to a higher, more universal sphere; this could be interpreted as meaning the level of humanity *tout court*, but was more likely intended to give symbolic content to panethnic Mauritianism. Classical European music is not very popular in Mauritius; it belongs to nobody's real or fictitious traditions (excepting perhaps increasingly marginal segments of the Franco-Mauritians), and can therefore easily be accepted as neutral by the entire nation.[8] The national anthem, which sounds much like any other national anthem, with lyrics in English written by a Francophile Creole poet, was, of course, also played at Pamplemousses. It should also be noted that the European classical music played was written by non-French composers, and the choice of works thus reflects Mauritius' past as a British colony rather than a society dominated by a French plantocracy. Like the English language, these works may therefore be seen as truly neutral.

The very visible parts played by the police and paramilitaries (*Special Mobile Force*, SMF) were not exclusively due to security measures. Uniformed rank and file had a highly prominent place both at Réduit and at Pamplemousses. Neither the police nor the SMF have a very strong position in Mauritius, compared with larger states.[9] The 500 men who make up the lightly armed SMF, which is the closest the state comes to having an army, are virtually never involved in violence; their most important duties are peaceful (guarding, fire-fighting, skindiving), although they have also been called upon during illegal demonstrations. Nobody perceives the threat of a military *coup d'état* as being relevant. Therefore the police and the SMF are alike fairly popular with the Mauritian population. Although there are inevitably rumours to the contrary, neither of them is dominated by one ethnic group. In thus displaying their uniformed and armed forces, the state representatives informed people that law and order was being maintained on a national level, and that this was being done in a just and impartial way, and not according to ethnic affiliation (uniforms are identical).

With respect to clothing, an important vehicle of ethnic demarcation, we have already noted that few high representatives of the state wore traditional Indian garb. Perhaps their wearing European-style suits was too obvious to be noticed, but had the prime minister (a Hindu) turned up in anything but a suit, people would certainly have taken account of it.

The form itself of the funeral, a long procession leading to a climax, is familiar to the majority of Mauritians. In February every year, the Hindus celebrate their Maha Shivaratree feast by marching to a small sacred lake;

while the Creoles in turn have their Père Laval pilgrimage in September: both annual events similar in form to Ramgoolam's funeral.

Had the ideological atmosphere been more *tiersmondiste* or anti-colonialist in Mauritius at the moment of the funeral, some might have reacted against the unwitting perpetuation of colonial symbolism in the decision to have the procession start at the Governor General's castle and end in the Gardens of Pamplemousses, the latter founded by Labourdonnais. However, this did not happen, and, anyway, alternatives would have been hard to come by: Mauritius has no precolonial history, and its postcolonial one is very short. Choosing sites, situations and historical persons associated with colonialism as symbols of nationhood conveniently overcomes problems of ethnically-specific symbols, although the solution cannot be permanent.

It is also a matter of interest that the most prominently placed foreign guests were the representatives of India and the South-Western Indian Ocean (Seychelles, Comoros, Madagascar and Réunion). The latter four are universally considered to be close neighbours, (in a non-geographical sense as well); but India is seen as an important ally by at most half the Mauritian population (the Hindus in a wide sense, including Dravidians); commodity exchange between the two countries is negligible, and geographically, Mauritius is if anything closer to mainland Africa. In placing the Indian representative in a position superior to that of, say, the French and British representatives, Ramgoolam's origins were emphasised in a fashion perhaps unfortunate for nation-building, but significant in showing the Hindu ethnic category's anxiety to maintain close ties with India.

The Kreol language, a potential symbol of nationhood, was not the only – or even the most important – language used during the event. In different contexts and by different speakers, Hindi, English, French and Kreol were employed; compromise being the only viable solution as long as the Mauritian population is divided on the language issue. Interestingly, the mother tongue of many of those opposed to Kreol as a national language, is Kreol.

• *Redefinitions of reality.* As in the 'composite cultural show', the meaning-contexts consciously produced during this event aimed at redefining cultural reality toward shared, national meaning, moving the common denominator to a more abstract level. But the *content* of the respective propositions differed. While the funeral defined Mauritianity as a quasi-religious, self-sustaining cultural system independent of the underlying mosaic, the definition inherent in the cultural show depicted Mauritianity as being identical with the mosaic itself. Both entail compromise, but in different ways: The funeral symbolised compromise between communal identity and national identity; the cultural show symbolised compromise between the

communal identities with no over-arching set of unifying symbols functioning at a higher logical level than the ethnic ones.

National Myths for a Nation with Many Pasts

Similar challenges obtain in the realm of national myths. Could a nation
like Mauritius, which has unfolded in the full daylight of recorded history,
develop credible myths of origin persuading the members of the nation
that they have a shared past? How distant does a past have to be in order
to be considered as *the* past? And in what way does Mauritian nationalism
relate to the past as a justification for the nation-state, and to what extent
is it on the contrary future-oriented, depicting the nation as *becoming* rather
than *being*? The creation of a shared mythical past is essential in the
legitimation of most nation-states. This seems not to be an available option
for Mauritian nationalists, who have since the beginning in the 1960s spoken
much, much more about the shared future than about the shared past. As
is obvious to anyone, the past of the Mauritian nation is neither evidently
mythical nor evidently shared. The entire history of Mauritian society has
been meticulously recorded by bureaucrats, statisticians, novelists, journalists and social scientists; the society has evolved from its point zero to
the present day in full daylight. It is true that oral traditions of storytelling
exist and that many of the stories have been recorded; but none of them
can be interpreted as expressions of embryonic nationhood. An example
is the story about the Malagasy prince Ratsitatane, who was exiled in
Mauritius in the nineteenth century, and who has since then, probably quite
undeservedly, become a symbol of black martyrdom; he may serve as an
appropriate symbol for the Creoles, but for nobody else. Most of the
officially endorsed historical research carried out at the Mahatma Gandhi
Institute, some of it of outstanding scholarly quality, aims at depicting the
history of single ethnic groups in Mauritius, thereby contributing to a
strengthening of ethnic boundaries. The only authoritative history book
encompassing the whole insular population was written by a Frenchman
(Toussaint 1971), while earlier histories of Mauritius, such as Unienville
(1838) and Hité (1897) were naturally written from a purely colonial (and
quite racist) perspective.
  • *A candidate for a national myth.* In its essence, Mauritian nationalism
in all its expressions is future-oriented; its main force in the 1990s lies in
the idea of economic progress, which clearly inspires sentiments of pride
and loyalty in the population. However, it may also draw upon the past,
and a fairly recent series of political events seems a likely candidate for a

national myth. In the spirit of the anthropological study of myth, I shall relate this story twice, first the way it is described in history books, and then the way it was told to me by an informant who was too young to have experienced it (see also Eriksen 1993d).

Version 1. 'The years around independence were marked by great uncertainty and economic crisis. The unemployment rate on the eve of independence was about 20 per cent, and many feared that the economy would deteriorate further with independence. Many non-Hindus also feared that an independent Mauritius would be strongly dominated by Hindus: that it would virtually become a Little India. There had been ethnic riots in 1965, and many feared a further deterioration of ethnic relations; and finally, the net growth rate of the population was among the highest in the world – in an island that was already considered overpopulated. In the 1967 elections, 44 per cent voted against independence. There was much communal tension, fear and anxiety in the country. In 1969, the year after independence, a prolonged feud between semi-criminal gangs in Port-Louis spread and took on the character of an ethnic riot between Muslims and Creoles. Several people were killed, and the situation in the country was so tense that the government felt compelled to declare a State of Emergency, which lasted a year. There have been no ethnic riots in Mauritius since then.'

Version 2.[10] 'I'll tell you about Mauritius, about the past, and how we got rid of [violent] communalism. Well, this was just after independence, in 1968 or 1969 I think, and there were two gangs in the Plaine Verte. In this part of Port-Louis, there were both Creoles and Muslims at that time, but today you won't see a single Creole there. Anyway, one of the gangs was Muslim and the other was Creole. The Creole gang was based in Roche-Bois [north-east Port-Louis], and it tried to take over some of the territory controlled by the Muslims. The Muslims for their part tried to take over some territory at Cassis [in western Port-Louis] which was controlled by another Creole gang. You know, there were fights and threats and quite a bit of trouble for a long while. (. . .) Then, suddenly one day, a Muslim from the gang at Plaine Verte killed a Creole kid outside Venus cinema [at Cassis],[11] and the other gang simply couldn't accept it. They went back to the Plaine Verte and killed a Muslim. Then the Muslims struck back, and this time they killed a member of the Creole gang. Anyway, by this time many people were involved on both sides, and a lot of [Creole] people who lived at the Plaine Verte began to stay inside their house all day. By now it wasn't just a gang fight, it was a war between the two communities. Even in Phoenix [another town] there was trouble. And quite a few people got killed. People were so terrified they even stayed home from work. They started to do nasty things to each other's churches [and mosques], you know, disrespectful things. Digging up graves, smashing windows, that kind of thing. And then Ramgoolam [the prime minister] said enough is enough, and he called in the Englishmen [the British army], who put a stop to the fighting. Quite a few people were sent to jail and all. And then he called off elections and said, "This is an emergency." You know, we Mauritians are really peace-loving people, and this was really scary. All the Creoles who used to live near the Plaine Verte moved away, to St Croix or even further away to Roche-Bois. (. . .)

What happened then? Well, I think people learnt their lesson and realised that we have to live together even if we are different. There has been no violence between Creoles and Muslims, or Hindus for that matter, later. You might say that this riot was the birth of the Mauritian nation.'

The myth exists in several other versions as well.

• *Time and nationhood.* Analysts who stress the importance of myths of ancestry for ethnic or national identity have shown that these myths refer to a starting-point somewhere in the dim and distant past. Sinhalese nationalism (Kapferer 1988), Québecois separatism (Handler 1988), Norwegian national romanticism (Österud 1984) and the ethnopolitical ideology of the Huron Indians (Roosens 1989) alike, to mention four otherwise very different examples, all depict the birth of the nation or ethnic group as an event in a dim and distant past. None of them implies that the nation has always been there. So, to paraphrase the question posed by the Creolophone Tamil quoted in an earlier chapter: How ancient does a myth of origin have to be in order to function as a myth of origin? How deep do the 'roots' of a people have to be in order for its members to consider themselves as 'a people'?

The Mauritian material points in two directions. On the one hand, it indicates that young nations that demonstrably do not have a shared past have to direct their national symbolism towards the future. This is evident not only in Mauritius, but also in many other postcolonial states, where the nation tends to be identified with progress, education and modernity. On the other hand, the Mauritian material calls attention to the analytical category of ethnicity, connecting it with notions of shared origins. All humanity ultimately descends from the same group; ethnic distinctions are, in other words, neither eternal nor natural. History and comparative anthropology have also shown us that ethnic groups or nations emerge and eventually disappear – they are split into several groups, are assimilated into dominant groups, or fuse. Ancestral myths are refashioned accordingly.

Nationalism, Ethnicity and Social Change

A shared national identity must, briefly, be compatible with the household field, accepted and reproduced in the locality and working-place fields, profitable in the national labour market, sanctioned by the political system and publicly reproduced in the fields of mass media and education.

The first is unproblematic, in so far as the 'Furnivallian' plural society ideology prevalent in Mauritius (see Furnivall 1948; M. G. Smith 1965) encourages cultural diversity at home. Whether or not national ideology is reproduced in the locality depends on the pattern of settlement and the nature of the institutions – the arenas for interaction present. It has been shown that several normative orientations may be linked to the shared system of representations (which is, naturally, itself evolving) in the course of practical interpretation. In the working place, the structure and nature of hierarchies, the composition of the labour force, and the spatial location of the enterprise seem to be the most important factors. This is discussed below. In the national labour market, then, where decisions affecting the total division of labour are taken, there can be no doubt that the ideology of meritocracy is most beneficial according to the internal criteria of the entire system of relations (efficiency, productivity). On the other hand, ethnic organisation (including nepotism) may pay off better locally (that is, to the individual owner of means of production). The political system as a whole is, in response to social change, inclining towards decisions strengthening the nation-state and influencing the other fields in this direction – although members of the state bureaucracy still widely practise ethnic strategies. In the national communicational systems, finally, particularly the larger media, political nationalism is as a matter of convention communicated overtly. Communalism is not considered *comme il faut* in this sector of Mauritian public life.

We now turn to discussing some consequences, hinted at earlier, of social change in Mauritius.

Tourism, Industrialisation and Bureaucracy in the National State

In earlier chapters, I have frequently alluded to the high rate of social change in Mauritius. Since 1986, the industrial 'zone' (EPZ or *Zone Franche*) has, as a unit, been the largest employer in Mauritius. More Mauritians are now industrial workers than agricultural labourers. Industrialisation does not take the shape of an exodus from the countryside: in fact currently the population growth rate is higher in 'rural' than in 'urban' areas. Parts of Port-Louis have actually experienced a *negative* growth rate during the 1970s and 1980s.

Rather, the change occurs, spatially located, in areas formerly dominated by a rural division of labour and local organisation, in newly established industrial estates outside the towns, and on selected sites along the coast (the establishment of hotels and *stations balnéaires*).

• *Tourism.* Some of the cultural effects of tourism were suggested in the comparison between the two coastal villages (Chap. 6). In La Gaulette, where most of the households had members working in hotels, people were up to date with European patterns of consumption; the young took great pains to adopt recent Western fashion in clothing and hairstyle; the adults invested much work in improving their dwellings; and many had bank accounts. In Case Noyale, on the contrary, where nobody was employed in the tourist industry, the dominant ethos was largely the classical, stereotyped Creole morality entailing short, unmeasured temporal units and accordingly, lack of commitment to long-term strategies. The social and cultural schism between these neighbouring villages, which might conceivably have developed regardless of tourism, has certainly been accentuated by it. The content of the cultural form emerging as the dominant one in La Gaulette (non-ethnic, 'progressive') is visibly inspired by the way of life encountered at the five-star hotels. The exigencies of the work itself include absolute punctuality, which is unimportant to the labourer and unknown to the fisherman. In La Gaulette, most of the men wear inexpensive wristwatches daily. In Case Noyale, watches are worn only at parties and at Mass, as jewellery.

Further, the employee at the hotel has the prospect – real or imagined – of promotion. The chairman of the Village Council, a poorly educated man, had begun as a waiter and was now, eleven years later, chief purser. Labourers and fishermen, on the contrary, have little or no prospect of 'promotion'. Nothing in their daily practices can, therefore, serve metonymically as a model of 'development' or 'progress', or even simply *change*.

• *Industrialisation.* Social change as industrialisation has slightly different effects, although this, too, entails a new structuring of time and social relations.

Many of the EPZ enterprises are small, family-owned textile factories, often located in the family's living quarters. One typical such factory, owned by a middle-aged, university-educated Hindu in Rose-Hill, has six employees: his wife, two of her sisters, one of his nieces and two of his female cousins. Only his wife is working full-time. The wages correspond to the national average.

In this kind of enterprise, no qualitatively new type of social relation arises from the organisation of production. Compared with a small planter with similar economic assets, the difference pertains to gender: in the small industrial enterprise, most or all of the employees are girls and women; in the fields, most of the labourers are boys and men. In other words, industrialisation on a small scale leads to the strengthening of horizontal female kinship bonds. But, as in the traditional small planter's enterprise, workers are recruited according to individual kinship bonds with the employer – and this ethnically based principle of recruitment thus remains unchanged.

In the larger factories, and especially in the industrial estates, the effects of change on local organisation are much more dramatic. Some immediate effects are obvious (and very visible):

• Increasing participation of women in the affected segments of the most numerous ethnic categories. Most of the workers in the textile industry are female. This increases their freedom of movement (many Indo-Mauritian women were formerly hardly allowed to leave the home unaccompanied) and their economic significance. There are many Mauritian households now where the women's factory work is the only source of money.[12] As yet, the man remains head of household, and his wife's and daughters' wages are allocated to him.

• Increasing interethnic contacts in a wholly shared meaning-context – a context introducing a new common denominator. Most of the larger factories are owned by foreigners, expatriates, Franco-Mauritians or Sino-Mauritians. All ethnic categories except Franco-Mauritians and Sino-Mauritians are amply represented among EPZ workers. The networks activated in these working places are much less dependent on ethnicity in the new industrial estates than elsewhere. Although collective syndical action is difficult in the EPZ, a certain awareness of shared interests is apparent. Many non-Creoles signed a petition defending *père* Diard (see Chapter 5). This signifies a class awareness that is in principle removed from gender, and definitely removed from ethnicity. Its relation to nationalism is less clear.

• The young age of the industrial workers is also significant. (A large percentage are under 20.) This means that most of them have reproduced non-ethnically based action sets in all social fields but the household, throughout their lives. I know several young industrial workers who are either engaged or married to men from ethnic categories other than their own, and intermarriage is believed to be more widespread in 'industrial' than in 'agricultural' villages, which has probably to do with the pattern of settlement as well as the social links formed in the working place.

The combined significance of social change as industrialisation and tourism can be summed up as follows.

• Workers are increasingly recruited according to universalist, not particularist criteria. This places the competitors for jobs in structurally equal positions, regardless of ethnic membership.

In abstract Parsonian terms, this can be understood as *achievement* replacing *ascription* as a leading principle of differentiation, and the process parallels those regularly described by 'classical' sociologists – from Tönnies, Simmel and Weber to Peter Berger and his associates – when they attempt to account for the changes in European society associated with the industrial revolution and the growing significance of the nation-state (see e.g. Weber 1981 [1922]; Berger *et al.* 1974).

• The working place is multiethnic, hierarchical and competitive. This leads to increased interethnic contacts and a widespread understanding of the workings of the (ideal-typical) meritocracy. The values associated with meritocracy and/or class struggle may present themselves as more relevant in daily life than those of ethnic organisation.

• The working place is also often composed of people from different parts of the island. Thus, workers establish non-localised networks founded on a shared experience as workers.

• The public participation of women is increasing as they begin to work with other women away from the home, and their representations of other ethnic categories change. This, along with the multiethnic character of the working place, contributes to removing some of the constraints formerly preventing widespread intermarriage.

• Modernisation brings Mauritius closer to the rest of the world. First, tourists are popular sources of information about Europe and Australia. Secondly, Mauritius has to compete with Oriental countries over markets for its clothing industry, and the workers know this (they are being told by the management, for example, that wages cannot be increased lest they lose the competition and thus their jobs). In other words, workers are being instructed to act in a *global field* – the world market. Further, the international exchange of goods is increasing, as is, accordingly, the local demand for 'Western' consumer goods – regardless of ethnic category.[13]

• *Principles of recruitment.* Social change, affecting Mauritian lifestyles and uniformising them in *some* respects (thus confirming Gellner's theory), creates new types of social relations in the working place. Of crucial importance is *the basis of recruitment to the labour force*. While pre-industrial wage workers were largely recruited on geographical and ethnic principles via the mediation of personal contacts, workers in the industrial and hotel sectors are recruited on basis of formal qualifications and sheer availability. Applications usually have to be in writing. New statuses or aspects of the social person gain relevance. Thus, Claude and Veerasamy (Chap. 3) can no longer take the ethnic status set-up of their working environment for granted.

This new situation in turn encourages the cultural reproduction of non-ethnic identities (although this is not the only possible effect). The new 'ideologies' need not be 'nationalist' in character, but the most important ones are – unlike ethnic identities as they are played out in the labour market – *compatible* with nationalism. Moderate class struggle denotes faith in the nation-state as benefactor. Career individualism, founded in a liberal belief in meritocracy, in principle implies equal opportunity and precludes ethnic particularism. The two are perceived as being complementary. Whereas the latter refers to the individual's right to progress unimpeded (and the state's duty to protect this right of unbounded freedom), the former emphasises the state's duty to establish social justice (and the individual's right to demand protection from certain aspects of the freedom of other individuals). In Mauritius, an emergent industrial society, the part played by the state bureaucracy and the organisations influencing the political system is in this sense an actor of increasing importance in the economy. Economic planning is perceived a public task by both main political blocs, and ambitious programmes of economic change are discussed in Parliament. Granted that Mauritius the nation-state is not a 'minimal state' but aspires to develop into a 'fully-fledged welfare state', taxation and social benefit schemes are also increasing activities of the state. This also serves to encourage the reproduction of individual identities as members of a nation in various contexts. In the end, then, it *does* make a difference to old L'Intelligent in Case Noyale (p. 29) whether he receives his monthly pension from his son or from the state.

I have now delineated some of the systemic parameters in the development of Mauritian nationhood. We now move to considering aspects of national identity seen from the perspective of the individual.

The Mauritian and the World: 'We' and 'Us'

Especially the fact of my being engaged with the others in a common rhythm to whose origin I contribute, serves to develop my experience of being engaged in a 'we-as-subject'. (. . .) I do not exploit the collective rhythm as a tool, nor do I regard it – in the sense I might, for instance, regard the dancers on a stage – it surrounds me and fascinates me

without being my object. (. . .) But this is, as one knows, only necessary if
I initially, through my acceptance of a shared aim and shared tools,
constitute myself as undifferentiated transcendence through relegating
my own aims to second place, after the collective aims now being
pursued.[14]

(Sartre, *L'Etre et le Néant* (1943), my translation)

The plurality of Mauritian society, if not manifest in the composition of
the social person, gives its inhabitants a sense of uniqueness, and is as
such a source of national pride (at least in conversations with foreigners).
'We are the tomato of the Indian Ocean,' say promoters of tourism, 'we go
with everything.' This implies an identity of *us-hood*. Mauritians are what
they are *as Mauritians*, relatively to what others are. Seen rather as members
of a collectivity of *we* (the system viewed from within), Mauritians tend
rather to experience the daily multiethnicity as a perpetual cause of anxiety
and frustration.

Self-awareness of being Mauritian *as opposed to* non-Mauritians implies a
redefinition, an expansion, of relevant systems boundaries: this encourages
Mauritianity as us-hood. Unity as we-hood, conversely, must be founded in
shared or complementary representations of shared practices. I will discuss
these two aspects of social identity separately for the sake of clarity; however,
every actual identity must encompass elements of both: internal criteria
for unity, as well as a *difference that makes a difference* (Bateson 1972),
contrasting the group with all who are *not* included.

• *Expanding system boundaries and us-hood.* Sports, widely studied as an
important carrier of national identity worldwide, have frequently been
invoked as focal points of ethnic unity in Mauritius, and this was until
recently considered legitimate. In 1982, several of Mauritius' leading football
teams changed their names (from Hindu Cadets, Muslim Scouts, etc. to
Cadets, Scouts, etc.), and the official policy is now to encourage non-ethnic
sports. Yet ethnic allegiances are still strong, despite the change in names
(and the inevitable odd player or two from an 'outside' ethnic category in
every team).

In March 1986 I attended the finals of a nationwide football tournament
at George V Stadium in Curepipe. I had arrived in Mauritius only a couple
of months earlier, and asked my companion, a young Creole, whether the
teams had any link with the 'communities'. He assured me that they had
not. 'Formerly, it used to be "Hindu Cadets"; now, it's only "Cadets", see?'
However, I couldn't help noticing the very visible ethnic clustering of
Creoles and Indo-Mauritians in different parts of the stadium. We took
our place amidst the Creoles, and predictably, when the Cadets scored,

cheers and handclaps soared from the other side of the stand, whereas the people surrounding myself silently lit another cigarette.

• *The unsuccessful tournament.* Lately, other foci of group allegiance have consciously been created (from the political-bureaucratic field, notably the *Ministère de la Jeunesse et des Sports*). In 1986, for example, the first *Jeux des Villes de L'Océan Indien*, an inter-town tournament with participation from Reunionan towns, Victoria (in the Seychelles) and Antananarivo, changed the focus from ethnic community to local territory. The interest in these new proposed allegiances was very low. In tiny Mauritius, where one town merges into another in urban Plaines Wilhems from Coromandel to Curepipe, and each town is spatially differentiated according to class and ethnicity, any Creole *cité* dweller in Beau-Bassin would rather identify with Creole *cité* dwellers in Curepipe twenty kilometres up the road (with whom he may well be linked by means of kinship or friendship) than with the bourgeois Sino-Mauritians and Francos a few streets off.

• *The unanticipated success.* Sometimes, however, these conscious redefinitions of systems boundaries may have social repercussions that are *stronger* than predicted. In August 1985 Mauritius was responsible for the second *Jeux des Iles de l'Océan Indien,* an international sports tournament. The event led to a sudden upsurge of national sentiment that could still be noticed a year later (people spoke fondly of Mauritian athletes belonging to ethnic categories other than their own, etc.). A schoolboy, quoted in *Le Mauricien* (February 1986), wrote in an essay that 'the country of Mauritius was born in 1968, but Mauritianity was born in August, 1985'. This is clearly a significant statement: from being 'us, the Hindus' and so on, one suddenly became, within a larger system of relevant relations, 'us, the Mauritians'. This system can be defined as the sum of the social relations created and activated during the *Jeux des Iles*; the important thing is nevertheless the tournament's enduring influence on the representations of many Mauritians. After the event, the system depends on certain representations shared by a certain number of Mauritians, in order to be reproduced as a relevant potential system ('model'). For this to happen, the mere sports event could never have been sufficient: in identity politics, as elsewhere, nothing comes of nothing. Like all successful rituals and symbols of community, the *Jeux des Iles* satisfied both the informal and the formal dimensions of nationalism: both the emotional, popular dimension and the legitimating dimension of the state; both meaning and politics; both the sensory and the ideological pole (to use Turner's terminology); both civil society and the state. It shows how powerful sports can be in unifying a nation; how sports, in complex modern societies, have taken over the traditional integrating functions of religious ritual.

The more recent *Jeux des Villes de l'Océan Indien*, as has just been noted, never led to town-based patriotism. There is, therefore, clearly an emerging self-awareness as *citizens* among Mauritians, as participants in a system of more ambitious scale than those reproduced locally; a self-awareness that became visible in the strong manifestations of national sentiments symbolically conceptualised as 'international sports'.

• *Underlying causes.* The underlying processes of expanding systemic boundaries, that is, those that made the nationalism following the *Jeux des Iles* possible at all, are those of internationally-linked social and economic change, notably the development of communications, tourism and industrialisation. Tourists bring knowledge and awareness of the greater systems where Mauritians potentially take part, and encourage the creation of representations of a rather loftier scope than those they potentially replace. Industrialisation creates, demonstrates and reproduces a variety of these representations in practice (cf. above). Mauritius is being served by an increasing number of international flights. In addition, many Mauritians emigrated, permanently or for shorter periods, during the first decade after independence.

The enthusiasm encountered during and after the *Jeux des Iles*, then, can be traced back to a self-awareness of 'us, the Mauritians' stemming from intensifying connections with the external world – in search, as it were, of a vehicle for its visible expression.

In the previous section, I noted that expansions of systemic boundaries are credibly interpreted (by the actors) as Mauritian *us-hood* in the social context of the industrial workers. From a different perspective than the factory owner's, the national authorities are painfully aware of Mauritian industry's dependence on the interest of foreign investors – and the presence of competing sources of cheap labour. Their implicit plea to the workers goes something like 'We've got to increase our productivity lest we, Mauritius Ltd, go bankrupt.' Let us now briefly consider two examples of us-hood caused by expanding systemic boundaries. In the first example, the new types of social relations emerge because of geographical, physical mobility; in the second, the ultimate cause consists rather in changes' having taken place *outside* Mauritius.[15]

• *Us-hood abroad.* When abroad, Mauritians (like members of virtually any other nationality) tend to cling together. A Muslim informant, definitely sceptical of the Creoles at home, told me this about his stay as an assistant nurse at a British hospital: 'And every Friday night, we'd have a huge *séga* party at somebody's place where we'd drink some rum – even I had a few glasses sometimes . . . Man, there were so many Mauritians there – Creoles, Hindus, you know; it's so nice to meet fellow Mauritians when you're far away from home.' This is a familiar expression of we-hood, caused by an *us-hood* resulting from expanding systems boundaries – when the difference that makes a difference appears at a level outside ethnicity because the outsiders are non-Mauritians. In Britain, being Mauritian as opposed to British is more important than being Muslim as opposed to Creole or Hindu.[16] As was pointed out by Anderson (1983), European nationalism was largely created in exile, and the same is true of African nationalism and *négritude*, an early movement of identity politics created by Africans and *Antillais* in Paris in the 1930s. This kind of movement is a result of the situational and relational dimension of identity.

• *Pan-Arabism in Mauritius.* The Muslim shift from Pakistani to Arab 'ancestral identity', which has taken place since the early-to-middle 1970s (cf. Chap. 5), can plausibly be interpreted as a wish to participate in a system of larger scale, rather than as 'ethnic revitalisation'. Embracing Pan-Arabism and later Pan-Islamism, local Muslim leaders stressed that they, as Mauritian Muslims, supported the Arab world in geopolitics, and, indeed, that they contributed to it. This international ideology is, unlike the *tiersmondisme* popular in the MMM of the 1970s, not compatible with Mauritian nationalism. Whether the 'quixotic expulsion' (Bowman 1984:8) of the Libyan embassy staff in 1984 (cf. Chap. 5) was due to 'a judicious accommodation to the sensitivities of Washington and Riyadh' or to 'an authentic revulsion toward Colonel Qaddafi's admonition to Christians to read the Koran' (ibid.), is still uncertain. Whatever the case may be, Pan-Islamism is neither compatible with Mauritian foreign policy nor with its internal ideologies, notably the rule of the highest common denominator and the concomitant policy of respecting ethnic boundaries.

Growing Areas of Shared Meaning

A nationalist ideology must have elements of the *we* aspect of unity ('pulling together', 'sharing the fruits of our labours', etc.), although the *us* aspect is perhaps always its *raison d'être* ('We're better than the *X*es' – put more directly: 'We, Mauritius the actor in international affairs, are competitive'). Nationalism becomes pervasively relevant the moment it is more interesting to a Mauritian to compare himself (his country, its products, etc.) with the foreigner than with his neighbour. Ultimately this is to do with expansions of the system considered most relevant at any given moment in the actor's life. If her status as an industrial worker, and the meaning produced therein, is more important (to her) than her status as a temple-going Tamil, then she is a Mauritian before she's a Tamil. This process cannot be measured,

and it appears difficult to infer from observation: When, after all, do we
know that Mlle Dimba's identity as a worker sets a deeper imprint on her
self, as it were, than her identity as a Tamil? We don't know.

What we can do, however, is to interpret what we do know: Sheila Dimba,
19, is the eldest daughter of a small planter near Petite Rivière, a large,
'rurban' village near Port-Louis with a rapidly growing industrial sector.
There are three more children; two girls and a boy. Sheila passed her CPE
five years ago, but there was no money to send her to secondary school.
For a while she helped her mother in the house and her father in the fields;
eventually, her father decided that she should work at one of the new
factories in the area. One of his sisters had a job there already, and she
could look after Sheila. At this time, there were still relatively few women
of Asian descent in the factories: the great majority were Creoles. Sheila
was sometimes harassed by some of the Creole girls, she says; but she also
made friends with some. Two years ago, she fell in love with a Creole boy,
working as a chauffeur at the same factory as herself. Since her aunt was
always nearby, she could never see him for more than a few minutes at a
time – but somehow they managed to agree to get married. Like virtually
anybody in a similar situation, she had to make a choice between her family
and her lover; she chose her family, and abandoned him; but she kept her
job – even though her aunt quit during this period. Today she comments,
'It's all very silly. To me, there's no reason that I should marry a Tamil
rather than anybody else. But I'm fond of my family, and don't want to
offend them. After all, I'm still young. Perhaps later I'm stronger and can
marry whomever I want.' About her religion, she says,

> I am a Tamil, but I don't know what that means. I go to the temple and I like it.
> Anyway, *Sakenn pe prie dan so fason* [Each prays in his/her way]. I dislike the
> Muslims because of their fanaticism; not as people, only their religion – but
> Christians are very nice. Did you know that some Catholics have done a lot of
> good for us girls at the factories?

Her identity as a Mauritian seems in several respects to be practically
prior to that as a Tamil. The chief criterion is her openness toward intermarriage. She also perceives her status as a factory worker as an important
one (referring to *nous, les filles dans les usines*, in French incidentally, as it
would clearly have been beneath her petit-bourgeois dignity to speak Kreol
to a European like myself). The fact that Sheila spends a significant part of
her day in a social context where the participants are mutually defined
through sharing a task horizontally seems to have liberated her from
consistent application of ethnic stereotypes altogether. There is no
relevant difference between herself and her Creole, Hindu and Muslim

workmates – on the contrary, they are united in 'we-hood' through the non-hierarchically shared work, and in 'us-hood' as underpaid workers. If we compare this with the division of labour in the sugar estate, the difference is obvious. Where Billy (Chap. 4) works, for instance, the director is Franco-Mauritian, the middle managerial positions are held by Sino-Mauritians and Coloureds, the artisans and mechanics are Creoles, and the labourers in the fields Hindus and Muslims: the division of labour is strongly ethnically correlated. At Sheila's job, a clothing enterprise employing some 90 people, the boss is an Indian from India, who uses a youngish Creole woman as interpreter when addressing his non-Anglophone workers. The white-collar positions are held by a Sino-Mauritian, a Mulatto and a Tamil. The majority of the employees, female *'machinistes'*, work together in a large, noisy hall; here, the four largest ethnic categories (Hindus, Creoles, Muslims, Tamils) are present, almost in statistically representative ratios.

• *Compatibility with non-ethnic nationhood.* An ethnically similar division of labour is found in the large hotels, too. Frequently, the upper managerial positions belong to foreigners, and Sino-Mauritians as well as Franco-Mauritians are often overrepresented among those of highest rank. But further down in the hierarchy, the pattern of employment does not reflect ethnic power asymmetries. This implies that the employees in question share a representation of meritocratic principles. This further means that they face each other in a competitive situation, unlike Sheila and her workmates at the factory. Unlike the factory worker, the hotel employee tends to consider the possibility of promotion, and no unity of the 'we' variety is viable here. However, the adoption of principles of meritocracy entails a weakening of cultural and social boundaries: an acknowledgment that everybody is up to the same thing – and here, too, there is no relevant difference between employees on roughly the same level in the hierarchy. The social context of the hotel, like that of the factory, provides a system of shared representations, confirmed in action, which is independent from ethnicity and which is – I have argued – compatible with nationalism. Through paying increasing income taxes to the state and receiving increasing welfare benefits in return, the worker and his/her family further develop a tangible understanding of the *we-hood* inherent in the abstract model of nation-building: '*We* take care of each other.' It eventually *pays* to be an abstract citizen. In addition, the workers earn their own money and become financially independent of their families; in this way, kinship becomes less important in social organisation.

• *The case for nationhood.* Areas of shared meaning are growing in many new and/or changing fields of interethnic interaction. In this final discussion of social change, I have focused on the working place; in the previous chapter, the rise in interethnic marriages was analysed. The spread of similar patterns of consumption, the role of higher education and social mobility have also have been analysed, and all point in the direction of stronger individualism and a weakening of ethnic ties. At the moment, the case for a successful panethnic *and* polyethnic nationalism may therefore seem a strong one. The national symbols are available and increasingly being perceived as relevant: colonial ones, economic progress and Ramgoolam as 'we' symbols, the Diego Garcia conflict, economic competition and ethnic diversity as 'us' symbols. Ethnicity and nationhood may be seen as the main rivals in the ongoing negotiation over identity. In order to be successful, any Mauritian nationalism must persuade citizens that they are first and foremost members of a nation and not of an ethnic group; it must have something to offer. I have argued that changes in the labour market may already have triggered a swing away from ethnic identity towards national identity based on individualism rather than kinship and religion. First, Mauritians increasingly imagine themselves as competitors on the world market. Secondly, and more importantly, individual merit is replacing kinship and ethnic membership as the most important principle for recruitment to the labour market. Thirdly, this entails social mobility, and thereby weakens that aspect of ethnicity that linked parents and children through an ethnically specific profession. Fourthly, following from this, many working places have become polyethnic, and people of different ethnic membership develop shared interests and have shared experiences. These and related processes encourage individuals to see themselves as members of an abstract nation rather than an ethnic corporate group. A general swing from collectivism to individualism is involved here: the importance of kinship diminishes, and the importance of individual choice and achievement increases. Nationalism postulates a direct link between the individual and the abstract, imagined community embodied in the state, while ethnicity, in Mauritius at any rate, functions at the level of interpersonal face-to-face networks. In this way, the increase in 'love marriages' among Indo-Mauritians contributes to strengthening nationhood at the cost of ethnicity, even if many of these marriages are intra-ethnic.

However, lest this study is misunderstood as a just-so story presenting a simple Weberian recipe for transcending ethnic tension, it must be emphasised that the Mauritian nation struggles with internal contradictions, not least those embodied in the dual model of universalism *and* multiculturalism, which is in principle self-contradictory, but which may, perhaps, not be so in practice. The next chapter will discuss this issue in greater detail.

Notes

1. Nor, it might be added, have South American nationalisms, which are in several interesting ways distinctive, been studied adequately in this comparative context: they predate most European nationalisms, emerged in non-industrial societies, and deal with ethnic variation in their own distinctive ways.
2. A rare example of a detailed analysis of a non-European nationalism, which brings out both similarities and differences in relation to European nationalisms, is Kapferer's (1988) analysis of Sri Lankan nationalist symbolism and practice.
3. The dictionary has a strong normative bias throughout.
4. Although it is a high caste in India, the Rajput caste is for various reasons (see Hollup 1994a) a *ti-nasyon* in Mauritius.
5. In 1985, the 150th anniversary of the abolition of slavery was held, after lobbying and planning by the Creole interest group *L'Organisation Fraternelle*. The government, sensing a possible conflict, rapidly ruled that the 150th anniversary of the arrival of the first indentured labourers from India should be celebrated simultaneously.
6. The national flag consists of four horizontal stripes; from top to bottom, they are red, blue, yellow and green. Officially, the colours symbolise (from below) the crops of the land, the tropical sun, the ocean enclosing Mauritius, and the struggle of the people. A popular interpretation holds that the red stands for the Labour Party (Hindu-dominated), the blue for the PMSD (General Population), the yellow for the Sino-Mauritians, and the green for the Muslims.
7. The most striking instance witnessed by me, admittedly bizarre to a European, was a police brass band playing Tamil religious music at a *Cavadee* in Mahébourg.
8. Note the parallels with the nearly universal acceptance of English as a national language.
9. Military expenditure in Mauritius amounts to 0.2 per cent of the GNP.
10. My questions have been omitted from this transcription. I first asked him what really happened in Port-Louis when there was fighting between Creoles and Muslims; then, I asked him if this was just a gang fight; and finally, I asked him what happened afterwards.
11. This detail is slightly inconsistent with the historical record. The narrator is a Creole.
12. I have found most instances of this in the Creole suburbs of Port-Louis, where the men traditionally worked on the docks. Since the opening of a sugar bulk terminal ('*vrac*') in 1980, many have been unemployed. During the same period, many of their wives and (particularly) daughters have found jobs in the new industries emerging in the mid- to late 1980s.

13. An Indian intellectual, *un Indien d'Inde*, a frequent visitor to Mauritius, com-
     plained about the average Indo-Mauritian: 'He's not an Indian, he just looks
     like it. What could his spiritual life possibly look like, when he spends all his
     time saving for a video machine! He doesn't speak like an Indian, nor think
     like one.'

14. Sartre's distinction between 'we-as-subject' and 'we-as-object' (French does not
     have a word for 'us') is illuminating, but his use of the concepts ('we-as-subject'
     as a 'subjective and psychological experience', his teachings on subject–object
     relationships, etc.) cannot usefully be applied here. I use the terms, then,
     inaccurately and tentatively, in referring (a) to *we*, the social and/or cultural
     unit held together chiefly through its internal workings, and (b) to *us*, kept
     together against the 'gaze of the Third (Tertius)'. He is looking at *us*, but *we*
     are producing meaning together. The two are, empirically, non-existent poles
     in a continuum.

15. The Rodriguan independence movement, existing since the mid-1970s and
     represented in parliament by the OPR party (*Organisation du People Rodriguais*),
     shows the importance of delineating changes in systemic boundaries. According
     to the OPR, tiny Mauritius has a *colonial problem* in (even tinier) Rodrigues,
     exploiting and underdeveloping the dependency much in the same way as the
     previous colonial powers (mis-)treated their colonies. Nobody proposed this
     view before independence, as the relevant system in question was then the
     British Empire or, more specifically, the system containing Mauritius-and-
     Rodrigues on the one hand, and the United Kingdom on the other. The new
     self-sustaining system of Mauritius-and-Rodrigues provided the structural
     conditions for a Rodriguan independence movement.

16. It should nevertheless be pointed out that even expatriate Mauritians frequently
     activate ethnic networks, and that ethnicity is not only being transcended but
     also reproduced abroad. In Strasburg, for instance, a large segment of the
     resident Mauritians are Tamils from a particular suburb of Rose-Hill, many of
     them relatives.

CHAPTER EIGHT

The Mauritian Dilemma

> You run on *ahead*? – Do you do so as a herdsman? or as an exception? A
> third possibility would be as a deserter . . .. *First* question of conscience.
>
> – Friedrich Nietzsche

The Swami Sivananda Yoga Ashram, set in a luxuriant garden in a lush
suburb of Rose-Hill, provides a striking image of multiculturalism. Facing
the street, statues and symbols representing a multitude of religious traditions are displayed: Mahayana and Hinayana Buddhism, Hinduism, Islam,
and Roman Catholic and Orthodox Christianity are represented. In the
meditation room, open to the public, a great variety of sacred scriptures
and holy books are available: the Gita, the Qu'ran, the Bible and many
others. In a certain sense, the ashram may be seen as a symbol of Mauritian
tolerance; it nonetheless represents an image of syncretism impossible to
accept for most Mauritians.

Compromise and Hegemony

Nowhere is the orthodox conceptualisation of the nation as an imagined
community more evidently valid than in the colonially created states.
Commonly invoked as examples of this are the postcolonial African states,
whose boundaries were randomly drawn a century or less ago. Even more
striking are the culturally constructed nationalisms of societies that were
never precolonial. Mauritius is such a nation. Its very society was created
through the mass imports of slaves and indentured labourers during the
modern era, and it has been independent for only three decades. Until the
1960s, the wider identities of the inhabitants of Mauritius were by and large
colonial; they knew that they were British subjects and that they owed their
dominant written language to France.

Mauritians are generally, this book has shown, self-conscious of ethnic differences. Their society is made up of groups originating from three continents and four major religions; there is no clear ethnic majority, and yet the Mauritian state has hitherto avoided public interethnic violence since the riots around Independence. Yet most Mauritians are, regardless of ethnic membership, subjectively concerned to retain their ethnic distinctiveness, although tendencies in Mauritian society indicate that this may be difficult in the near future. Religious ritual is widely attended, and there is currently – in the 1990s – an upsurge in popular interest in cultural origins. Simultaneously, there are strong forces at work, described in the last two chapters, encouraging a polyethnic or postethnic Mauritian nationalism that is identified with cultural uniformity in quotidian practices and a shared destiny: the emergent industrial system requires uniformly qualified, mobile labour, which in turn requires a standardisation of education; national radio, TV and the newspapers increasingly influence the form and topics of discourse about society, and there seems to have been a growth in the occurrence of interethnic marriages.

• *Particularism and universalism.* The Mauritian state, recognising the immanent dangers of the potential dominance of one ethnic category, has taken great pains to develop a set of national symbols that can be endorsed by anybody, and that are thus not associated with one particular ethnic category. Caught between different, sometimes conflicting ideological orientations, Mauritians choose situationally between universalist ethics of state nationalism, and particularist ethics of ethnicity or comparable ideological orientations. In formal politics, in matters relating to employment and marriage, and in some informal contexts of social interaction, ethnicity remains a major variable; but it is constantly being counteracted by discourse arguing the superiority of abstract justice and non-particularism. The openness of Mauritian discourse, public and private – in particular, the fact that ethnic tension and cultural differences are universally acknowledged as facts of social life, and the absence of a clearly hegemonic ethnic category – are some of the conditions for the kind of interethnic compromise realised in Mauritius. Although there may be important contradictions between ideologies of ethnicity and ideologies of nationalism at the level of individual agency, such contradictions can to a great extent be reconciled at the national, formal political level, where compromise, legalistic justice, equal rights and tolerance are emphasised. Ethnically based systems of segmentary oppositions are nevertheless encouraged officially, but only if they are enacted outside the educational, political and economic systems, where the virtues of meritocracy and individualism are stressed, although these principles are, as has been indicated, often violated. The Mauritian nation aims at striking a balance between the binary logic of the state (dividing the world's population into citizens and foreigners) and the segmentary logic of the ethnic mosaic, where *degrees* of membership and loyalty are made relevant (see Evans-Pritchard 1940; Gluckman 1982 [1956]; Eriksen 1993b on segmentary oppositions).

• *A non-ethnic nation?* The nation-building project in Mauritius is contradiction-ridden, even if the state does not represent a form of lineage organisation but rather a compromise between 'lineages', and requires continuous negotiation over the relationship between uniformity and diversity. The project is politically interesting, as it has successfully prevented interethnic violence for nearly thirty years; and also analytically interesting, because it seems to contradict central tenets in the academic analysis of nationalism, where cultural and ethnic diversity is generally seen as a threat to national integrity. However, virtually every country in the world is torn, in some way, between homogenisation and emphasis on shared values and culture on the one hand; and differentiation and ethnic or regional movements on the other. Mauritius is not unique in this.

In which sense can Mauritian nationalism truly be said to be non-ethnic? The answer is not as obvious as it might seem at a first glance. For although the official ideology of multiculturalism seems to 'freeze' ethnic distinctions, the Mauritian project of nation-building can also be seen, in its universalistic mode, as an attempt, more or less conscious, to create a new *ethnie* or ethnic community of people, whose ancestral language will eventually be Kreol. Since the entire population has already become integrated into a uniform system of communication, politics and economic exchange, it can be argued that the only ingredient missing is the self-definition: in other words, that Mauritians can be *a people* tomorrow if they decide to.

There can be no doubt that the majority of Mauritians do not wish ethnic boundaries to vanish altogether, although there are many views on what the relationship between similarity and difference ought to be. Since Mauritian nationhood must be defined as adherence to a unifying, non-ethnic ideology, it is difficult to invest any nationalism with substantive content, since most of the potential national symbols can be interpreted as expression of ethnic interests.

The Dilemma of Multiculturalism

Ethnic plurality poses a problem for the nation-state to the extent that the constituent groups communicate their distinctiveness in contexts where this distinctiveness is seen as incompatible with the requirements of the nation-state, notably those related to formal equality and uniform practices. In reminding the authorities of the possibility of segmentary systems of opposition within the nation-state, cultural minorities may seem to threaten its unity. The minorities are in turn usually faced with threats of more or less enforced assimilation. The intensity of such pressures to assimilate is usually contingent on the degree of modernisation and the level of state integration in national society. What about Mauritius?

• *Limits to plurality*. The 'cultural pluralist model', which is posited as an explicit ideal through Mauritian state nationalist ideology, sets clear limitations to the extent of the cultural plurality allowed: common denominators depend on cultural sharing. To the extent that the different population segments participate in the formal institutions of the state, their assimilation is likely at least in those respects to which these institutions are relevant. Thus the then Prime Minister Anerood Jugnauth commented on the Diard case (see Chap. 5): 'No religious body should think that it is a state within a state.' Responding to accusations of ethnic particularism, Jugnauth in this way redefined the conflict by maintaining that the expulsion was not caused by religious animosities, for religious pluralism had to be deemed legitimate; rather, it was the 'meddling' with the affairs of the *state* by the priest (who, like many Catholic clergymen in Mauritius, was a French citizen) that was considered illegitimate. The general issue pertains to the limits of shared imperatives and common denominators, and conversely, the scope of the cultural differences that are acceptable, seen from the state's perspective within the compass of the nation-state.

Between the Ethnic and the Post-ethnic

Let us look more closely at some of the problems, controversies, paradoxes and contradictions that inevitably arise in the course of the balancing acts between demands for similarity and homogenisation, and claims of difference and special rights justified ethnically.

Père Henri Souchon became famous overnight when, at the height of the legendary 'race riots' of 1968, he admonished his congregation in central Port-Louis to visit the nearby mosque in order to familiarise themselves with a Muslim way of thought and thereby mitigate the mutual suspicion between Christians and Muslims. He called for contact and a possible 'merging of horizons', to use Gadamer's term, between the antagonists.

More than two decades after the riots, Souchon, now fondly described as *l'homme-pont* (the human bridge, cf. Ahnee 1991), sees two possible scenarios confronting Mauritius in terms of the relationship between ethnic boundaries and the formation of identity categories oblivious of ethnicity. He calls them the *fruit salad* and the *fruit compote*, respectively. In the fruit salad, the components are clearly distinct; ethnic boundaries are intact, and reflexively 'rooted' identities are secure and stable. In the fruit *compote*, on the other hand, the different fruits are squashed and mixed together through a substantial use of force. (This metaphor, it may be noted, is reminiscent of the American 'melting pot' metaphor.) The result of the *compote de fruit*, in *père* Souchon's view, would be uprootedness, nihilism and confusion. He himself therefore supports the fruit salad variety, although he goes further than most in expanding the compass of the common denominators or, to stretch the fruit salad metaphor somewhat, thickening the syrup. In order to have a dialogue, Souchon argues, one needs a firm position to conduct it from. This kind of argument should be familiar from multiethnic societies elsewhere as well. The fruit *compote* corresponds to processes of creolisation and the merging of horizons; while the fruit salad corresponds to alternating policies of compromise and avoidance.

The world-view envisioned in the fruit salad metaphor, often phrased as a 'rainbow' metaphor, is hegemonic in Mauritius. Yet conflicts between equality and difference are inevitable given the complementary hegemony of ethnic identification of self and others. A few examples will make this clear.

• *The Catholic school.* Most Mauritian schools are public, but private schools also exist, many of them run by religious organisations. There are anti-discrimination laws. The Catholic Church runs some of the most prestigious secondary schools in the country, but as a condition for receiving state funding, a minimum of 49 per cent of the students have to be non-Catholics. (Only 30 per cent of the Mauritian population are Catholics.) It is nevertheless well known that Catholic schools have tended to prefer Catholic applicants for teaching positions, although they have also occasionally hired Muslims and Hindus. This policy was tested in court when an unsuccessful applicant filed a suit against a Catholic school in 1989 because she suspected that her application had been passed over on religious grounds. In court the following year, the defence argued that it was necessary to have devout Catholics in certain teaching jobs, because a part of their job consisted in turning the pupils into good Catholics. The prosecutor asked whether this policy was also relevant to subjects such as French, English and mathematics, which the school's lawyer admitted was not the case. In his testimony, the Archbishop, Mgr Jean Margéot, argued that the colours of the Mauritian rainbow had to be kept separate 'for the *arc-en-ciel* to remain beautiful'. The Catholic school won the case, and succeeded in this way in creating a precedent for differential treatment on religious grounds in a limited part of the labour market. The principle of difference was here victorious over the principle of equality. Instead of a common denominator defending a principle of meritocracy, a common denominator defending ethnic segregation was sanctioned.

• *The Muslim Personal Law.* Another nationally famous case from the same period concerned the controversial Muslim Personal Law, introduced during British rule, which allowed Muslims to follow customary Muslim law in family matters. A characteristic consequence of this law was that it became nearly impossible for women, but relatively easy for men, to obtain a divorce. In the course of the investigations of a Commission of Enquiry set up in the mid-1980s, it became clear that the opposition to the MPL was significant even among Mauritius' Muslims. Not unexpectedly, many women and young Muslims were against it, arguing that they were entitled to the same rights as other Mauritian citizens. In the end, the law was abolished, and universalistic principles won over particularistic ones.

This second example is the most interesting one in this context. Here, the fundamental paradox of multiculturalist ideology – Mauritian identity as identical with the 'cultural mosaic' – becomes highly visible: it presupposes that the 'cultures' are homogeneous and 'have values and interests'. The mere fact that the formal leaders of an ethnic category invoke particular values and traditions does not, however, imply that all members of the group support them. This is why many governments and social philosophers hesitate to accord special rights to *groups*, for groups inevitably consist of persons with often highly discrepant values and interests.

• *The syncretist intellectual.* A third example highlights the relationship between particularist identities and universalist principles in a somewhat different way. Some intellectual Mauritians, tending towards a 'fruit *compote*' as an ideal, have experimented with mixing religions and cultural conventions in novel way. One such is the radical music group Grup Latanier, which performs an essentially Creole *séga* music with strong Indian elements and politically radical lyrics. One leading Mauritian intellectual decided, at some time during the 1980s, to challenge the rigid boundaries between different religions, reasoning that the island needed a 'shared culture' for a proper national identity to come about. On Christmas day, therefore, he solemnly went to church, bringing bananas and incense as a sacrifice to the Hindu gods. This act was, naturally, frowned upon by Hindus as well as Christians, who both felt insulted by the blasphemous syncretism implied. If anything, they felt further apart after the experiment than before it. The ideal of the 'fruit *compote*' thus cannot be enforced against people's wishes. It should nevertheless be noted that universalist principles have been adopted by the Mauritian population with respect to political culture. In so far as discrepant religious or other cultural practices do not interfere with the universalism guaranteeing individuals equal rights, there is no good reason to chastise them.

Similarity and Difference

The Mauritian attempt at creating a synthesis between liberal principles of individual equality and a cultural relativist principle is remarkable and unusual, and it arguably deserves international attention at a time when identity politics is becoming a main political preoccupation in a great number of societies worldwide.[1]

• *Community and individual.* The examples sketched above suggest that *both* equal rights and the right to be different may in particular situations lead to discrimination and the violation of individual human rights. If one insists on shared civil rights as the basis of citizenship and nationality, as the French revolutionaries did, one will tend to oppress minorities by forcing them to assimilate to a public culture (language, rules, hierarchies and conventions) that they perceive as alien and intrusive. If, on the other hand, one opts for differential treatment on the basis of religion or ethnicity, the risk is the opposite: those afflicted may lose their equal rights. South African apartheid policies are a good example of this: South Africans were encouraged to use their vernacular languages at all levels, and the majority of blacks were thereby in practice excluded from national and international political discourse. This, in a nutshell, is the conflict between Enlightenment and Romantic social philosophers as well as that between communitarians and liberals, and it is *the* dilemma of multiculturalism (see Macintyre 1981; Lukes 1991; Taylor 1992; Rawls 1993, for the philosophical debate; see Lijphart 1977 for a classic statement from political theory). The hidden variable in this puzzle is power discrepancies (cf. Gledhill 1997): the unequal right to evaluate reified 'cultures', to define collective identities and social relations between them.

It should also be pointed out that political leaders are frequently prone to exploiting notions about cultural uniqueness strategically to strengthen their positions. In a critical study of ethnopolitics in the USA, Steinberg (1981) concludes that persons and organisations generally invoke principles of cultural relativism when they themselves have something to gain from differential treatment, and that they will otherwise support equality principles. 'Tradition', 'rooted culture' and similar catchwords are positively evaluated in many political discourses of our time, and they are often used rhetorically to justify privileges and political positions. On the other hand, this warning should not be taken to mean that there are never legitimate reasons for wishing to protect oneself against cultural domination (see Wilson 1997 for the anthropological debate over human rights and cultural rights; see Lijphart 1977 for a classic statement from political theory). The difficult task, handled more skilfully by Mauritians than by many others, consists in drawing the boundary between the right to a cultural heritage and particularistic politics, through flexible policies aiming at establishing common denominators for the resolution of common problems.

• *Do I have to have an 'identity'?* Another, related point, which is also relevant for all polyethnic societies, concerns identification with collectivities in general. As a matter of fact, many Mauritians feel quite at ease as members of what they see as an emerging 'fruit *compote*', and do not long for roots and purity. They would prefer to be cultural hybrids to the extent they wish, to be recognised as individuals and not as the representatives of a particular group. The legitimacy of this kind of strategy was tried out in practice by members of *Lalit* before the general election of 1991. When they stood for the general election in 1987, Lalit decided to demonstrate against the ethnic character of Mauritian politics, which is actually embedded in the Constitution. Owing to the ingenious 'best loser system', intended to ensure a fair representation of all ethnic communities in Parliament, every candidate in the general election has to state his or her ethnic membership. Lalit elected to decide their members' ethnic membership at random, by drawing lots. The result was not devoid of Theatre of the Absurd qualities. For example, one of their leaders, by all appearances a white Mauritian of foreign birth, re-emerged as a Hindu on the election rolls. In this way, they succeeded in calling public attention to a paradox in the prevailing multicultural ideology of Mauritius: it places a great stress on ethnic membership, and makes it difficult for anyone to be simply Mauritian. One virtually *has to* belong to a community, and one's community membership is necessarily something different from one's citizenship or nationality. Recall, in this context, Vishnu (Chap. 6), whose refusal to acknowledge Tamil as his ancestral language was contested by the census-taker.

The neo-Romantic ideological climate informing politics in many parts of the world today – either viciously nationalist (in the cultural sense) or equally viciously multiculturalist – is such that persons may be obliged to take on an ethnic identity whether they want to or not. Indeed, authoritarian culturalism may be just as oppressive in an ostensibly multiethnic and tolerant 'rainbow society' as in an ethnically hegemonic nation (as argued in a number of recent works, including Steven Lukes' wonderful philosophical novel about the adventures of Professor Caritat: Lukes 1995). The right to have an ethnic identity must also, according to the ideology of human rights, include the right not to have one. Here, perhaps, lies the greatest paradox of multiculturalism: in its apparently benevolent focus on 'the wealth of cultures and traditions' present in society, it neglects the Salman Rushdies of the world, so to speak; those persons who spend their entire lives midway between Bombay and London without wishing, or indeed being able, to land.[2] It excludes the 'mongrels', anomalies and idiosyncratic individuals who are numerous and necessary as interethnic brokers and in the forging of cross-cutting or non-ethnic alignments, and who arguably represent the possible future of many societies.

Creolisation and Revitalisation

Let us now move a step further, and reflect on the aforementioned tension in Mauritian society; the opposition between what Hannerz (1990) has labelled 'cosmopolitans and locals'. First, it should be emphasised that there is little to be gained from viewing this tension in evolutionary terms. Some individuals define themselves as, and act as, 'cosmopolitans' because their interpretations of their experiences and life-projects imply that they should do so; whereas others define themselves as 'locals' for the same kind of reasons. The point to be made in the context of current changes in Mauritian society is that an increasing number of young individuals experience the world and their own lives in ways encouraging a 'cosmopolitan' interpretation of their own identity and the surrounding social environment. To rephrase some points made earlier about social change in Mauritius: many Mauritians nowadays spend their Sundays in front of the TV set, in the shopping mall or at the beach instead of going to a place of worship; they read French *romans-photo* rather than the Bible, the Gita or the Qu'ran; they go to cafés and discos, where they meet others with a lifestyle similar to their own but a different ethnic identity; they compete on a par with everybody else for jobs and grades; and they end up working next to, and taking lunch breaks with, persons of different ethnic membership.

This 'cosmopolitan' tendency is underpinned at the institutional level by new forms of economic organisation, by the increasing application of principles of meritocracy in the educational system and the labour market (particularly in the private sector), by the growing secular public sphere (cafés, newspapers, magazines, professional organisations, etc.) and by increased contacts with the outside world through incoming tourism and economic diversification.

Equally importantly, the importance of kinship and family in the social organisation is decreasing in some milieux in Mauritius because of the individualistic and meritocratic tendencies in the labour market. Just like work, marriage is becoming a relationship between individuals rather than a relationship between groups.

One immediate outcome of this situation, which is no longer a mere scenario but visible (and quantifiable) in urban Mauritius, is the growth of the 'Creole' ethnic category. As remarked earlier, the Creoles make up an ethnic category that is not based on shared descent, but on 'family resemblances' (Wittgenstein 1983) pertaining to their general lifestyle. Ethnic anomalies therefore tend to be classified as Creoles. 'Creole' as an ethnic label in Mauritius is in practice a 'catch-all' label; a truly residual category absorbing everyone who does not fit well into the other categories, which are legitimised through references to notions of purity and descent. The children of Chinese–Muslim marriages tend to be categorised as 'a kind of Creoles', despite the fact that Creoles were initially defined as Mauritians of wholly or partial African or Malagasy descent.

Through this absorbent quality of the Creole social category, it may be remarked, the native term *Kreol* (when used about people, not about language) is superbly compatible with the analytic term 'creolisation' as used in the work of Hannerz (1992) and others, where it is conceptualised as a continuous process whereby distinctive 'packages' of cultural signification merge into new forms.[3] A possible redefinition of 'a Creole' in Mauritius, fitting the current situation of flux, could be 'an individual who holds that his or her ancestral language is Kreol', thereby acknowledging that his or her origins are mixed – if not genetically, then at least culturally. This option would, of course, be open to Hindus as well as Muslims, who thereby do not, however, become fully-fledged Creoles, but rather 'Creolised Indo-Mauritians', whose children may in turn be identified as Creoles. The Creole category is thus open in several respects; but it remains partly bounded, largely because most Mauritians define themselves as non-Creoles.

The next logical step, exemplified through Vishnu and Shalini (Chap. 6), transcends the ethnic logic altogether, would reject 'Creole identity' for being a residual category created by an obsolete ethnic logic, and claims Mauritian citizenship as the only rational basis for political identity. Within this world-view or structure of relevance, shared culture is caused by the ability to communicate rather than by shared origins. It would be possible to argue, in this respect, that the cultural distance between a rural, proletarian Hindu and an urban middle-class Hindu is greater than that between an urban middle-class Hindu and an urban middle-class *gen de couleur*. This identity discourse, which takes place in Mauritian society because of the very real tensions between the ethnic and the non-ethnic criteria for 'we-hood', is analogous to the debates over the concept of culture in anthropology and related disciplines (cf. Chap. 3).

Many thousands of Mauritians live within an experienced reality of this kind, which was unthinkable only thirty years ago, when the main social institutions of Mauritius were still tightly tied up with ethnic distinctions. In contemporary Mauritius, the boundaries have become fuzzy. Of course, most Mauritians still think and act largely within an ethnic mode of thought. Still, Creoles may bitterly complain that *tu pu malbar* when explaining why they can never expect to find employment in the civil service. And still, a Hindu may tell a visitor that 'it's funny, but nowadays, a lot of Creoles look almost like Hindus'. However, it can also be observed that a lot of Hindus look almost like Creoles, and this, perhaps, pertains especially to the young, who are constantly exposed to the same influences as Creoles in terms of music, dress, food and so on. On the other hand, it is also clear that not all parts of culture change in the same direction or at the same speed. Even if public culture becomes identical for all the ethnic categories in Mauritius, this (i) does not imply that ethnicity disappears as a socially organising principle, and (ii) does not mean that distinctive cultural values are not transmitted in the domestic and local fields. Be this as it may, it is clear that Mauritian ethnicity is in the middle of a phase of transformation in which its significance and relevance are changing. If the tendencies I have sketched here, some of which have been analysed more carefully in earlier chapters, were the only ones, the end of ethnicity might have been imminent. But there are other strong tendencies that strongly confront the processes of creolisation taking place in the economy, in the media and in the intimate sphere.

Until a few decades ago, ethnicity was firmly embedded in politics, the economy and informal social interaction in Mauritius. Ethnicity was *the* public discourse of Mauritius. Ethnicity was, also, strongly hierarchical. The changes in post-independence Mauritius have been no less than spectacular. The ethnic foundation of politics, although still strong, has repeatedly been challenged. Principles for recruitment to the labour market are no longer unambiguously ethnic. Educational opportunities have spread and have levelled out some profound (including linguistic) cultural differences. New arenas for informal networking, such as discos, have appeared. Most households now have a TV set, and follow the same programmes. Far from everybody views this development with delight, and the pressure towards conformity and cultural homogenisation is met with powerful counterreactions from different quarters.

• *Revitalisation*. Religious leaders from Hinduism, Christianity and Islam preach tolerance and simultaneously stress the importance of having one faith. Some high-profiled political leaders have also campaigned more or less openly for ethnic solidarity in recent years, and are gaining support. Hindu leaders speak at public meetings about the decline of Bhojpuri, linking it to urban decadence, the replacement of the sari and incense with jeans and the pill, and calls for a revitalisation of ancient Hindu values. In line with this logic, a Franco-Mauritian argues that in Mauritius, one has avoided violent ethnic conflict because one has – up to the present day and age – avoided mixed marriages. (A Creole who was present later commented, angrily, that this was tantamount to defending apartheid.) 'Traditionalism' and the search for roots take a number of other forms as well, within all ethnic categories.

These kinds of counterreactions against the homogenisation of identities indicate that many Mauritians today reflexively fashion ethnic identities as self-conscious responses to the tendencies towards blurring identity boundaries and cultural creolisation. Why?

There seem to be two distinct kinds of motivation for subscribing to essentialist ethnic notions of identity in the current situation.

Most obviously, there are large groups of people who have vested political or economic interests in some kind of ethnic segregation. A rich ethnic group such as the Franco-Mauritians is a very clear example – in their case, the very colour of their skin is a ticket to privilege; but among many Hindus, there is also fear that their privileged access to positions in the civil service is threatened by individualism and meritocracy. Through linking these tendencies to a moral decline, they try to gather the support of people who are concerned with leading a decent life in accordance with established values. During a recent electoral campaign, thus, a false rumour to the effect that Jugnauth's son was engaged to a Muslim girl (the Jugnauths are Hindus) circulated in many Hindu-dominated villages. It is not adequate to view this kind of rumour purely as an attempt to discredit the Prime Minister as a moral person, a good Hindu and so on. Economic and political interests are also involved, since rural Hindus remain socially and economically organised on the basis of lineage and kinship. To marry a Muslim, therefore, in this kind of context, implies selling out the ethnic estate of Hindus (seen as a metaphoric kin group), which would have a strong economic aspect.

This is not to say that purely instrumental motives underlie ethnicist counterreactions against individualism and meritocracy; but the lack of revivalist enthusiasm in urban parts of Mauritius, where the employment structure is different from the countryside, indicates that the economic dimension is an important one. If no economic and political resources were channelled through ethnic organisation, it is unlikely that calls for ethnic purity would have mass appeal.

A different context for ethnic revitalisation is nonetheless found in the urban middle classes. Often accounted for as nostalgia and romanticism in the professional literature, this kind of ideology has a strong appeal in urban areas in Mauritius. Many Mauritians, among them many urban 'cosmopolitans', feel an increasing attraction for their ancestral culture as they approach middle age, many even making pilgrimages to their areas of origin in India. The erosion of the past is countered by a reconstruction of the past, whose architects do not necessarily turn this into a political programme aimed at defending their rights at the expense of the rights of others.

This way of reasoning, which is symmetrical or complementary to creol- isation, globalisation and cultural homogenisation (see, for example, Friedman 1994), seems more difficult to undertake in Mauritius than in many other societies. For one thing, few Mauritians are able to trace their origins accurately. About three-quarters of the population are the des- cendants of either slaves or indentured labourers, and their genealogies usually vanish into the mists of oblivion after a few generations. Others, including many who are opinion leaders by virtue of being writers and journalists, have origins so mixed that any call for purity would seem patently meaningless to them. One of them actually sputtered indignantly, at the suggestion that he, too, might search for his roots: 'Should I search for my roots? I can count sixteen different origins in my ancestry. Perhaps I should begin in Brittany, or Canton, or on the Malabar coast? Should *I* search for my roots?' It nevertheless happens that representatives of the 'mixed' population, *les gens de couleur*, invoke notions of purity in their identity politics, arguing that they, *la population mixte*, are the only *vrais Mauriciens*, real Mauritians, as their category is the only one to have emerged on Mauritian soil. The two main criteria for political organisation, *Blut* (blood, kinship) and *Boden* (soil, land), thus meet in direct confront- ation.

Individualism as a Key Factor

Outsiders often ask why Mauritius is such a stable democracy, incorpor- ating, as it does, a vast number of religious groupings and people originating from different continents. The question is wrongly asked, and it reveals an inadequate understanding of culture. At the level of everyday representations and practices, Mauritian culture can actually be described as quite uniform, in the sense that there is a wide field of shared premises for communication encompassing most of the population: there is a shared political culture and a standardised and standardising educational system, there is considerable linguistic uniformity, and the recruitment to the labour market is increasingly based on individual skills. It is generally not difficult to argue the virtues of individual human rights among Mauritians; they tend to share similar, Western-derived notions of justice. It is, in other words, only superficially (if often noisily) multicultural, compared to most other societies, even if it may be profoundly multiethnic.[4]

It should be noted that the 'multiculturalist' model of coexistence, as practised in Mauritius and elsewhere, collapses unless the constituent groups share basic values of individualism and, in all likelihood, a shared *lingua franca*. For instance, it is widely believed, not least in that country itself, that the USA has been capable of absorbing a great number of different nationalities without homogenising them culturally. This is wrong, and generally, migrants to the USA have changed their language within two generations. One could perhaps say that immigrants to the USA have been assimilated to a degree of 90 per cent, and have been allowed to use the remaining 10 per cent to advertise their cultural uniqueness, which exists largely as a set of symbolic identity markers. As a Norwegian, I have often met Americans who identify themselves as 'Norwegians', but who seem to betray, in their verbal and non-verbal language, lifestyle and values, a strong attachment to the moral discourses of US society.

If political multiculturalists favour equal individual rights, the 'culture' in their rhetoric is either a thin cosmetic film, or rests on a strong division between public and private fields. If, on the other hand, they seriously defend the right of ethnic minorities to run their own political affairs according to a cultural logic of their own, they run the risk of defending practices that conflict with the human rights of individual group members – or that contribute to the reproduction of inequality between groups designated on an arbitrary (ethnic) basis. This, in a nutshell, is the classic predicament of Mauritian society, and it has been dealt with through a flexible application of policies of the lowest common denominator as well as policies of avoidance and policies creating merging horizons, trying to distinguish between the fields where the different policies are relevant. Particularism and universalism are confronted in many fields, from the household to the national mass media system, and the confrontations will doubtless continue, although their modes of expression will evolve. In this way, Mauritius, like many other contemporary societies, is facing a tension between modernism and traditionalism, or between communitarianism and liberalism. And there is no easy way out.

 • *Twenty-first-century identity politics.* There is something new to the current tension in Mauritian politics. While the classic model of reconciliation between ethnicist tendencies and universalist requirements accepted the omnipresence of ethnic loyalties, an emergent category of Mauritians see themselves as being beyond ethnicity: to them, ethnicity is irrelevant and provides them with few material or symbolic resources. In this context, it is interesting to note that a growing minority of Mauritians report to Census authorities that Kreol is their ancestral language (Mauritius 1991–2; see Chap. 5). This shift away from 'primordial' languages indicates that Mauritian identity is becoming the most important ancestral identity for many of the island's inhabitants.

The confrontation between a postethnic way of life, strengthened by consumerism, capitalism, secularism and individualism, and traditionalism will probably be the main challenge for Mauritian society in the twenty-first century. In this, Mauritius is, notwithstanding its degree of sophistication, similar to many, otherwise very different, complex modern societies facing an unpredictable but inevitable restructuring of the nation-state. The Aymara movement in Bolivia confronting the national élites of *criollos*, the anti-immigrant Front National in France confronting creolised *beurs* and a liberal tradition of citizen rights, politicised Islam in Algeria fighting a secular government, and Sami organisations in northern Scandinavia negotiating rights to natural resources with reluctant governments: notwithstanding the differences, these examples share several of the problems discussed in this chapter, concerning the balance between a politics of identity granting rights of belongingness to groups, and a politics based on individual rights where culture is, by definition, deemed irrelevant.

Notes

1. South African legislators and reformists have discovered Mauritius, and social theorists might benefit from following suit. For example, a consideration of Mauritian politics and ideology might have made a wonderful section in Charles Taylor's now famous essay on multiculturalism (Taylor 1992).

2. A journalist once asked Rushdie about his roots during a TV interview. He pointed downwards and said: 'What do I have at the end of my legs? Roots? What I see are feet.'
3. Archetti (1995) makes a number of interesting points regarding the Latin American term *criollo* in relation to the analytic term 'creolisation', referring to early twentieth-century Argentina.
4. This recalls a memorable passage by V. S. Naipaul, where he writes, bitterly: 'Superficially, because of the multitude of races, Trinidad may seem complex, but to anyone who knows it, it is a simple colonial philistine society' (Naipaul 1979 [1958]).

.

CHAPTER NINE

Conclusions and Prospects

'A l'Ile Maurice, on marche sur feu, on mange du feu, et on boit du feu.'[1]

– Proverb

It has been claimed that many readers of academic books start with the last chapter. Allow me therefore to state that the brief summary and conclusion that follow may make some sense to anybody, but they make more sense to those who have read the whole book. Let me first sum up the specific conditions for interethnic peace in Mauritius.

- *Its small size and uncontested boundaries*. This makes secessionism an impossible project. It is also widely understood that, since ethnic categories are not strictly spatially located, and since space is scarce, violent interethnic conflicts could not be won. In this, Mauritius differs from, for example, Sri Lanka, where Tamil secessionists have a firm territorial base.
- *The absence of an ethnic majority*. Although 52 per cent of the Mauritian population are Hindus by religion, they do not constitute a single corporate group in any relevant matter. Shifting political alignments along ethnic (and other) lines encourage compromise and caution in politics. In this, Mauritius differs from polyethnic societies such as Japan, France and Canada, where majority groups are politically (and culturally) hegemonic.
- *The absence of groups claiming aboriginality*. Unlike the situation in South Africa, where certain blacks may argue that they, as 'first-comers', have an exclusive right to the country, and unlike that in many other countries, where the notion of 'having been there first' is invoked in ideological justifications of particularist ideologies, no group can make a similar claim in Mauritius. All Mauritians are descendants of uprooted immigrants, and this is an established fact in ideological discourse. This shared historical destiny also facilitates the fashioning of polyethnic and panethnic images of the nation.

- *Division of power between different ethnic categories.* All the major ethnic categories have members who wield considerable power, economic or political, in national society. Although the Creoles are being marginalised in the ongoing process of industrialisation, there is no unambiguous power asymmetry along ethnic lines between the three largest main categories, Hindu, Muslim and Creole/Coloured: they all have their ethnically specific élites and their spokespersons. In this, Mauritius differs from most poly-ethnic societies.

- *The presence of a shared language* – Kreol – indicates cultural continuity in important respects; it also facilitates interethnic communication, com-promise and cooperation, as well as being a basis for an informal national identity. In this, Mauritius differs from most polyethnic nation-states: Lebanon, which is in certain other respects similar to Mauritius, may be a typical example.

- *Constitutional rights for minorities.* The Mauritian state actively encour-ages non-political assertions of cultural diversity, and has made 'the rainbow society' an issue that cannot be neglected in political practice. It is considered legitimate for an ethnic minority to demand public attention to its specific problems in so far as this does not contradict notions of individual human rights and notions of equal treatment. Other polyethnic states do not always distinguish between fields where the expression of cultural distinctiveness is politically unproblematic and fields where it may lead to fission or particularism. In addition, Mauritius has functioning democratic institutions guaranteeing political representation for every sizeable ethnic category.

- *Relatively even integration into instititions of the nation-state.* The primary educational system is nearly free and nearly universal, and most Mauritian households take part in capitalism both as wageworkers and as consumers. Mutual interdependence is thus evident. This also indicates that Mauritians of different ethnic identities have a great deal in common. In countries with large tribal populations, the differential participation in the modern institutions of the nation-state may be an important source of conflict, whether articulated or implicit. South American countries with large Amer-indian populations are obvious examples, as are African states such as Nigeria, where the Ibo ethnic category were for decades more thoroughly modernised than other major groups.

- *Emergent supra-ethnic career paths.* Particularly in the labour market, but also to some extent in politics and in the private fields, ethnicity is no longer necessarily the most important identity tag of an individual. It is increasingly possible to be recruited for a job independently of ethnic membership or kinship. In other words, meritocracy and individualism are, along with non-ethnic informal networks, emerging principles of social organisation. Systems of social stratification that are not based on ethnicity are of increasing importance.

• *Capitalism* and *parliamentarianism* are two institutional pillars of compromise, considered legitimate by the vast majority of Mauritians. So long as they are accepted, the contradictions of the system do not lead to socially disruptive breaches of common norms. The ethnic riots of the 1960s and the general strikes of 1970 and 1979 should nonetheless serve as a reminder of the vulnerability of Mauritian society; reminders that their remarkable success has required and still requires hard work and devoted negotiation about common denominators and their limits.

• *Symbolic ethnicity*, expressed, for example, through ritual, is encouraged; while *instrumental ethnicity* in some of its expressions, notably political communalism and economic particularism, is discouraged. In other words, the 'expressive' or 'meaningful' pole of ethnicity is accepted while the 'strategic' or 'political' pole is rejected. The role of ethnicity in the contexts of everyday life – from evening classes in Oriental languages to marriage practices and local interpersonal networks – is not considered a matter for the state. It is unclear to what extent symbolic ethnicity can reproduce itself without a political dimension; however, marriage and interpersonal networks have a political, or instrumental, dimension without necessarily interfering with the publicly sanctioned lowest common denominator.

Several of the points listed can be related to the relatively uniform degree of participation of the constituent populations in national Mauritian society and, arguably, to the high economic growth rate, which has virtually eradicated unemployment, and may thus have rendered certain notions of interethnic competition obsolete. However, ethnic tensions were also weak during the economic recession of the late 1970s and early 1980s. Nonetheless, recent Mauritian history is also a reminder that compromise between ethnic groups is notoriously difficult in a state where ethnicity is frequently the source of differences that make a difference. There is no easy way out, no *Endlösung* or simple solution. The problems relating to integration and equality on the one hand and cultural variation and ethnic incorporation on the other can only be solved through balancing policies of compromise with policies of avoidance and of creolisation, which requires considerable skills in the art of improvisation.

In which sense can it be said that the inhabitants in multiethnic societies 'live in different worlds'? If we compare it with African nation-states, Mauritius turns out to be a polycultural society only in a superficial way. There are adequate, and growing, fields of shared meaning available for

Mauritians of any origin. The interfaces of modernity provide a common language for the articulation of competition and cooperation. In addition, it should be stressed, Mauritians have *chosen* to give high priority to the resolution and prevention of ethnic conflicts. The conditions for interethnic peace listed above are, therefore, not sufficient conditions. In addition, some variant of the rule of the highest common denominator must be applied whenever necessary: a recognition of cultural differences, and a set of social techniques that efficiently prevent the escalation of conflict, must be agreed upon. We should in this context remember that Mauritius very nearly anticipated the breakdown of Lebanese national society in the late 1960s, when interethnic relations were tense and occasionally violent.

• *Ethnicity in Mauritius.* Ethnicity is in the Mauritius of the mid-to-late 1990s a fundamental ontology for historical reasons, connected with the division of labour, political organisation and career opportunities. It is now being reproduced in the household, through marriage practices, party politics, organised religion and, more recently, through modern identity politics, which self-consciously depicts and reifies the group as one with cultural continuity ('roots'), internal cohesion and group-specific needs, *as well as* linking personal identity tightly to ethnic identity. Countervailing forces are at work in all the fields studied in this book:

• Interethnic marriages contribute to blurring boundaries and presenting individualism and Mauritian nationhood as relevant alternatives to ethnic identity in the household field.

• Geographical mobility and consumerism contribute to the strengthening of interethnic informal networks in the locality field.

• Economic change creates new career opportunities not restricted by ethnic membership in the job market (seen from the individual viewpoint).

• International competition and domestic political pressure necessitate universalistic criteria for recruitment to the labour market (seen from the structural viewpoint).

• Educational homogenisation, required because of intensified job competition, erases ethnically specific differences in secondary socialisation.

• Cultural globalisation through increased consumption of foreign information commodities (from pop music to films) contributes to an awareness of cultural distinctions that do not follow ethnic lines.

• Increased international integration – economically, politically and through mass consumption, but also through migration and tourism – makes the Mauritian identity, as opposed to ethnic ones, relevant in many new situations.

• *Individualism and traditionalism.* And yet, ethnicity remains important in all the relevant social fields. Or rather: to many it does, perhaps even increasingly so; to others its importance has diminished tangibly over the past couple of decades. Perhaps it would make more sense to speak of ethnic *frontiers* (A. P. Cohen 1994) than ethnic *boundaries* in contemporary Mauritius. There is no doubt that cultural hybridisation or creolisation is taking place at an increased pace in the latter half of the 1990s. However, this blurring of cultural boundaries does not necessarily lead to the blurring of social boundaries: on the contrary, in many cases it leads to counter-reactions in the forms of politicised religion, traditionalistic identity politics and concerted efforts at reproducing the boundaries. To this point, familiar from many other societies, it should be added that cultural change, modernisation and homogenisation certainly do inspire traditionalism and revitalisation, but that they also lead to increased individualism, secularism and independence of 'primordial ties'. As Giddens says (1990, 1994), tradition no longer justifies itself automatically; it needs external justification, and individuals are to a greater or lesser extent free to choose *a* tradition or an alternative.

One may also state that there is a continuous swing between homogenisation and ethnic differentiation; indeed, that the two processes are taking place simultaneously. On the one hand, Mauritian sports have to a great extent been successfully decommunalised since the early 1980s. During the same period, however, the nationalist or panethnic Kreol movement has been weakened, and an increasing number of Indo-Mauritians now take evening courses in their ancestral languages in order to strengthen their ethnic or 'ancestral' identity. It would therefore be simplistic to state either that ethnicity is well and thriving in Mauritius, or that it is going to disappear because of economic and cultural changes, or that it is coming back with a vengeance. All three statements would be true. So far, Mauritian politics of common denominators and avoidance have been successful in dealing with the 'plural society'. A main challenge for the near future, not just in Mauritius but also in many other contemporary societies, consists not so much in reconciling different ethnic groups – methods for this are readily available, as Mauritius shows – but in reconciling the ideology of interethnic compromise with ideological orientations that reject the logic of ethnicity and its public reifications altogether.

The case of Mauritius might finally lead us to rethink our categories of ethnicity and nationalism. Being empirical generalisations rather than analytical concepts, they threaten to collapse when the facts on the ground fail to fit. Nationalism can perfectly well be reconciled with a multiplicity of myths and self-defined cultural groups provided common denominators exist in the shared public fields; the Mauritian brand of nationalism is neither ethnic, federalist nor civic in character; it is, in a certain sense, all three plus multiculturalist. So long as there are clear boundaries between the spheres where the different values are made relevant, this does not lead to conflict or 'cognitive dissonance'. As regards the Mauritian lesson on the concept of ethnicity, the different ethnic categories are bounded in different ways (from tight to extremely loose; from digital to analogue), and the degree to which ethnicity enters a person's life varies as well, although along different lines.

* * *

There are many stories about Mauritian society that are still to be told, and many possible analytical perspectives on the Mauritian miracle have not been encompassed in this book – some of them would surely be much more fashionable and dazzling than the modest analytical tools I have employed here. As promised in the introduction, I have concentrated on showing what works and why. It has become sufficiently clear, hopefully, that Mauritians are not saints. After two hundred years of self-conscious polyethnicity, they have nonetheless devised well-functioning ways of coping with tensions and conflicts caused by competition and value conflicts founded in ethnic differences: they have developed a political system difficult to monopolise by a single ethnic group, an openness about the perils *and* the inevitability of ethnic particularism, that provides Mauritian society with great flexibility and a very humane flavour. At its best, Mauritius embodies Claudio Magris' (1986) statement about what fascism is not. Fascism, he writes, is not tantamount to loving your family, your locality, your language and your folk customs, but consists in being unable to understand that other people, living in a completely different place, harbour the same feelings for their family, their locality and so on. Continuously struggling with dilemmas of nation-building and multiculturalism, and with the perennial tensions between universalistic ambitions and particularistic identities, Mauritian society is structured in such a way that tendencies towards disruption and fragmentation are contained and transformed.

The remarkable achievement of Mauritius does not essentially consist in replacing ethnic ontologies with non-ethnic ones. Rather, it consists in reconciling strong ethnic identities with democracy, peace and prosperity. However, there are currently strong tensions between ethnic and non-ethnic ways of conceptualising Mauritian society. Coping with multiethnicity may be relatively easy so long as the vast majority of a population agrees that ethnic identity is primordial. As soon as a sizeable category rejects ethnicity as an ontological basis for Mauritian society, the result may be mutual entrenchment and the loss of common denominators. If Mauritius is going to succeed in the future as well, it must find ways of acknowledging the non-ethnic identities as well as the ethnic ones. That will require new modalities of compromise.

Note

1. In Mauritius, one walks on fire, one drinks fire and one eats fire. In other words: One participates in firewalking (originally a Tamil ritual); one drinks rum; and one eats hot spicy food.

Bibliography

Abrahams, Roger D. (1983) *The Man-of-Words in the West Indies*. Baltimore: Johns Hopkins University Press.

Ahnee, Gilbert (1991) *Bonjour Île Maurice*. Montpelier: Editions du Pelican.

Allen, Richard (1983) 'Creoles, Indian immigrants and the restructuring of society and economy in Mauritius, 1767–1885.' Unpublished Ph.D. thesis. Urbana: University of Illinois.

Anderson, Benedict (1983) *Imagined Communities. An Enquiry into the Origins and Spread of Nationalism*. London: Verso.

Appadurai, Arjun (1990) 'Disjuncture and difference in the global cultural economy'. *Public Culture*, **2**(2):1–24.

—— (1993) 'Patriotism and its futures'. *Public Culture*, **5**(3):411–29.

Archetti, Eduardo P. (1995) 'Nationalisme, football et polo: tradition et créolisation dans la construction de l'Argentine moderne'. *Terrain* **25**:73–90.

Ardener, Edwin (1989) *The Voice of Prophecy and Other Essays*. Oxford: Blackwell.

Arno, Toni and Claude Orian (1986) *L'Ile Maurice, une société multiraciale*. Paris: L'Harmattan.

Baker, Philip (1972) *Kreol. A Description of Mauritian Creole*. London: C. Hurst.

—— and Vinesh Hookoomsing (1987) *Diksyoner kreol morisien*. Paris: L'Harmattan.

Banks, Marcus (1996) *Ethnicity: Anthropological Constructions*. London: Routledge.

Barnes, John (1954) 'Class and committee in a Norwegian island parish'. *Human Relations* **7**:39–58.

Barth, Fredrik (1969) 'Introduction'. In F. Barth, ed., *Ethnic Groups and Boundaries*, pp. 9–37. Oslo: Scandinavian University Press.

—— (1978) Conclusions. In F. Barth, ed., *Scale and Social Organisation*, pp. 253–74. Oslo: Scandinavian University Press.

Bateson, Gregory (1959) *Naven* (2nd edition). Stanford: Stanford University Press.

—— (1972) *Steps to an Ecology of Mind*. New York: Chandler.

Baumann, Gerd (1996) *Contesting Culture: Discourses of Identity in Multi-ethnic London*. Cambridge: Cambridge University Press.

Beaton, Patrick (1977[1859]) *Creoles and Coolies, or Five Years in Mauritius*. London: Kennikat .

Bébel-Gisler, Dany (1975) *Le Créole: Force Jugulée*. Paris: L'Harmattan.

Benedict, Burton (1961) *Indians in a Plural Society*. London: Her Majesty's Stationery Office.

—— (1965) *Mauritius: Problems of a Plural Society*. London: Pall Mall.

—— (1966) 'Sociological Characteristics of Small Territories and their Implications for Economic Development', in M. Banton, ed., *The Social Anthropology of Complex Societies*, pp. 23–36. London: Tavistock.

—— (1967) 'Caste in Mauritius'. In B. M. Schwartz, ed., *Caste in Overseas Indian Communities*, pp. 21–41. San Francisco.

—— and Marion Benedict (1982) *Men, Women and Money in the Seychelles*. Berkeley: California University Press.

Benoit, Gaëtan (1985) *The Afro-Mauritians: An Essay*. Moka, Mauritius: MGI.

Bentley, G. Carter (1987) 'Ethnicity as practice'. *Comparative Studies in Society and History*, **29**(1):24–55.

Berger, Peter, Birgitte Berger and Hansfried Kellner (1974) *The Homeless Mind*. Harmondsworth: Pelican.

Bissoondoyal, U. and S. B. C. Servansing, eds. (1986) *Indian Labour Immigration*. Moka: Mahatma Gandhi Institute.

—— and S. B. C. Servansing, eds. (1989) *Slavery in South-West Indian Ocean*. Moka: Mahatma Gandhi Institute.

Bourdieu, Pierre (1977) *Outline of a Theory of Practice*. Cambridge: Cambridge University Press.

—— (1980) *Le Sens Pratique*. Paris: Minuit.

Bowman, Larry (1984) 'Mauritius, 1984'. *CSIS Africa Notes* **34**.

—— (1991) *Mauritius: Democracy and Development in the Indian Ocean*. Boulder: Westview.

Braithwaite, Lloyd (1960) 'Social Stratification and Cultural Pluralism'. In *Social and Cultural Pluralism in the Caribbean*. Annals of the New York Academy of Sciences, **8**, Art. 5.

Bunwaree, S. S. (1994) *Mauritian Education in a Global Economy*. Rose-Hill: Editions de l'Océan Indien.

Carter, Marina (1995) *Servants, Sirdars and Settlers: Indians in Mauritius, 1834–1874*. Oxford: Oxford University Press.

Chatterjee, Partha (1993) *The Nation and its Fragments: Colonial and Postcolonial Histories*. Princeton: Princeton University Press.

Chaudenson, Robert (1979) *Les Créoles Français*. Paris: F. Nathan.

Chazal, Malcolm de (1979 [1951]) *Petrusmok*. Port-Louis: Editions de la Table Ovale.

Christie, Nils (1972) *Fangevoktere i konsentrasjonsleire*. (Prison guards in concentration camps) Oslo: Scandinavian University Press.

Clifford, James (1988) *The Predicament of Culture: Twentieth-Century Ethnography, Literature and Art*. Cambridge, Mass.: Harvard University Press.

Cohen, Abner (1969) *Custom and Conflict in Urban Africa*. Berkeley: University of California Press.

—— (1974a) 'The Lesson of Ethnicity'. In A. Cohen (ed.), *Urban Ethnicity*, pp. ix–xxiv. London: Tavistock.

—— (1974b) *Two-Dimensional Man*. Berkeley: University of California Press.

—— (1981) *The Politics of Elite Culture*. Berkeley: University of California Press.

Cohen, Anthony P. (1985) *The Symbolic Construction of Community*. London: Tavistock.
—— (1994) *Self Consciousness*. London: Routledge.
Connor, Walker (1974) 'A nation is a nation, is a state, is an ethnic group, is a . . .'. *Ethnic and Racial Studies*, 1(4):378–400.
Corne, Chris and Philip Baker (1983) *Isle de France Creole*. Ann Arbor: Karoma.
Davidson, Basil (1978) *Africa in Modern History*. Harmondsworth: Pelican.
Despres, Leo (1975) 'Toward a Theory of Ethnic Phenomena'. In L. Despres, ed., *Ethnicity and Resource Competition in Plural Societies*, pp. 187–207. The Hague: Mouton.
Dinan, Monique (1983) *Une île éclatée*. Port-Louis: Best Graphics.
Dumas, Alexandre (1974[1843]) *Georges*. Paris: Gallimard.
Dumont, Louis (1983) *Essais sur l'individualisme*. Paris: Seuil.
Durand, J.-P. and J. Durand (1978) *L'Ile Maurice et ses populations*. Paris: P.U.F.
Eidheim, Harald (1971) *Aspects of the Lappish Minority Situation*. Oslo: Scandinavian University Press.
Elster, Jon (1983) *Explaining Technical Change*. Oslo: Scandinavian University Press.
Emrith, Moomtaz (1967) *The Muslims of Mauritius*. Port-Louis: Editions Le Printemps.
Epstein, A. L. (1958) *Politics in an Urban African Community*. Manchester: Manchester University Press.
—— (1978) *Ethos and Identity*. London: Tavistock.
—— (1992) *Scenes from African Urban Life: Collected Copperbelt Essays*. Edinburgh: Edinburgh University Press.
Eriksen, Thomas Hylland (1986) 'Creole culture and social change'. *Journal of Mauritian Studies*, 1(2): 59–72. Moka, Mauritius: MGI.
—— (1988) *Communicating Ethnic Difference and Identity. Ethnicity and Nationalism in Mauritius*. Oslo: Department of Social Anthropology, Occasional Paper no. 16.
—— (1990) 'Linguistic diversity and the quest for national identity: the case of Mauritius'. *Ethnic and Racial Studies*, 13(1): 1–24
—— (1991a) 'The cultural contexts of ethnic differences'. *Man*, 26(1):127–44.
—— (1991b) *Languages at the Margins of Modernity. Linguistic Minorities and the Nation-State.* Oslo: PRIO, PRIO Report no. 5/91
—— (1991c) 'Ethnicity and two nationalisms. Social classification and the power of ideology in Trinidad and Mauritius'. Doctoral thesis, University of Oslo.
—— (1992a) *Us and Them in Modern Societies*. Oslo: Scandinavian University Press.
—— (1992b) 'Multiple traditions and the problem of cultural integration'. *Ethnos*, 57(2):5–30.
—— (1992c) 'Modernity and ethnic identity: Fragmentation and unification in Europe seen through Mauritius'. *L'Express Culture & Research* (Port-Louis), no. 5, Spring 1992.
—— (1993a) 'Formal and informal nationalism'. *Ethnic and Racial Studies*, 16(1):1–25.
—— (1993b) *Ethnicity and Nationalism: Anthropological Perspectives*. London: Pluto.
—— (1993c) 'In which sense do cultural islands exist?' *Social Anthropology* 1b(1): 133–47.

—— (1993d) 'A non-ethnic, future-oriented nationalism?' *Ethnos,* **58**(3–4):197–221.
—— (1994a) 'Nationalism, Mauritian style: Cultural unity and ethnic diversity'. *Comparative Studies in Society and History* **36**(3):549–74.
—— (1994b) *Kulturelle veikryss. Essays om kreolisering* (Cultural Crossroads: Essays on creolisation). Oslo: Scandinavian University Press.
—— (1995) 'We and us: two modes of group identification'. *Journal of Peace Research,* **32**(4): 427–36.
—— (1997a) 'Mauritian Society between the Ethnic and the Non-ethnic'. In Hans Vermeulen and Cora Govers, eds., *The Politics of Ethnic Consciousness,* pp. 250–76. London: Macmillan.
—— (1997b) 'Multiculturalism, Individualism and Human Rights'. In Richard Wilson, ed., *Anthropology and Human Rights,* pp. 49–69. London: Pluto.
Evans-Pritchard, E. E. (1940) *The Nuer.* Oxford: Clarendon.
Friedman, Jonathan (1990) 'Being in the World: Globalization and Localization'. In Mike Featherstone, ed., *Global Culture. Nationalism, Globalization and Modernity,* pp. 311–28. London: Sage.
—— (1994) *Cultural Identity and Global Process.* London: Sage.
Furnivall, J. S. (1948) *Colonial Policy and Practice.* Cambridge: Cambridge University Press.
Geertz, Clifford (1973) *The Interpretation of Cultures.* Chicago: Chicago University Press.
Gellner, Ernest (1983) *Nations and Nationalism.* Oxford: Blackwell.
Giddens, Anthony (1979) *Central Problems in Social Theory.* Cambridge: Cambridge University Press.
—— (1984) *The Constitution of Society.* Cambridge: Polity.
—— (1990) *The Consequences of Modernity.* Cambridge: Polity.
—— (1994) *Beyond Left and Right.* Cambridge: Polity.
Gledhill, John (1997) 'Liberalism, Socio-economic Rights and the Politics of Identity: From Moral Economy to Indigenous Rights'. In Richard Wilson, ed., *Human Rights, Culture and Context,* pp. 70–110. London: Pluto.
Gluckman, Max (1955) *The Judicial Process among the Barotse of Northern Rhodesia.* Manchester: Manchester University Press.
—— (1958 [1940]) *Analysis of a Social Situation in Zululand.* Manchester: Manchester University Press.
—— (1982 [1956]) *Custom and Conflict in Africa.* Oxford: Blackwell.
Goodman, Morris F. (1964) *A Comparative Study of Creole French Dialects.* The Hague: Mouton.
Grillo, Ralph (1980) 'Introduction'. In Ralph Grillo, ed., *"Nation" and "State" in Europe: Anthropological Perspectives,* pp. 1–30. London: Academic Press.
Grønhaug, Reidar (1974) *Micro–Macro Relations.* Bergen: Bergen Studies in Social Anthropology, **7**.
—— (1978) 'Scale as a Variable in Analysis'. In F. Barth, ed., *Scale and Social Organization,* pp. 78–121. Oslo: Scandinavian University Press.
Hancock, Ian (1979) *Readings in Creole Studies.* The Hague: Mouton.

Handelman, Don (1977) 'The organization of ethnicity'. *Ethnic Groups*, **1**:187–200.

Handler, Richard (1988) *Nationalism and the Politics of Culture in Quebec*. Madison: Wisconsin University Press.

— and Daniel Segal (1992) 'How European is Nationalism?' *Social Analysis* **32**(1): 1–15.

Hannerz, Ulf (1990) 'Cosmopolitans and Locals.' In Mike Featherstone, ed., *Global Culture*, pp. 237–52. London: Sage.

— (1992) *Cultural Complexity*. New York: Columbia University Press.

— (1996) *Transnational Connections: Culture, People, Places*. London: Routledge.

Heiberg, Marianne (1989) *The Making of the Basque Nation*. Cambridge: Cambridge University Press.

Hité, Evenor (1897) *Histoire de l'Ile Maurice*. Port-Louis: Engelbrecht & Cie.

Hobsbawm, Eric (1992) *Nations and Nationalism since 1780* (2nd edition). Cambridge: Cambridge University Press.

Hollingworth, Derek (1965) *They Came to Mauritius*. London: Oxford University Press.

Hollup, Oddvar (1994a) 'Changing conceptualization of Indian ethnic identity in Mauritius.' Doctoral thesis, University of Bergen.

— (1994b) 'The disintegration of caste and changing concepts of Indian ethnic identity in Mauritius'. *Ethnology*, **33**(4):297–316.

— (1995) 'Islamic revivalism and political opposition among minority muslims in Mauritius'. Bodø: Nordland Research Institute Working Papers.

Holy, Ladislav and Milan Stuchlik (1983) *Actions, Norms, and Representations*. Cambridge: Cambridge University Press.

Hookoomsing, Vinesh Y. (1986) 'Langue et identité ethnique: Les langues ancestrales à l'ile Maurice'. *Journal of Mauritian Studies*, **1**(2): 126–53.

Horowitz, Donald (1985) *Ethnic Groups in Conflict*. Berkeley: University of California Press.

Humbert, Marie-Thérèse (1979) *A l'autre bout de moi*. Paris: Stock.

Hutchinson, John (1994) *Modern Nationalism*. London: Fontana.

Jourdain, Anne Marie (1956) *De français aux parlers créoles*. Paris: C. Klincksieck.

Joyce, James (1984 [1922]) *Ulysses*. Harmondsworth: Penguin.

Kalla, Abdool Cader (1986) 'The Language Issue: A Perennial Issue in Mauritian Education'. In U. Bissoondoyal and S. B. C. Servansing, eds., *Indian Labour Immigration*, pp. 165–78. Moka: Mahatma Gandhi Institute.

Kapferer, Bruce (1988) *Legends of People; Myths of State*. Washington: Smithsonian Institution.

Keng, Jean-Claude Lau Thi (1991) *Inter-Ethnicité et Politique à L'Ile Maurice*. Paris: L'Harmattan.

Klass, Morton (1991) *Singing with Sai Baba. The Politics of Revitalisation in Trinidad*. Boulder: Westview.

Kouwenhoven, Arlette (1988) 'A Study of the Integration of the Chinese Community into Mauritian Society'. In A. Kuper and A. Kouwenhoven, eds., *Contributions to Mauritian Ethnography*, pp. 39–70. Leiden: ICA Leiden.

Leach, Edmund (1954). *Political Systems of Highland Burma*. London: Athlone.

Leffler, Ulrich (1988) *Mauritius: Abhängigkeit und Entwicklung einer Inselökonomie*. Hamburg: Institut für Afrika-Kunde.

Lévi-Strauss, Claude (1955) *Tristes Tropiques*. Paris: Plon.

Lijphart, Arend (1977) *Democracy in Plural Societies. A Comparative Exploration*. New Haven: Yale University Press.

Little, Kenneth (1978) 'Countervailing Influences in African Ethnicity: A Less Apparent Factor'. In Brian du Toit, *Ethnicity in Modern Africa*, pp. 175–90. London: Sage.

LPT (1978) *Alfa Ennbuk: Liv Profeser*. Port-Louis: LPT.

—— (1985) *Diksyoner Kreol–Angle*. Port-Louis: LPT.

—— (1987) *L'histoire d'une trahison. MMM so sosyalism*. Port-Louis: LPT.

Lukes, Steven (1991) *Moral Conflict and Politics*. Oxford: Clarendon.

—— (1995) *The Curious Enlightenment of Professor Caritat: A Comedy of Ideas*. London: Verso.

Ly-Tio-Fane Pineo, Huguette (1985) *Chinese Diaspora in Western Indian Ocean*. Port-Louis: Editions de l'Océan Indien.

McDonald, Maryon (1989) *'We are not French!' Language, Culture and Identity in Brittany*. London: Routledge.

Macintyre, Alasdair (1981) *After Virtue*. Notre Dame, Ind.: University of Notre Dame Press.

Magris, Claudio (1986) *Danubio*. Milan: Garzanti.

Mannick, A. R. (1978) *Mauritius: The Development of a Plural Society*. Nottingham: Spokesman.

Masson, André (1986) *La Divine Condition*. Paris: Karthala.

Mauritius, Government of (1953) *Population Census of Mauritius, 1952*. Port-Louis: Government Printer.

—— (1968) *Constitution of Mauritius*. Port-Louis: Government Printer.

—— (1984–6) *Housing and Population Census of Mauritius* (6 vols). Port-Louis: Central Statistical Office.

—— (1986) *Report of the Select Committee on The Certificate of Primary Education*. Port-Louis: Government Printer.

—— (1991–2) *Housing and Population Census 1990* (7 vols). Port-Louis: Government Printer.

Mayer, Adrian (1966) 'The Significance of Quasi-Groups in the Study of Complex Societies'. In M. Banton, ed., *The Social Anthropology of Complex Societies*, pp. 97–122. London: Tavistock.

Mayer, Philip (1961) *Townsmen or Tribesmen*. Cape Town: Oxford University Press.

Meade, J. E. *et al.* (1961) *The Social and Economic Structure of Mauritius*. London: Her Majesty's Stationery Office.

Miller, Daniel (1994) *Modernity – An Ethnographic Approach*. Oxford: Berg.

Mitchell, J. Clyde (1956) *The Kalela Dance*. Manchester: Manchester University Press.

—— (1966) 'Theoretical Orientations in African Urban Studies'. In M. Banton, ed., *The Social Anthropology of Complex Societies*, pp. 37–68. London: Tavistock.

—— (1974) 'Perceptions of Ethnicity and Ethnic Behaviour: An Empirical Exploration'. In Abner Cohen (ed.), *Urban Ethnicity*, pp. 1–36. London: Tavistock.

MMM (1985) *L'Histoire d'Un Combat*. Port-Louis: MMM.

Naipaul, V. S. (1973) *The Overwrowded Barracoon*. Harmondsworth: Penguin.

—— (1979 [1958]) London. In Robert D. Hamner, ed., *Critical Perspectives on V. S. Naipaul*. London: Heinemann.

Nash, Manning (1988) *The Cauldron of Ethnicity in the Modern World*. Chicago: University of Chicago Press.

Nave, Ari (n.d. 1) 'Communalism as conflict. Examples from Mauritius'. Unpublished ms., University of California, Los Angeles (1997)

—— (n.d. 2) 'Marriage and the maintenance of ethnic group boundaries: the case of Mauritius'. Unpublished ms., University of California, Los Angeles (1997)

Oodiah, Malenn (1986) 'Le développement du mouvement syndical à L'Ile Maurice'. *Afrika Spektrum* **21**(1):77–100. Hamburg: Institut für Afrika-Kunde.

—— (1989) *MMM 1969–1989: 20 ans d'histoire*. Rose-Hill: MMM.

-, ed. (1992) *Les années décisives: 1982–1992*. Rose-Hill: Océan.

Österud, Öyvind (1984) *Nasjonenes selvbestemmelsesrett. Søkelys på en doktrine* (The Right to Self-Determination of Nations. A Critical View of a Doctrine). Oslo: Scandinavian University Press.

Quenette, L. Reynald (1985) *La Fin D'Une Légende*. Port-Louis: Monoprint.

Ramdoyal, Ramesh (1977) *Education in Mauritius*. Réduit: MIE.

Rauville, Camille de (1967) *Mauricianismes à éviter*. Port-Louis: Le Livre Mauricien.

Rawls, John (1993) *Political Liberalism*. New York: Columbia University Press.

Revi Lalit (1985) *Lalit Kont Kominalism*. Port-Louis: LPT.

Roosens, Eugen E. (1989) *Creating Ethnicity*. London: Sage.

Rosaldo, Michelle Z. (1974) 'Woman, Culture and Society: A Theoretical Overview'. In M. Z. Rosaldo and L. Lamphere, eds., *Woman, Culture and Society*, pp. 17–42. Stanford: Stanford University Press.

Sahlins, Marshall D. (1972) *Stone Age Economics*. London: Tavistock.

St. Pierre, Bernardin de (1983[1773]) *Voyage à L'Ile de France*. Paris: Maspero.

Sartre, Jean-Paul (1943) *L'Etre et le Néant*. Paris: Gallimard.

Schütz, Alfred (1972 [1932]) *The Phenomenology of the Social World*. London: Heinemann.

—— and Thomas Luckmann (1979) *Strukturen der Lebenswelt*. Band 1. Frankfurt: Suhrkamp.

Selvon, Sydney (1984) La culture euro-créole à Maurice: quel avenir? *Le Mauricien*, 6 March 1984.

—— (1985) *Histoire – La Génèse d'une Ville: Vacoas-Phoenix*. Vacoas: La Municipalité de Vacoas-Phoenix.

—— (1986) *Ramgoolam*. Rose-Hill: Editions de l'Océan Indien.

Selwyn, P. (1983) 'Mauritius: The Meade Report Twenty Years Later'. In R. Cohen (ed.), *African Islands and Enclaves*, pp. 249–75. London: Sage.

Simmons, Adele Smith (1982) *Modern Mauritius: The Politics of Decolonization*. Bloomington: Indiana University Press.

Smith, Anthony D. (1983) *State and Nation in the Third World*. Brighton: Wheatsheaf.
— (1991) *National Identity*. Harmondsworth: Penguin.
— (1995) *Nations and Nationalism in a Global Era*. Cambridge: Polity.
Smith, M. G. (1965) *The Plural Society in the British West Indies*. Berkeley: University of California Press.
SOFRÈS (1977) *L'Opinion publique à Maurice en avril 1977*. Paris: Sofrès/Groupe Métro.
Souchon, Henri (1982) 'Le mythe des quinze langues pour un million'. In H. Unmole, ed., *Proceedings, National Seminar on the Language Issue in Mauritius*, pp. 78–83. Réduit: University of Mauritius.
Southall, Aidan (1961) 'Introductory Summary'. In A. Southall, ed., *Social Change in Modern Africa*, pp. 1–66. London: Oxford University Press.
Stein, Peter (1983) *Connaissance et emploi des langues à l'Ile Maurice*. Hamburg: Helmut Busche Verlag.
Steinberg, Stephen (1981) *The Ethnic Myth: Race, Ethnicity, and Class in America*. New York: Atheneum.
Strathern, Marilyn (1991) *Partial Connections*. Savage, MD: Rowman & Littlefield.
Sussman, Linda K. (1983) 'Medical pluralism on Mauritius: a study of medical beliefs and practices in a polyethnic society'. Ph. D. thesis, Washington University. Ann Arbor: University Microfilms.
Taylor, Charles (1992) *Multiculturalism and "the Politics of Recognition"*, ed. Amy Gutmann. Princeton: Princeton University Press.
Tinker, Hugh (1974) *A New Form of Slavery: The Export of Indian Labour Overseas 1880–1920*. Oxford: Oxford University Press.
— (1977) 'Between Africa, Asia and Europe: Mauritius: cultural marginalism and political control'. *African Affairs*, **76**: 321–38.
Tönnies, Ferdinand (1912) *Gemeinschaft und Gesellschaft* (2nd edition). Berlin: Karl Curtius.
Toussaint, Adolphe (1971) *Histoire des Iles Mascareignes*. Paris: Berger-Levrault.
Turner, Victor (1969) *The Ritual Process: Structure and Anti-Structure*. Ithaca: Cornell University Press.
— (1974) *Dramas, Fields, and Metaphors*. Ithaca: Cornell University Press.
Unienville, Baron de (1838) *Statistiques de l'Ile Maurice*. Paris: Gustave Barba.
Varma, M. N. (1981) *Profiles of Great Mauritians*. Quatre-Bornes.
Vermeulen, Hans and Cora Govers, eds. (1994) *The Anthropology of Ethnicity: Beyond "Ethnic Groups and Boundaries"*. Amsterdam: Het Spinhuis.
Virahsawmy, Dev (1983) 'Quel Mauricianisme?'. *MIE Journal*. Réduit: MIE.
Virahsawmy, Raj (1979) 'Le Développement du Capitalisme Agraire et l'émergence de petits planteurs à l'Ile Maurice'. *Africa Development*, **IV**: 2/3.
— (1986) A Form of Liberation (From the Camp to the Village). In U. Bissoondoyal and S. B. C. Servansing, eds., *Indian Labour Immgration*, pp. 145–51. Moka: Mahatma Gandhi Institute.
Walker, Ian (1986) *Zaffer pe sanze*. Vacoas: KMLI.
Weber, Max (1981[1922]) *Wirtschaft und Gesellschaft*. Tübingen: J. C. B. Mohr.

Wilson, Godfrey (1941–2) *An Essay on the Politics of Detribalization in North Rhodesia*, Part II. Livingstone: Rhodes–Livingstone Institute, Rhodes–Livingstone Papers, no. 5–6.

—— and Monica Wilson (1945) *The Analysis of Social Change*. Cambridge: Cambridge University Press.

Wilson, Peter J. (1978) *Crab Antics* (2nd edition). New Haven: Yale University Press.

Wilson, Richard, ed. (1997) *Human Rights, Culture & Context*. London: Pluto.

Wittgenstein, Ludwig (1983 [1958]) *Philosophical Investigations*, trans. G. E. M. Anscombe. Oxford: Blackwell.

Woolf, Virginia (1928) *Orlando*. London: Hogarth Press.

Worsley, Peter (1984) *The Three Worlds*. London: Weidenfeld & Nicolson.

Yelvington, Kevin (1991) 'Ethnicity as practice? A comment on Bentley'. *Comparative Studies in Society and History*, **33**(1):158–68.

Yeung, D. Ha and Pierre Yin (1986) 'La zone franche: essai d'évaluation économique'. *Le Mauricien*, June 20–21.

Index

Abdul and Françoise, a mixed couple
124–5, 127
Africa: nationhood and ethnicity 138
African Mauritians *see* Creole
Mauritians
age: idealism 120; youth networks
118–21
Ainu people 139
alcohol 57–9
All-Mauritius Hindu Congress 41
Anderson, Benedict 190
Anquetil, Emmanuel 104
anthropology: shifting connotations of
ethnicity 24–6; structure and flow of
culture 22–3
Arab language 77, 80
Archetti, Eduardo 132–3
Ardener, Edwin 25
Aymara movement 181

Baker, Philip 21n, 71
Barth, Fredrik 25, 30–1
Baumann, Gerd 130
Beaton, Patrick 9
Benedict, Burton 1, 19
Bérenger, Paul 68–9, 107
Berger, Peter 156
Bhojpuri language 71, 142; link
between Creoles and Hindus 112;
revitalisation movement 178
Billy, a Creole 64–5
black culture 134
Boodhoo, Harish 112–13, 135

Bourdieu, Pierre 23
Britain 9–10, 143
buildings and houses 3–4

Case Noyale 114–15, 117; effect of
tourism 154
caste: Kreol connotations 140, 141–2
Catholicism: the Catholic school case
171–2; the Diard affair 95–6; factor
in ethnicity 97; not a defining
category 142; Sino-Mauritians 81, 82
Chazal, Malcolm de: *Petrumsok* 47
children: from intermarriage 125, 127
China *see also* Sino-Mauritians
Chinese Chamber of Commerce 43, 65
Chinese languages 80–1
Chopin, Fredrik 147
Christianity 15–16, 17–18, 50; converts
to 92–3; divergence of French and
Creole 91; liberation theology 91;
paid conversion to Islam 93–4;
pragmatic role 90–1; revitalisation
movement 178; stereotypes 162;
syncretism 172–3
Christie, Nils 46
cinemas 44
class: cultural identity first 109–10;
Hindu structure 177; marrying
'down' 125; neo-Trotsky abstraction
110–11; overrules ethnicity 106–7;
trade unions and Dr Curé 104–5;
worker recruitment 157
Claude, a Creole 33–4; networks and

identity 36–9
clothes 148, 154
cocoa 13
Cohen, Abner 25; particularist and
    universal intentions 42
Cohen, Anthony P. 25, 116–17
Coloured Mauritians 9, 50, *51*;
    Catholicism 142; defining 16, 75–6;
    intermarriage 60; stereotype 54;
    trade unions and class 104–5;
    traditional labour 13, 62
common denominators 18, 28; shared
    culture 98–9, 179–81, 185–8; unity
    in diversity in public only 121
competition 115–16
compromise and conflict 5–6
Connor, Walker 137
Creole Mauritians 3, 20, 149 *see also*
    Kreol language; absorbent category
    176–7; attitudes towards wealth 109;
    category shifting 75–6; class and the
    MMM 106–8; Claude's case 33–4;
    divergence in Catholicism from
    Franco-Mauritians 91; ethnic riots at
    Independence 151–2; Hindu
    influence in La Gaulette 115;
    intermarriage 60, 123–4; kinship
    network shallow 66; labour
    stereotypes 64–5; language 81–2, 84;
    networks and identity 36–9; politics
    25, 42, 69–70; regional identity
    111–12, 113; stereotypes 53–4;
    taxonomy 15–16, 50, *51*, 52;
    traditional labour 13–14, 62, 67;
    women's roles 118
culture: duality 23–4; flowing 22–3;
    globalisation 186; homogenisation
    175–6, 177; relativism versus
    equality 173–4
Curé, Dr Maurice 104–5
Curepipe 3

Darwin, Charles 9
Dev, a Hindu: idealism and

disappointment 119–20
Diard, Père 95–6, 155
Diego Garcia 11
Dimba, Sheila, a Tamil 162–3
dodos 8
Dravidian Hinduism 79, 92
Durand, J.-P. and J. Durand 85
Durkheim, Emile 24, 27, 32
Duval, Gaëtan 94, 107; Dionysian
    lifestyle 109; joins Ramgoolam's
    government 146; praises Boodhoo
    for political gain 113; rhetoric 105

economy *see also* industrialisation;
    sugar; tourism: agriculture 12–13;
    capitalist norm 185; international
    trade 12; nationalisation fears 94;
    planning 157; rupee currency 4;
    rural and urban 19; social patterns
    13–14, 43
Edheim, Harald 25
education: the Catholic school case
    171–2; free and universal 184;
    homogenisation 19, 180, 186;
    language controversies 82–5;
    national system 70; post-
    independence youth 119; power and
    control 70–1
Elizabeth I of Mauritius 143
Emrith, Moomtaz: *The Muslims of
    Mauritius* 80
English language: global culture 132;
    growth of influence 71–2; official
    use 4, 17; Ramgoolam's funeral 149;
    schools 84
Epstein, A. L. 25, 27–8
EPZ/Zone Franche: Diard Affair 95, 96;
    industrialisation 153–5
ethnicity 1–2 *see also* common
    denominators; nationhood;
    assimilation or plurality 169–70;
    categories 15–16, 75–6; and class
    107–8; contextual 97–9; creolisation
    176–9; defining 48, 49; ethnic riots

at Independence 151; field and scale
30; field-dependent identities 39;
football loyalties 158–9;
homogenisation 19–20; imperative
and situational identity 32;
intermarriage 60–2, 121–2; kinship
networks 67–8; labour roles 13–14,
62–7, 63–8; language issues 16–17;
Mauritian concepts 49–50;
modernity 48–9; multicultural
independence celebrations 144–5;
nationhood 48, 163–4; network 98;
no majority in Mauritius 183; notion
of differences 14–15; obligation of
identity 174–5; peace in avoidance
47–8; post-ethnic fruit salad 170–3;
predicaments caused by
polyethnicity 17–18; public versus
private 121; regional 2–3, 14; as a
relationship 25; relativism versus
equality 173; and religion 96–7;
revitalisation 178–9, 187; shared
culture 98–9, 179–81, 185–8; shifting
anthropological connotations 24–6;
significance of identity 99–101; skin
colour 128–9, 134–5; stereotypes
52–60; symbolic over instrumental
185; tangled roots 179; taxonomies
15–16, 31, 50–2, *51*, *53*; trade
unions 38; youth clubs 119–20
Evans-Pritchard, E. E. 27

family and kinship: Claude's case 33;
defining aspect of ethnicity 49;
disapproval of intermarriage 122;
individual histories 40; working
place networks 64, 66–7
fascism 188
feminism 117
fields and scale 29–31
fishing industry 62–3, 113–14
Floréal 3
football 158–60, 187
Fortes, Meyer 27

France 8–9, 181
Franco-Mauritians 3; Catholicism 91,
142; deep kinship network 66;
economic power 63, 155, 163; fear of
nationalisation of sugar plantations
94; Hindu political pressures 42;
intermarriage 60, 124–5; labour
movement against 106; labour roles
13; politics 69; Port-Louis 2–3;
professions 65; stereotype 54;
taxonomy 15, 16, 50, *51*, 52, *53*
Françoise and Abdul, a mixed couple
124–5, 127
La Francophonie 11
French language: instruction in schools
84; and Mauritian nationhood 85–6;
media 71–2; power relations 87–8;
Roger's preference 134; shop signs
4; status 17, 19, *88*, *90*

Gandhi (Mahatma) Institute 127, 150
La Gaulette 114–15; tourism 154
Gellner, Ernest: *Nations and
Nationalism* 138, 139
Gérard, a Sino-Mauritian 57–9
Giddens, Anthony 23–4, 187;
structuration 26, 32
globalisation: industry 154–7;
participation and consumption
130–5
Gluckman, Max 27, 30, 103
Grand-Port, Battle of 144
Gronhaug, Reidar 29–30
Grup Latanier 172

habitus 23; defining aspect of ethnicity
49; shared cultural universe 98–9
Handel, George Fredrick 147
Handelman, Don 25
Hannerz, Ulf 175, 176
Hart, Robert-Edward 9
Hegel, Georg W. F. 42
Hindi language 149; mass media 71
Hindu Mauritians 50, *51*; attitudes

towards wealth 109; campaign of
Telegu Federation 78–80; caste
140–2; class 106, 177; dominance in
politics 68–70; influence Creoles in
La Gaulette 115; intermarriage
123–4, 125–7; labour roles 13–14,
62, 67, 154; political concerns 42;
power relations 63; Runglall's
history 39–42; stereotypes 53–4;
taxonomy 15; use of term *malabar* 8;
women's roles 118
Hinduism: aspects of tolerance 94;
Maha Shivaratree feast 148; Port-
Louis 2, 3; pragmatic role 90–1;
Ramgoolam's funeral 146–7, 147;
revitalisation movement 178;
syncretism 172–3; various beliefs
and practices 92
Hité, Evenor 150
Hobsbawm, Eric 139
Hookoomsing, Vinesh Y. 21, 82
Horowitz, Donald 25
households 43, 61–2
Hutchinson, John 138

identity 99–101; culture over class
109–10; and identification 23;
necessity 174–5; post-ethnic 181;
process 161–3
Ilois ('Islanders') 11
immigration and emigration *see also*
slavery: Aline's fears 132; indentured
labour 9–10, 12–13; labour
improvement lowers emigration 19;
majority want to leave 13
India 138
individualism 164, 168–9, 187; cultural
rights 173–4; obligation of identity
174–5; post-ethnic shared culture
179–81; threat to privileged access
178
Indo-Mauritians: Christians 142;
defining the group 50, 52;
indentured labour 9–10, 12–13;

intermarriage 60–1, 129; languages
17, 77, 78, 85; population taxonomy
16; Tamils' distance 36; trade unions
104
industry 13, 18–19; EPZ/*Zone Franche*
153, 154–5; factory working place
62; globalisation 186
International Peace Research Institute
(PRIO) 6
Islam 16; Arab language 80; Christian
attitudes 124–5; Jummah mosque 2;
paid converts 93–4; Pan-Arabism
161; pragmatic role 90–1;
revitalisation movement 178

Jackson, Michael 133
Jacqueline, a Creole 56–7, 59
Janata Dal Party 109–10
Japan: the Ainu 139
Jean and Marie-Claude, a mixed couple
123–4, 127
Jean-Pierre, a Franco-Mauritian 65
Jeux des Villes de L'Océan Indien 159–60
Joyce, James: *Ulysses* 137
Jugnauth, Anerood 10, 69, 84, 105,
170; on Père Diard 95
Jummah mosque 2

Klass, Morton 136
Kreol language 21; connotations of use
88, 90; dialects 76; mass media 71;
and MMM politics 88–9; '*nasyon*'
concept 140–2; and nationhood
85–90; not taught in schools 84;
shared by Mauritians 17, 19, 169,
181, 184; social status 85, 87, 162;
spoken by Sino-Mauritians 80–1;
statistics on use 77, 78; town identity
111–12; use in Ramgoolam's funeral
149
Kurdish people 139

labour *see also* slavery; working place:
emergent supra-ethnic career paths

184–5; employment rise lowers emigration 19; ethnic relationships 37–8, 162–3; ideology of meritocracy 153; individual histories 33, 34; political left on exploited *110*; professional and white-collar 126–7; recruitment 156–7; roles of ethnic groups 13–14, 108–9; social relations in industry 154–6; stereotypes 63–8; tourism 163; women 118

Labour Party/*Parti Travailliste* 10

Labourdonnais, Mahé de 8–9, 144, 149

Lalit 110–11, 174

L'Alliance Française 88

languages *see also* individual languages: campaign of Telegu Federation 78–80; cinemas and films 44; connotations *88*; defining aspect of ethnicity 49; development of Kreol 8–9; in education 82–5, 100; isolation of the vernacular 173; issues of ethnicity 16–17; Mauritian shared language 184; media 71; multilingualism 4; percentages of use *77*; and religion 82; types 76–7

Laval, Jacques Désiré (Père) 144, 149

Leach, Edmund 25

Ledikasyon pu Travayer/Lalit 110–11, 174

legal system 68

leisure: ethnic relationships 37; individual histories 33–5, 40

Lévi-Strauss, Claude: *Tristes Tropiques* 132

Ligue Feministe 117

Ligue Ouvrier d'Action Chrétienne (LOAC) 41, 91, 95

Little, Kenneth 117

local context *see* regional context

Luckmann, Thomas 73

Lukes, Steven 175

magic and occult 93

Magris, Claudio 188

Mahmood, a Muslim 56–7, 59

malabar 8

Manchester University 5

Margéot, Mgr Jean 171–2

Marie-Claude and Jean, a mixed couple 123–4, 127

Marie-Josée, a Creole 128–9

marriage: arranged 118; articulation between public and private 121–2; blurring of boundaries 186; choosing by skin colour 128–9; endogamy 61–2; gender differences in intermarriage 128; individuals rather than groups 176; industrial workers and intermarriage 155, 156; intermarriage 121–2, 129–30; Jean and Marie-Claude 123–4; 'selling out' 178; Shalini and Vishnu 125–7; suicides over forbidden love 61; taxonomic distance 60–1

Marx, Karl and Marxism 42; agents and intentions and social conditions 28; structural-functionalism 26

Mascarenha, Pedro de 7

Mauritian Labour Party/*Parti Travailliste Mauricien* 104–5

Mauritius: aspiration to welfare state 157; British colonisation 9; capitalist norm 185; character of ethnicity 183–5; constitutional and institutional rights 184, 185; contextual ethnic relationships 97–9; early history and Portugese discovery 7–8; foreign relations 11–12; French colonisation 8–9; historical events as symbols 144; immigrants and no aboriginal peoples 183; independence celebrations 144–5; interethnic compromise 168–9; multiethnicity 1–2, 4–5; national myths 150–2; nationhood and Kreol language 85–90; no contested territory 183;

non-colonial history short 149;
political system 10–11; post-ethnic
shared culture 179–81, 185–8; riots
at Independence 106, 151; rural and
urban 19; self-awareness as nation
157–61; structure and flow of
culture 22–4; territory-based
nationhood 143–4; uncertainties at
Independence 94
Mauritius Alliance of Women 117
Mauritius Broadcasting Corporation
(MBC) 44
Maurits van Nassau, Prince 8
Mauss, Marcel 24
Mayer, Philip 38
media: global culture 130–5;
homogenisation 19–20, 175, 177;
languages 71; as national social field
44
men: male-dominance in Mauritian
society 5
meritocracy 153, 168, 175–6, 178
Mitchell, J. Clyde 25, 27–8, 46
modernity 48–9
moral values 55, 59–60
Mouvement Militant Mauricien (MMM)
10, 68–9, 135; abandons ethnic
taxonomy 15; class politics and
strikes 105–8; Kreol as symbolic 88–
9; '*nasyon*' concept 140–2; trade
unions 33; young support 118–19
Mouvement Socialiste Militant (MSM) 10,
84, 105
music: Chopin and Handel for funeral
147, 148; mixtures 172; national
anthem 148; pop 130–1, 133, 134;
séga 88–9, 134, 172
Muslim Mauritians 50, *51*; business
power 63–4; in conflict with café
over alcohol 57–9; ethnic riots at
Independence 151; intermarriage
124–5; Pan-Arabism 161; Personal
Law 172; politics 69; predicaments
in polyethnic culture 17; rural

identity 113; stereotypes 54, 162;
taxonomy 15, 16; traditional labour
13, 62
Muslim Personal Law 172
The Muslims of Mauritius (Emrith) 80
Muvman Liberasyon Fam 117

Naipaul, V. S. 13
nationhood: assimilation or plurality
169–70; colonial past 143–4, 149,
167–8; defining 142; European
paradigm 138–9; football 159–60;
independence celebrations 144–5;
the Kreol '*nasyon*' 140–2; Mauritian
self-awareness 157–61;
multiculturalist 137–8, 144, 164;
myths 150–2; non-ethnic 138, 163–4,
169; particularism and universalism
168–9, 180–1; post-ethnic fruit salad
170–3; process of identity 161–3;
Ramgoolam's funeral 146–50;
territory-based 143
Nations and Nationalism (Gellner) 138,
139
Nave, Ari 136
New Commonwealth 11
newspapers *see* media
Newton, Sir William 144
Nietzsche, Friedrich 167

Organisation for African Unity (OAU)
11
L'Organisation Fraternelle 115
Orlando (Woolf) 1

Pamplemousses: Ramgoolam's funeral
147, 148, 149
Parson, Talcott 156
Parti Mauricien Social Démocrate
(PMSD) 10, 68, 105, 113
Parti Socialiste Mauricien (PSM) 68,
135; Boodhoo establishes 112–13
particularism and universalism 180–1
Petite Rivière Noire 114

Petrumsok (de Chazal) 47
physical appearance: ethnicity 49, 177; skin colour 128–9, 134–5
politics: democratic system 5, 11–12; ethnic pressure groups 98; Hindu dominance in government 68–70; Labour Party's foundation 104–5; nationhood 140–1; neo-Trotsky account of class 110–11; particularist and universal intentions 42; regional 112–14; religion 93–4; Runglall's activity 39, 40, 41; state and system as social field 43–4; strange bedfellows 69–70
Port-Louis 2–3, 8; regional identity 111–12
Portugal 7–8
poverty 111; the *Ilois* 11
power relations *see also* politics: constitutional and institutional rights 184; education 70–1; ethnic division and distribution 63–4, 184; French language 87–8
PRIO *see* International Peace Research Institute

Radcliffe-Brown, A. R. 27
Ramgoolam, Sir Seewosagur 10, 48, 69; funeral 146–50; life and career 145–6; religion not a topic for discourse 93; replaces Queen as symbol 144
Ramgoolam (son) 146, 147
Ratsitatane, Prince 150
regional context: collective action 116–17; competition 115–16; Mauritian context 111–12; politics 112–14; rural life 112–13; social field 43; stereotypes and conflict 57–9
religion: Diard affair 95–6; diversity 1, 167, 168; as ethnic category 15–16, 49, 96–7; and language 82; only one factor in ethnicity 97; political

context 93–4; pragmatic diversity 90–3; revitalisation movement 178–9; syncretism 92, 97, 172–3
La Réunion 7
Rhodes-Livingstone Institute 27
Rioux family 131–3
ritual symbols 143
Robert, a Sino-Mauritian 65–6
Rodrigues 7, 166
Roger, a Creole 133–5
Rosaldo, Michelle Z. 29
Rose-Hill: industrialisation 154; youth networks 120
Runglall, a Hindu 39–42; levels of interaction 44–5

St Pierre, Bernardine de 9
Samajism 92
Sami people 181
Sanatanism 92; Ramgoolam's funeral 147
Sartre, Jean-Paul 157–8, 166
Schütz, Alfred 73
séga music 134, 172; and Kreol language 88–9
Selvon, Sydney 146
sexuality 118
Shalini and Vishnu, a mixed couple 125–7
Simmel, Georg 156
Simmons, Adele Smith 13, 104–5
Sino-Mauritians 3, 50, *51*; Christians 92, 142; deep kinship network 66; immigration 10; intermarriage 60; labour roles 13, 62; languages 80–1; more tolerant of daughters intermarrying 128; owners 155, 163; retail trade 63; stereotypes 35, 54; taxonomy 15, 16; traditional labour 65–6
slavery: colonial period 8; French Creole language 8–9; indentured labour from India 9–10
Smith, A. D. 143

Smith, Dr Dan 6
Smith, M. G. 23
social organisation: deconstruction of
    traditional concepts 27–8; field-
    dependent identities 39; fields and
    scale 29–31; identity 99–101;
    integration of agency and structure
    26; languages and fields 86–7; local
    and national fields 43–5; public and
    private spheres 28–9; shared
    meaning 55–6; status 31;
    structuration 31–3; structures of
    relevance 73
Souchon, Père Henri 76; the human
    bridge 170–1
Southall, Aidan 28
Special Mobile Force 148
sport: global culture 132–3
status: diversity within social fields 45
Steinberg, Stephen 173
stereotypes: flexibility 55–6;
    interpretation of others 54–5; local
    public conflict 57–9; religious
    groups 162; self-fulfilling prophecy
    63–7; shared cultural universe 98–9;
    symbolic systems 52–4; values 59–60;
    working place 56–7
structuration 31–3; theory 32–3
sugar 8, 62; dominance 1, 12–13, 19;
    fear for nationalisation 94; Franco-
    Mauritian control of plantations 63;
    imported Asian labourers 9–10;
    multiethnic working place 162–3
suicides 61
Sussman, Linda K. 93
Swami Sivananda Yoga Ashram 167
syncretism 92, 97, 172–3

Tamil Mauritians 50, *51*; Christians
    142; Dravidians 79, 92;
    intermarriage 60, 125–7; networks
    and identity 36–9; politics 69–70;
    population taxonomy 15–16; Port-
    Louis 3; rural identity 113;

separated from Indo-Mauritians 52;
    Sheila's identity as Mauritian 162–3;
    stereotype 54; taxonomy *53*;
    traditional labour roles 13;
    Veerasamy's case 34–5
tea 12
television 19
Telugu language: National Telugu
    Federation campaign 78–80
Telugu Mauritians 60
Tönnies, Ferdinand 45, 73, 156
tourism 2, 13; avoiding mass tourism
    19; cultural effects 154; enhances
    'us-hood' 160; hotel work 163
Toussaint, Adolphe 150
trade unions 33, 38
Tristes Tropiques (Lévi-Strauss) 132
Turkey 139
Turner, Victor 143

Ulysses (Joyce) 137
Unienville, Baron de 150
United Nations 139
United States: absorbs different
    nationalities 180

Varma, M. N. 104
Veerasamy, a Tamil 34–5; networks
    and identity 36–9
La Vie Catholique (weekly) 95–6
Vishnu and Shalini, a mixed couple
    125–7

wealth: attitudes towards 109;
    transcends ethnicity 111
Weber, Max 156
Week-End (weekly) 95–6
Wilson, Godfrey 27, 29–30
Wilson, Monica 29–30
witchdoctors 93
women: multiethnic working relations
    156; new careers 118; supra-ethnic
    ties 117–18; wages of wives and
    daughters to man 155

Woolf, Virginia: *Orlando* 1
working place: ethnic and kin networks
    66–7; ethnicity 62–7; factories 62;
    fishing boat 62–3; industry and
social relations 154–6; plantations
62; self-fulfilling prophecy 63; as
social field 43; stereotypes in
practice 56–7